UNDERSEA WARRIOR

THE WORLD WAR II STORY OF "MUSH" MORTON AND THE USS *WAHOO*

DON KEITH

NAL
CALIBER

NAL CALIBER
Published by New American Library, a division of
Penguin Group (USA) Inc., 375 Hudson Street,
New York, New York 10014, USA
Penguin Group (Canada), 90 Eglinton Avenue East, Suite 700, Toronto,
Ontario M4P 2Y3, Canada (a division of Pearson Penguin Canada Inc.)
Penguin Books Ltd., 80 Strand, London WC2R 0RL, England
Penguin Ireland, 25 St. Stephen's Green, Dublin 2,
Ireland (a division of Penguin Books Ltd.)
Penguin Group (Australia), 250 Camberwell Road, Camberwell, Victoria 3124,
Australia (a division of Pearson Australia Group Pty. Ltd.)
Penguin Books India Pvt. Ltd., 11 Community Centre, Panchsheel Park,
New Delhi - 110 017, India
Penguin Group (NZ), 67 Apollo Drive, Rosedale, Auckland 0632,
New Zealand (a division of Pearson New Zealand Ltd.)
Penguin Books (South Africa) (Pty.) Ltd., 24 Sturdee Avenue,
Rosebank, Johannesburg 2196, South Africa

Penguin Books Ltd., Registered Offices:
80 Strand, London WC2R 0RL, England

Published by NAL Caliber, a division of Penguin Group (USA) Inc. Previously published in an NAL Caliber
hardcover edition.

First NAL Caliber Trade Paperback Printing, November 2012
10 9 8 7 6 5 4 3

NAL Caliber Trade Paperback ISBN: 978-0-451-23810-8

The Library of Congress has catalogued the hardcover edition of this title as follows:

Keith, Don, 1947–
Undersea warrior: the World War II story of "Mush" Morton and the USS Wahoo/Don Keith.
p.   cm.
Includes bibliographical references and index.
ISBN 978-0-451-23488-9
1. Morton, Dudley W. (Dudley Walker), 1907–1943. 2. Wahoo (Ship: SS-238).
3. Submarine captains—United States—Biography. 4. United States. Navy—Officers—Biography.
5. World War, 1939–1945—Naval operations—Submarine—Biography. 6. World War,
1939–1945—Naval operations, American—Biography. 7 World War, 1939–1945—Campaigns—Pacific
Area. I. Title. II. Title: World War II Story of "Mush" Morton and the USS Wahoo.
D783.5.W3K45 2011
940.54'41092—dc23   2011026913

Set in Minion Pro
Designed by Ginger Legato

Printed in the United States of America

This book is dedicated to John Crouse, Bob Robison, Jon Jaques, Paul Sniegon, Douglas Morton, Edna Morton Thirsher, Mayna Avent Nance, Bryan MacKinnon, Ken Henry, George Wallace, Bill Isbell, Charlie Rush, Charlie Odom, David Glaser, and Larry Maggini, and, by the way, to every man and woman who has ever pinned on the dolphins.

We rode on the winds of the rising storm.
We ran to the sounds of the thunder.
We danced among the lightning bolts
and tore the world asunder.

—Robert Jordan, from *The Dragon Reborn*

The torpedo wake headed right for his stack. The explosion blew his midships section higher than a kite. Troops began jumping over the side like ants off a hot plate. Her stern went up and she headed for the bottom. . . . [Later] we surfaced to charge batteries and destroy the estimated twenty troop boats now in the water. There were boats of many types, scows, motor launches, cabin cruisers, and other nondescript varieties. At 1315 made battle surfaces and manned all guns. Fired 4" gun at largest scow loaded with troops. Although all troops in this boat apparently jumped in the water our fire was returned by small-caliber machine guns. We then opened fire with everything we had.

—Lieutenant Commander Dudley W. "Mush" Morton, from his official patrol report about an incident in January 1943, during the third war patrol of the submarine USS *Wahoo* (SS-238)

CONTENTS

UNDERSEA WARRIOR

PREFACE

*W*as that thunder? Was God about to backhand them again?

A misleading calm had settled on the surface of the sea where only minutes before stormy hell had raged. A 7,200-ton Japanese troop transport ship that had been steaming for the Solomons was now simply gone. Only debris, a haze of thick smoke, and a roil of oily water marked where she had suddenly disappeared, nose down. She sank so quickly it was hard to fathom for those now floating in the warm waters north of New Guinea.

A vessel that big could not have gone down so fast.

Once the torpedo punched a hole in her side, there had hardly been time for the prisoners of war crammed into her hold to get off the ship. Some, not so lucky, rode her down. Even then, many of the fortunate ones did not have life vests. Their captors did not provide them. They were forced to jump and swim frantically away from the inevitable suck as their ship broke apart and plunged downward.

The Japanese, on the other hand, had launched lifeboats. Then, from somewhere, a fleet of small vessels appeared and began taking on survivors. Japanese survivors.

The prisoners of war had to fend for themselves, frantically searching for any bit of floating wreckage. Some struggled for their lives with the Japanese, using their last bit of strength trying to wrest away a plank or life vest. There were echoless cries as men fought one another for anything buoyant. All were aware that sharks swam in these waters.

The Japanese had no doubt about what took their ship out from under them. Those on deck had seen the track of the torpedo that did them in. Saw another ship in their convoy go down. A third get wounded.

They fired their deck guns at the point from which the torpedoes came. Now that stealthy warship was almost certainly chasing after the heavily damaged vessel that had limped away wounded, disappearing over the horizon. She would make an easy target.

Then those in the water far enough away from the noisy motors of the scows and launches heard an ominous sound. It was a distinct clap of distant, grumbling thunder. It was not an explosion, not a storm. No, it sounded more like the deep-throated rumble of a powerful engine. Then, when the gentle roll of the waves lifted them high enough, they could see something dark gray on the horizon, its position marked by a smudge of smoke above it.

It was a submarine. The same one that had sunk them? Or maybe there had been more than one all along. A wolf pack.

The POWs who saw it, who realized what it was, cheered. The Americans were coming back to rescue them. To end their months of hell, their days of being jammed together in the fetid, stifling hold of the troopship, swimming in their own waste and vomit, a truck parked over the hatch cover to prevent them from getting to the deck and fresh air.

But how could such a cramped vessel take on so many men? Hundreds of Indian prisoners of war. Maybe they would chase away the Japanese boats and summon help, though.

Maybe their ordeal was finally over.

Then the submarine was close enough that they could see men scurrying about on her decks, manning her deck guns. Others perched on her bridge, looking their way through binoculars.

As the slick gray iron eel drew closer, the Indian prisoners frantically waved anything they could find that might serve as a white flag, shouting, "POW! POW! Indian POW!"

Suddenly the biggest deck gun on the submarine belched smoke and launched a shot toward one of the canopied motor launches. Japanese soldiers dived overboard even though the shell was a miss.

Then, from behind them, the staccato ack-ack-ack of a machine gun drowned out their cries. Some could hear the sizzle of the bullets as they passed mere feet over their heads. The Japanese were firing back at the American boat. There were also a few cracks of sidearm or rifle fire, too, though the submarine was well out of their range.

All three deck guns on the submarine swung to the direction of the machine-gun fire, as if they were needles of a compass tugged by some strong magnetic pull. One of the guns snarled. The bigger one again, coughing, spitting fire and smoke. Then all three deck guns were barking, aiming at the assortment of boats that held many of the surviving troops. Aimed, too, at the men in the water, Japanese and prisoner of war alike. Sailors with automatic rifles were also on the submarine's deck, firing methodically, repeatedly, at men who floated in the sea.

The men in the water looked for cover. They found none.

INTRODUCTION

"When a natural leader and born daredevil such as 'Mush' Morton is given command of a submarine, the result can only be a fighting ship of the highest order, with officers and men who would follow their skipper to the Gates of Hell."

—Admiral Charles Lockwood

*S*uccess *in war often comes through improvisation. Enemies, technology, geography, timing, and other factors dictate how a war is to be fought. The American Revolution is a prime example of what happens if warriors do not adapt to the nature of combat in which they find themselves. Those who introduce new tactics and develop better methods of blowing things up and killing people usually prevail, even if outnumbered. That is especially true if the other side in the conflict is slow to react, loath to change, or simply unable to do either one.*

Even if we accept the argument that the involvement of the United States in a world war was inevitable in the early 1940s, we must still acknowledge as well that our country was far from ready for the type of war in which we suddenly found ourselves.

Even as fires still raged on the U.S. naval base at Pearl Harbor, Hawaii, President Franklin Roosevelt issued the order to units scattered around the Pacific to wage unrestricted warfare against Japan. For the first time in our nation's history, our ships had orders to attack any enemy vessel. That included merchant and noncombatant shipping.

There was little or no preparation for that level of conflict, and obviously no experience in conducting such warfare among those who would have to do it.

Much of our naval fleet was damaged at Pearl Harbor and other bases that were attacked by the Japanese around that same time. That was the intention of Japan in the first place, to neuter the ability of the Navy to wage a sea war in the Pacific. This meant that most of the naval war in the first months would be fought by aircraft carriers—all three Pacific-based carriers were away from Pearl Harbor at the time of the attack—and submarines. Those submarines based at Pearl were not attacked, and others were away on patrol when the dive-bombers thundered in out of a peaceful sky that morning.

In the decade prior to World War II, most naval brass assumed the submarine to be a defensive weapon. Submersibles were best suited to guard shorelines and harbors or to accompany ship convoys as a protective screen. Those who trained submarine crews and who ran the submarine squadrons almost uniformly instructed their captains and crews to avoid detection if at all possible. They were specifically told to not attack a target unless it was reasonably safe to do so. They were supposed to risk firing their limited number of torpedoes on targets only if they were almost a sure kill.

There were good reasons for this cautious strategy, based on previous wars and the capabilities of the submarines that helped fight them. Rely on the stealth of the vessel. Do not allow the enemy to know the vessel was there unless a sure target was identified. Save the precious torpedoes for only the best targets. Keep the enemy guessing about where the submarine might attack next.

Though the vessels were also typically armed with a limited complement of deck guns and a cache of ammunition, submarine captains were taught to avoid their use. Man them and fire them only if the ship was surprised on the surface. Then use them only to defend yourself.

In short, the submarine skippers were ordered to use the stealth of their vessels to run away from trouble and hide in the depths—to live to fight another day. Dive deep, hide, then flee.

In the first months of the war, American submarine captains did pretty much as they had been taught. It was difficult at first for some skippers, as well as for their more traditional squadron commanders, to adapt to this new thing, this unrestricted warfare. They tended to pass up tankers and freighters, fishing boats and transports, electing instead to remain hidden until a warship happened by, if one ever did. That was what had been expected of them for decades.

It is also true that most submarines in service at the time of the beginning of the war were older, smaller, less habitable, unable to dive to great depths, and limited in the amount of firepower they could deploy. Torpedo technology was still lacking as well. Sonar and radar, too. Though they immediately began taking a toll on enemy shipping, the submarine service was not yet the awesome destructive force it would eventually become. Certainly not the equivalent of the German U-boats.

Those were some of the reasons why the Japanese had not even tried to destroy submarines at Pearl Harbor, concentrating instead on the battleships. And why many American commanders were distressed when they realized how much they would have to rely on the creaky, dirty old "plunging boats" and their conservative skippers until the battleships could be salvaged or constructed.

There are two primary reasons American submarines would eventually become such a major contributor to victory in the Pacific. Reasons why submarines would ultimately account for over half the Japanese shipping destroyed in the war, although America's sub force was never more than a small fraction of the total naval assets at work there.

First, forward thinkers in the Navy—men who early on felt the rising winds of conflict and anticipated the storm on the western horizon—had designed and begun production on a far superior submersible warship. This was the much more advanced *Gato*-class submarine.

Assuming a Pacific war with Japan was inevitable, and with the Navy well aware of the damage that was being done by the Germans in their U-boats, construction on USS *Gato* (SS-212)—a program that was almost two decades in the making—began in earnest in 1940. The first-in-class boat was launched in August 1941 and officially commissioned a mere three weeks after Pearl Harbor. She and her seventy-six sisters that followed her to war would eventually sink more than 1,700,000 tons of enemy shipping.

The *Balao*-class boats soon followed in early 1943. These submarines were capable of diving even deeper than the *Gato*s. They had a much sturdier hull and included more improvements in firepower, technology, and crew habitability. With 122 *Balao* boats built, they eventually became the largest class of submarines in the history of the Navy.

These vessels were arguably the most advanced war machines created by man to that point. With their massive diesel-fuel-powered railroad locomotive engines, banks of storage batteries, and sophisticated torpedo data computers, they were a most formidable weapon. They proved perfect for the decidedly different kind of war in which the United States now found itself. During the conflict, these new warships would also be the catalyst and platform used to introduce ever newer technology, such as improved radar, better listening devices, wakeless and acoustic torpedoes, and even VHF radio systems.

Once some of the more innovative squadron commanders such as Charles Lockwood began equipping the submarines with larger, more powerful deck guns, these ships demonstrated a totally new and unexpected capability. They also became effective surface gunboats, but with the added advantage of being able to pull the plug and disappear if the battle became too hot or enemy help suddenly arrived on the scene.

In almost every way, the *Gato* and *Balao* boats were superior to the legendary German U-boats. And they were perfectly suited for a new kind of submarine warfare that was about to be developed on the fly by a different kind of submarine commander.

That, of course, is the second reason for the remarkable success of submarines in the war effort. The arrival of a new breed of younger, free-wheeling skippers who either ignored or disdained the old way of running the submersibles. These men took "unrestricted warfare" beyond the limits of its typically accepted meaning.

It should be noted, and it is certainly true, that the brashness and daring of these commanders were not always prized or supported by all of their superiors. At times that lack of appreciation even applied to their otherwise admiring crews. However, the astounding results of this new breed of commander soon began making a difference in the war, much to the consternation of U.S. Navy brass and the enemy alike.

With the winds of the rising storm blowing hard, though, America needed this special breed of warrior like never before. They were soon relieving experienced but old-line skippers, sending them on to other ways of helping fight the war. The mayhem set loose by these new submarine "aces" quickly made a major difference in the war for the Allies.

Like airplane fighter aces, these captains took every advantage of the capabilities of their unique state-of-the-art hardware, and even found new ones nobody anticipated. Using tactics that were unorthodox—if not downright foolhardy—they immediately made their presence in the war known. And they quickly became the "stars" of the war, the "golden boys" of some of the top commanders.

Even as many in the higher command accused this bunch of being "cowboys," of taking unnecessary risks, of exaggerating their exploits to get the fame and glory, the Navy was only too happy to feed the media back home the exciting tales of their exploits and successes. Their faces, images of their submarines and crews, and photos of exploding enemy ships taken through their periscopes often graced the pages of national magazines and big-city newspapers. They were featured in the newsreels that flickered on movie screens around the nation. The news of their achievements in the Pacific and among the sweltering islands between Australia and the Japanese Home Islands was also fed to the Allied troops wherever they fought, in order to boost their morale.

Here was a bright spot in an otherwise dismal war. They did not need actors or models. Here were actual handsome, smiling faces to show to the public, central-casting characters who happened to be real, living people out there striking a mighty blow against the fanatical enemy.

For the first time in history, the stealthy Silent Service was front-page news on a world stage. The daring acts of their photogenic leading men could be displayed for all—friend or foe—to get to know better, to admire, to rally around, to fear.

With matinee-idol names like Dick O'Kane, "Mush" Morton, Slade

Cutter, Walt Griffith, Creed Burlingame, Gene Fluckey, Gordon Underwood, "Moke" Millican, and "Red" Ramage, they soon caught the fancy of all who heard about them, even as they caused some of the Navy brass heartburn. But they were also creating great consternation in the inner sanctum of the Imperial Japanese Navy as they claimed their terrible toll.

With their swashbuckling tactics, they were dispatching to the deep not just warships, but vessels that were loaded with rubber and petroleum and other natural resources unavailable on the Japanese Home Islands. The enemy was losing precious fuel for the insatiable war engine. Though not as sexy as a battleship or aircraft carrier, these American submarine commanders each inflicted a significant blow to the empire's hopes of winning the war they had started.

The most colorful skipper of the lot, though, was a handsome Naval Academy graduate with the unflattering nickname of "Mush."

Dudley "Mush" Morton was certainly the first real submarine ace of World War II. He left in his wake a long list of other submarine warfare firsts and is arguably the most innovative and inventive skipper in history.

In his very short tenure, he shared the wardroom of his submarine—USS *Wahoo* (SS-238)—with and tutored other officers who went on to make their own indelible marks on the enemy. Each of them employed his inspiring style and nonconformist but effective tactics. They acquired as if by osmosis Morton's unique ability to bring out the best in a crew. To inspire his men to follow him willingly into some of the most harrowing situations any one of them could have imagined. And to do it over and over again.

Admiral Charles Lockwood, who became commander of the Pacific submarine fleet during Morton's short time on the bridge of *Wahoo*, wrote of his star skipper, "When a natural leader and born daredevil such as 'Mush' Morton is given command of a submarine, the result can only be a fighting ship of the highest order, with officers and men who would follow their skipper to the Gates of Hell. And they did."

The big boss of the Pacific submarine fleet was not shy at all in telling people around him what he thought of Morton. Lockwood routinely referred to him as "Mush the Magnificent."

His men idolized their skipper and were loyal to him, even as he all too often scared the wits out of them with his lightning-bolt attacks. His commanders—for the most part, including some who had once tried to drum him out of submarines—loved him, too. Still, they gritted their teeth at times and looked the other way when they heard about something amazing that he had done or the audacious way he had done it.

The enemy knew who he was, too, and they feared him and his diving boat, dreading the sight of *Wahoo* rumbling and grumbling out of the sunrise, zooming along on the surface, her deck guns belching lightning bolts.

Mush Morton's actions and tactics were often as controversial and debatable as they were appreciated and admired. His rabid and freely expressed hatred for his enemies has been labeled as everything from laudable and inspiring to racist and inhuman.

How did an officer who was almost jettisoned out of the submarine service in disgrace become its most famous warrior in a matter of only a month, after only one war patrol? Why is it that this man who sits near the top of most lists of submarine heroes has never received the Congressional Medal of Honor?

How did this complicated, controversial man become one of the war's most influential fighters? And how did Morton accomplish all this in a bottle-rocket submarine career that effectively lasted only ten months? A history-altering run in which he really only took one submarine to war?

I will attempt to answer some of these questions and likely create more as I examine the short life of the man who was the epitome of a submarine commander, Dudley W. "Mush" Morton, the first and most famous submarine ace of World War II.

CHAPTER 1

Pinky and Mush

"Tenacity, Dick. Stay with the bastard till he's on the bottom!"

—Lieutenant Commander Dudley "Mush" Morton to
Richard O'Kane, his executive officer on USS *Wahoo*

*S*ome men are fortunate enough to be able to do in life exactly what they were born to do. Others find themselves cursed, locked into a situation for which they were never intended intellectually, emotionally, or by previous experience.

Lieutenant Commander Marvin "Pinky" Kennedy must be placed firmly into the latter group.

On the other hand, Lieutenant Commander Dudley "Mush" Morton was a man who was born to do exactly what he ended up doing: helming a submarine against a frenzied enemy force. He was born to be a submarine commander.

When the two men ended up inside the hull of the same submarine at the same time for a few weeks, it was the perfect metaphor for the conflict that was raging at all levels of the U.S. Navy's submarine force at the time. It was also a flashpoint within the cramped spaces of one of the Navy's newest and most fearsome warships, USS *Wahoo*.

Kennedy was not the only one who found himself showing up for a ball game with the wrong ball. Others who skippered American submarines at the beginning of World War II quickly realized they were not prepared in any way for what they were now being called upon to do.

Many of them had chosen submarines for what turned out to be all the wrong reasons. Some went to the boats because command experience was supposed to be the most direct route to making admiral. Many were trained as engineers, and the complicated submersible vessels gave them the opportunity to practice the theory they learned in the classroom and prepare for a career after the Navy. Others saw it as relatively easy duty, with a smaller crew to shepherd, higher pay, and decidedly better chow than other sea duty in the Navy.

While submarine service has always been voluntary—and still is—the nature of that duty changed dramatically when World War II started. Submarines were suddenly called upon to fight a different kind of war, one in which the role of submersibles changed radically. And the job not at all what many had anticipated when they joined up. They were no longer expected to hover just beneath the surface and attack by sound and, in extreme circumstances, employing their periscopes.

This left many experienced, trained submarine commanders and officers ill prepared, either by training or temperament, to do what had to be done. Still, the United States had no choice but to go to war with the men and resources they had.

America showed up at a gunfight with a knife.

Within the first two years of the war, a majority of the skippers who first responded to the Japanese had gone elsewhere and were no longer at the helms of submarines. That was either by resignation or purposeful shove. Or because they, their crews, and their warships were at the bottom of the Pacific forever.

This should not necessarily reflect negatively on the bravery, dedication, or capabilities of these men. The nature of this war caught them in a situation for which they were not prepared. Submarine commanders would be called upon to adapt. Some did. Most could not.

Many went to desk jobs. Others moved to surface duty. Most contributed to the eventual victory, and for that, we owe them a huge debt, not our scorn.

Fortunately for the Allies, and whether it was by design or a lucky happenstance, a new breed of submarine officer emerged. In an almost Darwinian manner, these remarkable commanders adapted, evolved their tactics to fit the needs of the conflict, learned to take every advantage available in the new class of vessels available to them, and eventually inflicted a staggering amount of damage on Japanese shipping, both military and commercial. Damage in stunning proportion when compared to the relatively small number of submarines and crews that fought in the Pacific. And a success rate that greatly contributed to the eventual victory over Japan.

Marvin Granville Kennedy and Dudley Walker Morton came to be in the same submarine at the same time by very similar routes. However, their personalities, style, and personal appearance, as well as their theories and opinions on how to drive a submarine in battle, could not have been any more different.

Kennedy was born in 1905 in a small town in Middle America, Huntsville, Missouri, halfway between St. Louis and Kansas City. His hometown was a long way from the nearest salt water. Morton, too, was born far from the sea, in Owensboro, Kentucky, in 1907.

Kennedy won an appointment to the U.S. Naval Academy in Annapolis, Maryland, directly out of high school in 1925. Morton's mother was ill, hospitalized most of the time, and his father had sent him and his brother to Miami, Florida, to live with relatives during their high school years. He went to the academy out of Miami High School in 1926 after a brief time at a prep school.

Both midshipmen were athletes at the academy. Kennedy played varsity soccer and lacrosse. Morton was a football player and was also a star on the varsity wrestling team.

As so often happened at the service academy, both men earned distinctive nicknames during their time there. The monikers bestowed on midshipmen were not always flattering.

Kennedy was a tall, skinny man with very pale skin. His classmates naturally dubbed him "Pinky."

It is not nearly so clear how Morton earned the nickname "Mushmouth," which was usually shortened to "Mush." Morton himself confirmed several versions of the story and actually seemed to enjoy bearing the name and helping perpetuate the various myths of where it came from. He later urged his officers to call him "Mush" instead of "Captain," a request that made some of them uncomfortable.

He did have a decided Southern accent, and some said he talked as if he had a mouth full of mush. Morton jokingly told some that mush was his favorite breakfast dish. He certainly had a great time impressing the ladies and his classmates by putting four or five golf balls in his mouth and quoting Shakespeare. With his prominent lantern jaw, he did bear some resemblance to a cartoon character named "Mushmouth," a regular in the *Moon Mullins* comic strip. The strip debuted in the newspapers in 1923 and was quite popular while Morton was at Annapolis.

Kennedy graduated and was commissioned as an ensign in June of 1930. So was Morton.

It is unknown whether either man knew the other during their time at the academy, but it is likely that they would have at least had a passing acquaintance. Of course, neither would have dreamed that their paths would eventually cross in the conning tower of a submarine in the midst of a war storm in the Pacific Ocean.

The country was reeling from the Great Depression in the summer of 1930, so it was a good time for a young college graduate to have the security and enjoy the prestige of being an officer in the peacetime Navy. Both new ensigns headed off to sea duty on the West Coast, Kennedy to the wardroom of the battleship USS *Idaho* (BB-42) and Morton to serve as an officer aboard the aircraft carrier USS *Saratoga* (CV-3), the Navy's first "fast" carrier.

Again, the two young men remained on a parallel course. Both ships were home-ported in San Pedro, California, in the Los Angeles area. Once more, we do not know whether or how often the two men's paths crossed. We do know Morton enjoyed being in Southern California and was soon attending Hollywood parties when off duty and in port, spending time with people in the movie industry, who were impressed with the dashing young officer's sea stories and ebullient personality.

Early in 1932, Pinky Kennedy was the first of the pair to make a significant course correction. He volunteered for and received orders to go to the Navy's submarine school, back east on the banks of the Thames River in New London, Connecticut. There he would prepare for duty as an officer aboard a submersible vessel.

Meanwhile, Morton had been reassigned to help launch a newly built heavy cruiser, the USS *Chicago* (CA-29). That ship was already undergoing sea trials out of Mare Island Naval Shipyard, up the California coast and on the northern shores of San Francisco Bay.

A year and a half later—in June 1933—Mush Morton also volunteered to go to New London and to submarines, just as Marvin Kennedy had done. He liked the prospects of being a submarine officer for many of the same reasons that led others to volunteer.

There was the quicker route to command, better pay and food, a smaller crew, and a closer bond with such a small, tightly bound group of men. But he also liked the adventurous aspect of serving aboard such a ship, too. The deep, almost sexual throb of the engines as they reverberated beneath his feet. The warm rush of the wind and kiss of spray in his face as he stood on the bridge, the submarine racing along on the surface. The ability to simply disappear if things got tangled up, to circle around and creep up on an unsuspecting enemy and take them by surprise. To be the aggressor, the silent warrior, the almost feline stalker of unsuspecting prey.

The excitement of it all was impossible for Morton to resist.

Wahoo and her tense second war patrol were still nine years away for both men, but they were already on a converging course. A collision course, just as surely as the old and accepted way and the new and daring way of conducting submarine warfare were.

When that coming-together ultimately took place, the U.S. Navy and the manner in which submarines were used to fight a war would never be the same again.

CHAPTER 2

A Mind of His Own

"There was never anything halfway about Dud Morton."

—Unidentified classmate, quoted in an article in the Evansville,
Indiana, *Courier & Press*

"*He was built like a bear but he was as playful as a cub.*" That is how George Grider, a junior officer who served under Mush Morton on Wahoo, *described his skipper. "He was constantly joking, laughing, or planning outrageous exploits against the enemy.*"

His classmates back in Madisonville, Kentucky, paint a similar picture of a young man with a true zest for life, well liked, a good but not great student who did not always trust or appreciate what his textbooks and teachers told him.

"He had a mind of his own," one classmate remembers in a 1963 article about Morton in the Evansville, Indiana, *Courier & Press.* "But he was a hail fellow well met and had a world of friends."

"There was never anything halfway about Dud Morton," another former classmate told the reporter.

He was athletic as a boy—"mostly muscle but not a big fellow," yet another one of his classmates remembers in that article—but for some reason, when Morton tried out for the football team at Madisonville, he failed to make the squad. He later grew a couple of inches and rectified the situation by making the football team, first in high school after moving to Miami, Florida, and then at the U.S. Naval Academy. He was not an exceptional football player. Wrestling would be his sport, and he excelled there.

Morton's father, William Dix Morton, was a native of Owensboro and worked as a superintendent at the Norton Coal Company there. His mother, the daughter of a prominent lawyer and politician, was born Elizabeth Rebecca Rowe, but everybody called her "Bessie." He also had an older brother, William Junior, who followed in his maternal grandfather's footsteps and became an attorney in Boston, Massachusetts, after attending Harvard. William later served in the Massachusetts state assembly.

When Dudley was growing up, Bessie was often ill and was regularly hospitalized at a health care facility in the Owensboro area, then later in the small town of Pewee Valley near Louisville. With his work at the mines, his father was simply unable to manage two high-spirited teenage boys. Dudley and William were packed up and sent to live with their aunt and uncle in Miami.

Edwina Botts was Bessie's sister, and Edwina's husband, Fred Botts, was relatively well-off and politically connected. That would direct young Dudley in a direction he may not have taken—or been able to follow—without that money and influence.

Morton played center on the Miami High Stingaree football team for three years. He was also secretary of the senior class, president of the French Club, secretary of the MiHiSci Club, and snapshot editor of the *Miahi*, the school's yearbook. "He was ever ready to crack a joke and caused everlasting merriment among his companions," someone wrote of Dudley in the *Miahi*.

Like many others his age, young Dudley spent much more of his time carousing with his friends, pursuing sports, and wooing young ladies than he did getting serious with his studies. His schooling went somewhat better once he moved to Miami. Uncle Fred was able to channel some of the boy's energy toward his studies, and was a guiding force in persuading his nephew to pursue his education at Annapolis. Botts was also able to use his connections to secure the necessary appointment.

But when it came time to attend the Naval Academy, it was determined by his father and uncle that Dudley needed a bit more polish. He spent time at a prep school in Maryland, as many others bound for service academies have done. That would not have been possible without his uncle's financial help. William Morton had no money for prep school or college for his boys, so the appointment to the service academy was Dudley's only hope for college.

Morton was a handsome young man with a strikingly broad smile, big hands, and a shock of thick, wavy hair, but it was his outgoing personality and sense of humor that most people who knew him remember. That was true both in high school and during his time at Annapolis. From his earliest days, he enjoyed good-natured roughhousing, wrestling with friends, classmates, and, later, even his submarine crews.

Some even thought he was a bully at times, too vigorous in his playful attacks on some of his crew. With his strength and size, he could—and did—inflict some minor injuries on some of the men he tussled with. That even included enlisted men, who were reluctant to fight back when their captain grabbed them from behind and put them in a sudden and powerful headlock.

However, his personality was magnetic, his style engaging. This would stand him in good stead later, when he inherited a disappointed and dispirited crew on *Wahoo*, eager for a commanding officer with Morton's inspiring leadership and daring style.

There was little in his time at Annapolis to indicate that he would eventually become such a dynamic naval officer. On the contrary, he continued to be high-spirited, preferring to "go over the wall" for fun in Baltimore to staying in Annapolis and poring over the schoolbooks. He also chose to indulge in his early passion for sailing, spending more time out on Chesapeake Bay than in the library studying. At a school that would one day name a building for him, young Dudley Morton was not a standout midshipman.

He was notorious for being willing to do anything for a laugh. One of his favorite stunts was to practice his ventriloquism when a substitute teacher was overseeing one of his classes. He had a knack for throwing his voice and simulating a dogfight in the back of the classroom. He frustrated more than one substitute with his antics, all while keeping his fellow students entertained.

Dudley's laugh was legendary. Some described it as "starting in his toenails," and regardless of how unpleasant the practical joke might have been for its victim, or how frustrated the instructor or the other serious students might have been with his disruptions, it was hard for any of them to stay mad at him for long.

While he did make the football team, it was in the sport of wrestling where young Dudley Morton was a star athlete. He almost qualified for the U.S. wrestling team in the 1932 Olympics in Los Angeles. But in the trials, Mush was beaten out by another wrestler whom he had already subdued the previous thirty-two straight times they had met each other.

In the *Lucky Bag*, the Naval Academy's yearbook, the description next to Morton's first-class (senior year) picture says, "Everybody's happy! And 'Mushmouth' seems to have brought along a goodly supply of that same Florida sunshine and happiness. A cheery 'wha' d'ye say, Tillie,' and his famous smile is enough to drive away any case of the blues."

The write-up continued, "Dud's ever-ready sense of humor and charming personality have made him admired of many; while a heart of gold and a vast appreciation and understanding of others have made Dud beloved of those who are so fortunate as to really know the man behind the smile."

After his service aboard *Saratoga* and *Chicago*, Morton made his own fateful decision to volunteer for submarines and headed for the Navy's sub school at New London, Connecticut. It did not take the cocky young officer long to run afoul of the powers that be there. One day there was an unannounced inspection of the officers' quarters at the school. Though he really had nothing to hide, Mush Morton was livid.

"Dammit, I am an officer and a Naval Academy graduate. I will not have my room inspected like I'm some damned convict!"

He promptly persuaded a couple of other officers to go in with him and rent a house in nearby Mystic, within sight of Long Island Sound. All the others in their class predicted disaster with this move. And especially when they heard that Morton and his buddies had dubbed their house "Stud Manor."

But amazingly, the test scores of the guys from "Stud Manor" actually improved. Improved to typically perfect grades. Some of the other officers finally asked Morton the secret. They could only imagine what was going on out there in Mystic, yet those guys were suddenly model students.

"It's simple, boys," Morton drawled. "We got a ban on women and booze from midnight Wednesday night until after exams on Friday. We cram, we take the tests, and then we throw a victory party!"

In October 1933, after completing submarine training at New London, Mush Morton was commissioned a lieutenant (junior grade). In early 1934, he was sent back across the country for duty with Submarine Squadron Five as part of the Navy's Asiatic Fleet. His first assignment was aboard the submarine tender USS *Canopus* (AS-9).

A tender is a ship that supports and supplies other vessels. Since World War II–era submarines were not blessed with much storage or transport space, they were unable to carry a large amount of food, supplies, repair gear, or spare parts. Tenders would rendezvous with submarines at sea—a decidedly dangerous operation in wartime—or be available at ports where the subs could meet with them for restocking, to pick up parts, or to complete repairs. The *Canopus* did not end up the way its builders intended. She had been constructed by the New York Shipbuilding Company in Camden, New Jersey, for W. R. Grace and Company. Upon her launch in 1919, she was supposed to become the ocean liner SS *Santa Leonora*, but the Navy had other ideas. She was taken over by the Navy to be used as a troopship, making runs from the United States to Europe, which was still recovering from World War I. She later became the property of the U.S. Army for a time before coming back to the Navy and being refitted as a submarine tender. After plying the Atlantic for a few years, she went through the Panama Canal to California, to Pearl Harbor in Hawaii, and eventually to Manila in the Philippines, where she would became flagship for Submarine Squadron Five for a while.

That was where Mush Morton joined her.

From the Philippines, *Canopus* visited many ports around the Pacific, servicing the old S-boats that then made much of the U.S. submarine fleet. Each summer, she followed the boats to Tsingtao, China, for exercises along the eastern Chinese coast, west of Korea and Japan. This became one of the sailors' favorite stops.

"Tsingtao" means "lush green island," and, considering its beauty, the name was most appropriate. With its strategic location on the Yellow Sea, the city has had its share of foreign occupation. The Germans were there from 1897 until 1914, and during that time, they built modern buildings and greatly enhanced the natural seaport. They also established a beer-making facility in the city, which eventually became the famous Tsingtao Brewery. That was just another reason the sailors loved visiting there.

By all accounts, Mush Morton enjoyed his duty aboard *Canopus* and his life in Manila, as well as time spent during this period as an officer aboard one of its S-class submarines, *S-37* (SS-142). This was an exciting and exotic part of the world for a young man from Kentucky to be, truly a different environment from the one where he grew up. He also reveled in the camaraderie of the submarine service. As others discovered, with the very small crews and the extremely close quarters in which they lived, an officer soon knew the names and abilities of every man on his boat. And the crews quickly learned the mettle and temperament of their officers—including their skipper—as well.

Life aboard *Canopus* was not unpleasant at all. *S-37*, though, was hardly a pleasure craft.

Like most of the S-boats, this early submarine was just over two hundred feet long and typically carried a crew of forty-two enlisted men and officers. Boats in her class had been designed primarily to patrol shorelines and harbors. They were built for stealth, not for crew comfort. They were not expected to make long runs or submerge for long periods of time. That made for cramped living inside a dark, steamy, dank ship. These vessels were called "diesel" or "electric boats" because their propulsion actually came from a complicated combination of electric motors and diesel engines. Those electric motors drew their power from a huge bank of storage batteries that occupied most of the belly of the boat. And those batteries had to be kept charged by loud, smoky diesel engines that were originally designed, in most cases, to propel railroad locomotives.

The storage batteries were not only smelly but downright dangerous. If not properly vented or if charged too rapidly or too long, they became potentially explosive because of the gas they emitted during the process. Early in her life, *S-37* had experienced this danger firsthand, and the results were tragic.

In October 1923, while Mush Morton was still a schoolboy, *S-37*'s crew was busy recharging her batteries one day as she floated gently in the harbor at San Pedro. Suddenly, the submarine was rocked by a massive explosion. Two crewmen died instantly in the blast. Others were overcome as dense, black smoke and gas fumes filled the lower part of the boat. Rescue operations began as men were pulled from the battery compartment, one of whom died of his injuries before medical help arrived. Two of the rescuers were seriously injured.

The captain decided no one in the battery could still be alive, so the compartment was sealed to starve the roaring flames of oxygen. The next morning pressure was so great that the main hatch blew open and had to be resealed. Later, when it was cautiously opened, the blaze reignited with the inrush of air.

Almost a full day after the initial explosion in the battery compartment, the area was finally ventilated and cooled enough so that the crew could enter and assess the damage.

Fire. The element most feared by all submariners. Not flooding, as most would assume. Fire and its resulting smoke. If a blaze sparks when the vessel is submerged and she cannot quickly reach the surface, it is especially dangerous.

Mush Morton knew only too well that this ever-present danger had already visited the vessel on which he found himself serving in the mid-1930s.

There were other worries, too, that were not lost on a happy-go-lucky young submarine officer. Hitler had become chancellor in Germany in 1933 and abolished democracy. The rearming of Germany had begun. Many believed another war in Europe was inevitable if not imminent, and it would be difficult for the United States to avoid entanglement there.

Meanwhile, Japan had marched into Manchuria in 1931. The Japanese were intent on spreading their empire around the Pacific, beyond the limited geography and natural resources of their Home Islands— so much so that they were willing to go to war with a China that was fragmented by warlords. The Japanese knew it would be in the empire's best interests to ensure a government there that would be stable and friendly to them. They were also aware that the United States and its allies were pushing back in response to what they saw as dangerous imperialism.

But despite those storm clouds, Mush Morton was having himself one great time. One submariner who knew him in those days described Morton as the kind of officer nobody noticed—unless he got into trouble or a fight. And he apparently did both on multiple occasions.

Another described him as "kind of rough, kind of loud, not the kind of officer that seemed to be at home in the officers' club. Truth is, he would probably get his ass thrown out."

One man who served with him during this time noted that he was far from a by-the-book officer. "Mush didn't give a damn about the book," he remembers. "He would have given an ulcer to the public information officers back then." The PIOs were charged with keeping the locals pacified when sailors did too much damage while ashore.

"Mush was the kind of guy that you either went with him all the way or you didn't go," another brother submariner recalls.

There were signs that Morton had aspirations for a more respectable naval career. He loved to sail and took every opportunity when off duty to be out on the water in whatever craft he could round up. He told friends that one day, when he retired from the Navy as an admiral, he would buy a sailboat—and not just a sailboat, but a ninety-foot sailboat—and spend his later years skimming over the wave tops of not only his favorite body of water, Chesapeake Bay, but all the great seas of the world.

Morton also talked of how much he admired the fine homes of the admirals that overlooked the harbor at Manila. He decided to get a head start on furnishing the home he and his future wife would one day have. He commissioned a local furniture maker in Manila to build a beautiful table and chairs from mahogany, complete with ornate rope carvings in the backs of the chairs. He hoped that by the time they were finished, they would be his wedding gift for his bride.

For the rest of his career, that table and chairs were shipped—at great trouble and expense—from one place to another, wherever he was based at the time or where his family awaited his return from sea.

Some would later charge that Morton was a fatalist, that he had no future envisioned for himself beyond the next enemy target, the next attack. However, the lovely, hand-carved mahogany table and chairs strongly counter that conjecture. They became a symbol of a future he envisioned, a full life made happier by a wife to love and fully share it with. That was a life that had been denied his father due to his mother's illness, and something Morton openly talked about. He simply had not found that wife yet, but he was having one hell of a good time looking for her.

(The table and chairs today are in the home of Morton's son, Douglas.)

Lightning flashed ominously on the horizon, and the storm of war was threatening as young submarine officer Dudley Morton took every advantage that he could to have a good time, making the most of this part of his naval career in Manila and the Far East as he plied the South Pacific, the Yellow Sea, and the Sea of Japan, and visited other exotic, colorful ports of call around Asia.

One of those exotic ports was Tsingtao. He made stops there while serving on both *Canopus* and *S-37* as they conducted summer maneuvers. Morton would have been fully aware during those summers that trips to that colorful port—across the Yellow Sea from the southwestern coast of Japan—would almost certainly end if Japan pressed its war effort against China.

The young officer had no way of knowing, though, that he would find more in that ancient Chinese harbor city than just a good time with his fellow submariners and an exceptional German-influenced Oriental beer.

By coincidence, he would find the love of his life.

Some may call it an omen, but that chance encounter, one that resulted in a whirlwind romance, actually began with a fatal automobile accident half a world away.

CHAPTER 3

Ice Cream and Sailor Suits

"This was the most exciting day of my life. My beloved aunty Harriet and Uncle Mush were getting married!"

—Mayna Avent Nance, Dudley Morton's niece

*H*arriet Rose Nelson had no plans to run off to China, of all places. And she certainly had no idea she would meet a handsome, fun-loving naval officer there and fall in love.

She got drafted for the visit to China. Mushmouth Morton simply swept her off her feet.

Harriet was a slim, pretty girl with a fashionable hairstyle, dark eyes, a fetching smile, and plenty of boyfriends around DeKalb, Illinois, west of Chicago, where she lived. She was also an accomplished artist and was attending art school. But then, her sister, Jeanette, and Jeanette's husband, James Avent, were heading out to the other side of the world. Avent, a veteran of World War I from Murfreesboro, Tennessee, was an executive with Standard Oil, and had been assigned to the company's office in Tsingtao, China, since 1919.

Preparations were well under way for the family to make the trip back to China after being in the States for a while. James and Jeanette and their three small children—Jacqueline, four, Mayna, two, and Jimmy, eight months—planned to make the drive across the country from Illinois to San Francisco, turning it into something of a grand adventure. They had a brand-new automobile, and the trip to the West Coast to catch the boat for the voyage across the Pacific would give them the chance to see the great American West before they departed for the Far East.

Harriet was happy for them, but she knew she would miss her sister and her nieces and nephew when they were so far away in the exotic Orient. China seemed like a distant planet, not just a country on the far side of the world.

Then a terrible accident changed everyone's plans.

Jeanette was riding in an automobile that was hit by a drunk driver. One person died and several were critically injured. Jeanette suffered a broken elbow that was stubborn in healing. It was finally determined that the doctor who set the break did a bad job, and it had to be rebroken and set again.

That was a problem for someone about to take a long automobile trip and an even longer ocean voyage. The young mother was unable to drive, and she certainly would not be up to taking care of her three children on a cross-country trek. Everyone knew that getting their home back in shape in a distant country would be difficult enough, even if Jeanette had not had an arm bound up in a plaster cast. They decided that James would drive the car to the coast with the assistance of one of Jeanette and Harriet's uncles. Jeanette would take the train cross-country with the kids. And Harriet was asked to go along to help her sister on the trip. Go along all the way to Tsingtao to help out in getting them all settled there.

Harriet's mother gave her daughter an option: Go back to art school as she had planned or accompany her sister and her family to China. On a whim, Harriet opted for China.

"Just promise me one thing," her mother told her.

"Yes, ma'am?"

"Don't have anything to do with any of those Navy men."

"Yes, ma'am."

And so it was that the family met up in San Francisco and boarded an ocean liner for the long voyage to China.

Theirs was a beautiful place above the beach, with picturesque mountains in the background. As a reminder of home, they flew a big American flag in the front yard, visible to ships entering and leaving the ancient harbor.

Then, when Harriet was finally getting ready to return to Illinois and go back to school, James suggested to his sister-in-law that she stay just a little while longer. The Navy fleet visited Tsingtao each summer while in the area for drills, he told her. It was always a fun time when the sailors came to town. And who knows? She might meet someone interesting.

Why not? she thought, conveniently forgetting her promise to her mother. Once again, on a whim, she postponed packing and put off art school just a bit longer.

Within an hour of the arrival of *Canopus* in Tsingtao, there was a knock on James Avent's door. When he opened it, there two stood two naval officers decked out in their best dress uniforms.

"Good day, sir," the big one with the dazzling smile said. "We are here to call on Mr. Jimmy Avent."

Avent, of course, knew how it worked. Within moments of tying up their vessels, Navy men found out the whereabouts of any single American women in a foreign port city. Clearly, these two had heard about Avent's sister-in-law, Harriet. He shook their hands and invited them into his home.

In their quaint way, the officers got around to politely asking Avent's permission to take out the young lady they had heard about. The one named Harriet, his sister-in-law. He granted their request after obtaining Harriet's okay.

The big officer with the engaging smile and Southern drawl was Dudley Morton. The other officer was James A. "Caddy" Adkins, Morton's roommate back at Annapolis and his current shipmate.

The courtship was on. Morton, though, seemed to be courting not only Harriet Nelson but the entire family.

Almost kidlike himself, he enjoyed taking Harriet's nieces and nephew out to the *Canopus* and even aboard the old S-boat submarine. The children liked the surface ship. However, they remember the submarine as being dark, wet, and smelly, an ugly thing, like some kind of deep-sea beast unaccustomed to sunlight.

Mayna remembers well what an easy relationship Morton had with everyone—sailors and officers alike—aboard the *Canopus* and *S-37*. One day while they were visiting the sub tender, Mayna needed to go to the bathroom.

"Uncle Mush, I have to wee-wee!" the youngster shouted, dancing.

All the sailors thought it was hilarious, and from then on, when they—sailors and officers alike—saw Morton, they shouted, "Uncle Mush, we have to wee-wee!"

The Avent kids also remember that when "Uncle Mush" came over to visit them after being out for a few days on maneuvers on the old diesel boat, he would not only smell of diesel fuel but he would also have a voracious appetite for ice cream. He would eat bowl after bowl until it was all gone. Jacqueline Avent later speculated that duty aboard the hot submarine with its poor ventilation must have left her uncle dehydrated, famished for something cold to eat.

The children enjoyed Morton's affiliation with the Navy, and not just for the trips down to the pier to climb aboard the warships. Mush often brought them things when he came over to visit with their aunt. Once he had the tailor aboard *S-37* sew together little sailor suits for them. Only later did they learn that Morton himself had helped sew the outfits together, that he not only enjoyed sewing but was quite accomplished at the craft.

He enjoyed taking them out to the flagpole in the Avents' front yard and helping them run the Stars and Stripes up so it could be seen by approaching ships from far out in the Yellow Sea.

Mush had also bought a roadster with a rumble seat during a previous visit and kept it garaged in Tsingtao. It was not unusual to see Mush and Harriet in the front and the Avent children in the rumble seat, all tooling around town, enjoying the nice weather and great views.

Much of the courtship took place on a small sailboat. A sailboat with a story.

The summer before he met Harriet, Morton had brought a mahogany log lashed to *Canopus* all the way up from the Philippines. Once in China, he had hired some local craftsmen he had heard about to saw the log up and make it into a sailboat.

It was a beauty! And fast. He loved to race other sailboats, but because of the sleekness of his boat and his skill as a mariner, none of the locals could beat him. Ultimately he was given a handicap: Only when he gave everyone else an hour's head start did he begin to lose the races.

And it was on that boat that the romance with Harriet Rose Nelson blossomed.

There was one small snag, though. Mush had named his beloved sailboat the *Gabway*. The reason was that he had once dated a girl back in Coral Gables in the Miami area with the last name of Way. Thus Miss Way of Coral Gables was shortened to *Gabway*.

"Shoot, Harriet," Morton explained to a miffed Harriet. "That was a long time ago and a long damn way from Tsingtao. You're my first mate now."

Morton loved China and the Chinese people. He spent hours talking with James Avent, who had been in China for a decade and a half by that time, learning about the culture. They visited with residents and talked with the international community who lived there. The foreigners often came over to the Avents' home for meals and events, or simply to visit and chat about what was going on in the region.

It was a worrisome time. James Avent and the others in the community shared their concerns about the Japanese presence in the country, relating reports of brutality against anyone who objected. He showed Morton photos of everyday activities and otherwise happy events that were shadowed by the ominous presence of armed, uniformed, unsmiling Japanese soldiers keeping an eye on things.

Avent was already anticipating the day when he would have to send his family back to the States while he remained behind and sold kerosene for Standard Oil. Their idyllic life in Tsingtao was not going to last much longer, he feared. Avent, like many others in the city, was certain war was inevitable, and their area would be in the middle of the fray.

Mush Morton and Harriet Nelson were soon very much in love, though both knew that Mush would have to leave at the end of the summer to return to his home port in Manila. So it came as no surprise to anyone when Morton proposed and Harriet accepted. The Avents adored Morton and were thrilled. They scheduled the wedding for the next spring and, in the meantime, saw one another when Mush had leave and could catch a ride to Tsingtao.

Mush and Harriet were married on May 16, 1936. It was a big, beautiful wedding, taking place at the Community Church in Tsingtao, a central gathering place for the Americans who lived in the area.

When it was time to secure the marriage license, Harriet produced the passport she had obtained for the trip to China to prove her American citizenship. Morton's was obvious, since he was by then a lieutenant in the U.S. Navy. The American consul in Tsingtao signed their marriage certificate, and the church's pastor, Reverend Courtland Van Denson, performed the ceremony.

Harriet's mother traveled over from Illinois to help with all the elaborate preparations. Many of Mush's shipmates and academy friends attended, including Caddy Adkins, who served as best man. Jeanette's children remember what an elegant and exciting affair it was, a top social event for the American community in Tsingtao. They recall crawling on their hands and knees among all the grown-ups' legs at the big reception, held at the Avent home overlooking the harbor.

(Caddy Adkins, Morton's shipmate, former roommate, and best man, had his own up-and-down submarine career. He, as would Morton, had a bad time aboard an old submarine during an Atlantic patrol, but it resulted in Adkins's being subsequently disqualified from submarines. He was later brought back to the boats by a former skipper of his who saw great promise in the young man. Adkins eventually became skipper of USS *Cod* (SS-224), taking her on three successful war patrols.)

Pictures of the wedding show Morton in his best dress uniform, with a chest full of buttons and epaulets at the shoulders, and Harriet in a simple dress with a long train, holding an armful of flowers.

Jeanette's children are in the photos as well, Jacqueline and Mayna pretty in their white dresses and huge hair ribbons, and Jimmy in his white suit. Mayna is frowning, though. She recalls that her uncle Mush—already the commanding officer regardless of the occasion—warned her about fidgeting so much and ordered her to stand still for the camera. He then put a strong hand on her shoulder until the photographer was ready to snap. That hurt her feelings, and she pouted for the pictures.

Harriet Nelson, who had unexpectedly relocated to China for a few months to help her sister, and who had made her mother a solemn promise, was now married to a Navy man. She had also accepted the uncertainty that goes along with such a union. She had no idea where he might next be stationed or what his duty would be. She would soon find out.

They honeymooned at a chalet at Mount Lao in the Laoshan coastal mountain range, a lovely place that belonged to friends of the Avents. By Chinese custom, it was considered good luck to allow a newly married couple to spend their wedding night in someone's home. That was not necessarily so if half of the couple was Mush Morton. He took issue with a big cuckoo clock in the chalet that kept him awake at night, squawking every hour and half hour. He finally decided to take it apart to try to temporarily silence it. No matter what he did, though, he could get it only to the point that it would emit a shrill "Kook! Kook!" Harriet had to threaten her new husband to keep him from tearing the clock to pieces.

Then, after the honeymoon, it was back to the Philippines for six months. Harriet enjoyed living there for the most part. She did not like the flying cockroaches and other tropical bugs that inhabited their home. She was also doing all she could to civilize the sailor she had married. He had a habit of referring to the bathroom as the "head," the kitchen as the "galley."

"This is my house, too," she told him. "And in my house, that's the bathroom and that's the kitchen!"

He just grinned, hugged her, and went on about his business.

Harriet, too, was concerned about the constant rumors of war. She watched the airplanes coming and going from the nearby airfield, the ships and submarines making their way in and out of Manila Bay past the formidable isle of Corregidor. All that getting ready simply confirmed the war rumors, and she knew her husband and his many friends would be called upon to fight in it, if and when it happened. And most of the other wives she talked with were convinced it would.

Then, just as she was getting accustomed to the routine, everything changed. Morton's orders next took him to a far less colorful location, the Navy Yard in Philadelphia, Pennsylvania. Never one to do things in a mundane way, Mush came up with the idea of going back to the States in style and giving his bride a real honeymoon journey. He and Harriet caught and rode the storied Trans-Siberian Railway across China, Mongolia, and Russia, going back to the States the long way around the globe after shipping belongings, including the completed mahogany chairs and table, by the more conventional route.

They stopped over in Tsingtao for a few days and then made a visit to Japan. Morton admired the ancient culture of the Japanese, too, and showed no particular animosity toward the country's people. His only problem with them was their threats against China, the Philippines, and the rest of the region he had come to love.

It was a glorious trip across Asia and Europe, but not without its revealing moments. The railroad provided a "translator," who was probably more realistically a guard, considering Morton was an American military officer. He was a Russian national, ostensibly there to assist passengers during the transit. Morton, ever the conversationalist, soon struck up a dialogue with him. In the course of it, he asked whether it was true that Joseph Stalin, the general secretary of Russia's Communist Party, was conducting a "great purge," brutally removing anyone he saw as a threat to his government.

"No!" the translator answered. "Is nothing but fascist propaganda."

But only moments later, Mush and Harriet were gazing out the train window and saw, sitting on a sidetrack waiting for them to pass, two cattle cars packed with raggedly dressed people, almost certainly headed for a gulag. It was something Morton never forgot and talked about often afterward. From that point on, he openly expressed distrust of the Russians, and even vowed—when the possibility was on the minds of everyone aboard his vessel at the time—that he would not even consider ditching a ship of his on a Russian beach, even in the direst of situations.

The sleeping car on the Trans-Siberian Railroad had individual bunks, one over the other. One morning, Harriet awoke to see a beautiful sunrise over a stunning snowscape outside her window. She leaned out, awoke her husband in the bunk above her, and told him to come down and watch the sun coming up with her. He did.

But the conductor stuck his hand inside the curtain and shook his finger at them, telling the still relative newlyweds to behave themselves. They got the giggles and laughed about it all the way across Russia.

There was another unnerving event in Italy. They noticed a huge cheering crowd outside the train station. The throng seemed mesmerized by a man giving a speech. It turned out the speaker was Benito Mussolini.

Even though rumors of a pending world war continued unabated, Morton and his wife settled into a pleasant life once they were back in the United States. In the summer of 1939, Morton was named executive officer (XO) of the destroyer USS *Fairfax* (DD-93), a World War I–era vessel that had escorted troopships halfway across the Atlantic during the war. There she rendezvoused with British ships that took the troop carriers the rest of the way. By the time Morton became second in command on the *Fairfax*, she was used primarily for training midshipmen from Annapolis. She traveled up and down the Atlantic seaboard and into the Caribbean Sea, giving the students a chance to get their sea legs and begin to learn the basics of seamanship firsthand.

The Mortons enjoyed entertaining and often invited their many Navy friends over. One of the highlights of a visit with Mush and Harriet was their dog, named Trouble. Mush had taught his dog an interesting trick. When anyone asked the mutt the question, "Would you rather be in the Army or would you rather be dead?" Trouble would instantly roll over, stick all four of his feet in the air, and pretend to be deceased.

It was also during this time that the Mortons started their family. Their first child was a son, Douglas Nelson Morton—his middle name from his mother's maiden name—born in October 1939, and christened in nearby Swarthmore, Pennsylvania. Their daughter, Edwina Rowe Morton—named after Dudley's aunt in Miami and his mother's maiden name—came along not long after, in November 1941, after Mush had returned to New London for more schooling in submarines. She was born in Boston, almost exactly one month prior to the Japanese attack on Pearl Harbor.

All was not totally pleasant for the Mortons during this time. In addition to the continued threat of a worldwide military conflagration that would pull the young family apart, the stout, athletic Mush Morton developed a nagging health problem, one that would be with him the rest of his life. It has typically been described as some form of prostate disease—probably prostatitis—and it caused him much discomfort. It also affected his kidneys. He was hospitalized for treatment of the condition at the Naval Hospital in Boston from May 27 until June 23, 1939, though little else has surfaced to give us any additional information about the problem.

In the summer of 1940, Morton was ordered back to submarines—and to submarine command for the first time—after his tour on the surface aboard *Fairfax*. He was slated to become the skipper of USS *R-5* (SS-82), a small submersible vessel, which, like most submarines of the time, was designed for defense of shores and harbors and for shielding other vessels in convoys. Designed for that and little else.

R-5 was in the process of being recommissioned and refurbished for a second life after being in mothballs for the previous eight years. At less than two hundred feet in length and with a typical crew of fewer than three dozen men, she was a far cry from the newer, much larger submarines that were already or would soon be under construction at Portsmouth, New Hampshire; Manitowoc, Wisconsin; Mare Island, California; as well as right there in Philadelphia.

Morton was delighted to be back in submarines and to be spending time in company with submariners. They were his kind of people and he missed them, missed the camaraderie and close brotherhood the submarine service created.

Mush quickly dubbed his new ride, the *R-5*, "the Nickel Boat."

R-5 had been built way back in 1918 and commissioned the next year, but she had mostly served as a training ship all her life. She had one claim to fame, though: She had a starring role in the 20th Century Fox silent adventure movie *The Eleventh Hour*, starring Alan Hale, which was shot mostly around San Pedro, California. Coincidentally, Hale would have another role in another submarine movie twenty years later, one that would have a strong Mush Morton connection.

But in June of 1940, the old boat had a new skipper, and a legendary if all too brief submarine career had begun in earnest. We have no reason to believe that Lieutenant Morton gave any early indications of his dynamic tactics or trademark aggressive style in the year and a few months that he was at the helm of the "Nickel Boat." But with U-boats plying Atlantic and Caribbean waters, it was not long before the young commander finally found himself at war, and he did take his ship into harm's way.

R-5 primarily patrolled along the Atlantic Coast and down into the Bay of Panama, protecting that vital passage through the isthmus that separated the Atlantic and the Pacific. That duty became even more serious when the war began on December 7, 1941.

Harriet, with new son Douglas in tow, moved down to Panama to be near her husband while his boat was temporarily based there. Then, in October of 1941, *R-5* went back to be home-ported in New London, with orders to patrol the shipping lanes between New England and the island of Bermuda.

That transfer worked out well for Mush and Harriet, and a little girl named Edwina. Harriet arrived back in Connecticut just in time to give birth to their daughter in Boston, where medical care was better and her husband could spend more time with them. That also meant that she and the growing family would already be back in New England when the war started. Mush moved his growing family into a big house—a really huge house, according to Harriet—in Mystic and they settled in.

That is where they were in December 1941.

It was not long after that that Mush Morton and his crew had occasion to actually fire torpedoes at what had so recently become the enemy, though it was not the Japanese.

In February 1942, late one afternoon and with night quickly approaching, Morton and *R-5* were running on the surface in the waters of the Atlantic Ocean off the Virginia capes. Morton suddenly spied through the periscope exactly what they were out there looking for.

It was a German U-boat. She was sitting boldly on the surface, pretty as she pleased, almost daring someone to shoot at her.

The U-boats had been doing far more damage than the American public was aware of, against shipping bound for Europe or the Panama Canal. Much of that destruction occurred shockingly close to shore, but the government covered up the mayhem. Officials were worried about what it would do for morale so early in the war if the general public knew how dangerous it was out there just beyond the beaches.

Morton knew it, of course. And now here was the skipper's first real opportunity to shoot back, even if he was in a boat that was no match in any way for the enemy vessel. At least he could finally put some of that learning, drilling, and practicing he had done to good use.

Morton assumed *R-5* had not yet been spotted by the U-boat. He steered closer, trying to get the right angle and range to give them the best chance of a successful attack. Surprise was about the only thing he had going for him, but failure to get the Germans on the first attack could leave his own boat in considerable peril.

Mush managed to get his clunky old boat to within about four thousand yards—two and a quarter miles and as close as he dared—just before it was too dark for him to even see his target anymore. The enemy submarine had decided to move by the time he was in position to launch an attack. Morton quickly sent his crew to battle stations and submerged for a periscope attack. By that time, the target was moving quickly on the surface. However, with a decent enough angle to justify shooting, *R-5* sent a spread of four torpedoes toward the U-boat.

Not surprisingly, all four missed. Morton immediately moved his boat away from their firing point and went deep. Or at least as deep as the old tub could safely go without springing leaks and starting to come apart.

He was never sure whether the U-boat crew suspected that they had been fired upon. But Mush knew one thing for certain: That damn U-boat was much better equipped than his ancient vessel. The German would be far more able to chase down the American boat than the decrepit old *R-5* was of pursuing and sinking the German. That was especially true when considering the murky darkness.

Later, Morton caught serious heat from his superiors when they wrote the patrol endorsement—the commanders' comments on the submarine's patrol report. They strongly criticized Morton because he did not bring his boat to the surface immediately after launching the torpedoes and go muddling around, looking to once again engage the German submarine. Go after him in the deepening night.

The way Morton looked at it, anyone with any experience or an ounce of common sense would have known that looking for an elusive U-boat while on the surface and in the dark of the night would have been foolhardy. And just plain stupid. *R-5* would have instantly gone from being the hunter to becoming the prey.

It especially rankled Morton because the way he read the comments, his superiors were hinting that he was not aggressive enough. No one else knew yet just how aggressive Mush Morton could be. He already longed for the day when he could show them.

Outwardly, Morton took the criticism in stride, considering that it came from commanders who had never fired a torpedo in wartime. But he shared with a few friends how disgusted he was with the indelible stain that had now been placed on his first submarine command. He knew he was right, that he had done the only prudent thing, considering the situation, but he would never have the opportunity to make his case.

Someday, though, he would show them. Should the time come when he had the proper equipment and a similar opportunity, he would demonstrate for them the damage he could do. That is, he had to concede, if he was ever granted a submarine command again after the disappointing first "action" aboard *R-5*.

The storm of war that had been building for so long had finally blown up with the Japanese attack on Pearl Harbor. The United States was immediately dragged into a war, not only against Japan, but with Germany and Italy as well, because of the Tripartite or Axis Pact among the three countries.

Life was about to change for millions of families, and that included the Mortons. Most of Mush's duty since he and Harriet had married sent him to sea for only a few days or weeks at a time. He was home often, roughhousing with the kids, spending time with Harriet, having dinner with the family, entertaining a plethora of friends. It was a life that was not so much different from that of most other family men who went to a plant or office each day to work. Like his father in the coal mines back in Kentucky.

But that lifestyle changed rapidly for everyone the day after the "day that will live in infamy."

America needed warriors as never before. That especially applied to naval officers. Naval officers with command experience. Naval officers with submarine command experience.

Less than a month after Pearl Harbor, Mush Morton took the oath and was promoted to the rank of lieutenant commander. In April, he was whisked off the bridge of *R-5* and ordered back to New London for still more training, to get him ready to take the helm of another submarine. In June 1942, the Navy told him to head for Hawaii.

He was now officially a PCO—a "prospective commanding officer"— presumably of a more modern and effective submersible warship than the one he had been overseeing for the past year and a half.

"Prospective commanding officer" may sound odd to some when considering Morton's experience. After all, he had already been a skipper on *R-5*. But the kind of ship he was preparing to eventually helm would be radically different from the tiny harbor craft and convoy screener.

He and Harriet left the kids with Harriet's sister and her husband for a few days. The Avents were now living in Scarsdale, New York, after fleeing China. Mush and Harriet wanted to get away for a few days together before he departed for Hawaii and serious warfare.

Harriet's niece Mayna still remembers that visit, even though she was only ten years old at the time.

"I can remember so strikingly how changed Uncle Mush seemed. He was grave and distracted, not the fun-loving uncle I had always known. There seemed to be a distance between us that I could not understand, but I knew it was serious and it worried me."

Morton made arrangements to move his family to Los Angeles, to a small home on Highland Avenue. That would get them as close as they could safely be to where he was going, and there were plenty of other Navy wives headed that way, too. Mush also convinced his father—now called "Grampy" by Doug and Edwina, so he was "Grampy" to everybody else—to follow along. Mush had found him a job in a steel mill in California, where the blast furnaces were running around the clock to meet the need for steel for the war effort. The job paid better than the one in the coal mines, and besides, it would get him out there to help watch over Morton's wife and two children while he was off fighting the Japs. If something should happen to him, it would be good for his father to be there.

Of course, that did mean his father had to leave his mother behind in the nursing facility in Pewee Valley. However, by then Bessie's mental condition had deteriorated to the point that she was not even aware of what was happening with her husband or son.

Once he had them settled, Morton kissed Harriet, Doug, and Edwina good-bye and took off for his next assignment. He would be attached to Submarine Squadron Four in the Pacific, based at the site of the travesty, Pearl Harbor. If things followed the usual course, as a PCO he would first have the opportunity to ride along on patrol on a boat with an experienced skipper, helping and observing. That would give him a month to six weeks to learn the right way to do things from the veteran captain before the PCO ultimately assumed command of his own submarine. That was almost always another boat, and not the one on which he took the PCO cruise.

The Navy had taught him all they could in the classroom in New London. He had considerable experience diving and surfacing the old "sewer pipes," *S-37* and *R-5*. Now he hoped to have the opportunity to operate in the newer boats, the vastly superior *Gato*-class submersible ships. The chance to watch a captain who had already been to real war beneath the sea operate and to learn firsthand how it was supposed to be done. Then the chance to show everybody that what had happened on *R-5* was not an indication of what he could do with a good submarine and a well-trained crew.

He was about to experience one big hiccup in that plan.

Pearl Harbor was a beehive of activity, with workmen getting as much of the damage repaired as they could, even as a good portion of the war was being managed from that strategic location. It was amazing to see, but some of the damaged ships, including some that had actually been sunk, were in the process of being salvaged. Several of them would live to fight, to exact their own revenge.

But the sight of the Navy facility, the thought of the men and women who died there—some of whom he had known, either from the academy or previous service—left Mush Morton incensed. He had also heard plenty of news and scuttlebutt about the vicious attack by the Japanese on Manila and the Cavite Navy Yard there, a sneak attack overshadowed by Pearl Harbor, which came three days before. That Philippine bombing claimed the lives of even more people Morton knew from the time when he was stationed there. Over five hundred men had died during that attack. One submarine, USS *Sealion* (SS-195), was destroyed in the assault. Four of his fellow submariners died there.

Morton had told many people how anxious he was for the opportunity to strike back at the Japs, for whom he had by now developed a strong and vocal hatred. And he was convinced that a submarine with a full load of torpedoes was the ideal weapon to seek revenge for the loss of his friends, brother submariners, and fellow Americans.

As Mush Morton made his way into Pearl Harbor, though, there were two defining encounters that awaited him. Each of them would threaten to end his plans to sink enemy ships as the skipper of a submarine. Nip his career before he even had the chance to show his commanders what he could do.

One encounter would be with another dank, dirty, and antique submarine.

The other meeting would be with a former classmate at Annapolis named "Pinky."

CHAPTER 4

The New Fleet Boat

"I left the Navy Yard thinking [*Wahoo*] surely must be getting the best officers and chief petty officers."

—Richard O'Kane, executive officer and
plank owner, USS *Wahoo*

*M*arvin Granville Kennedy was clearly an officer on the rise in the submarine service. After graduating from sub school in New London in 1932, he served over the next four years aboard S-35 (SS-140), S-34 (SS-139), and S-45 (SS-156), in that order. The first two vessels had been built before 1920. The S-45 was launched in 1923. They were about the best submarines the Navy had at the time, but that was not saying much.

Kennedy was an able engineer, spending most of his time aboard S-34 while she was based at Pearl Harbor. During that period, the submarine received several awards for excellence. In 1936, Kennedy was selected to attend the course in General Line at the Navy's postgraduate school in Annapolis, the equivalent of going back to a well-respected and exclusive graduate school. That further confirmed that the Navy brass had their eye on Kennedy and that he was bound for command, maybe taking the first big step toward making admiral someday.

Upon graduation, he was back on surface ships, coincidentally aboard the cruiser USS *Chicago* out of San Pedro, California, the same ship on which his former classmate Dudley Morton had briefly served seven years prior. From there, he went back east in August 1939 to New Jersey, to the Federal

Shipbuilding & Dry Dock Company near Newark, to help launch USS *Hammann* (DD-412), a new destroyer. He served as her engineering officer, but his duty there was cut short by the Japanese attack on Pearl Harbor.

Men with submarine experience were suddenly at a premium. Partly taking their cue from the German U-boats, many in the U.S. Navy had already realized that the type of war that might erupt in the Pacific would require a different strategy—different warships and different commanders, too—from anything that had come before. Submarines, with their unique capabilities, would play a major role in the effort. That was especially true when the Japanese caught much of the Pacific fleet at the docks in Pearl Harbor and, a few days later, at Cavite Naval Base in Manila Harbor, the Philippines. They damaged or destroyed most of the surface ships that were in port at the time at both places.

That meant an engineering officer with Kennedy's experience and his considerable command training would be reassigned to submarines immediately—so long as they were willing to volunteer, of course. Kennedy was.

In March 1941, he was transferred to USS *Narwhal* (SS-167) as her executive officer. *Narwhal* had been the first boat in her class, designated as "V-boats." Her name at commissioning in 1930 was *V-5*, but she was renamed *Narwhal* in the summer of 1931.

She was one of the five submarines sitting at the dock in Pearl Harbor on December 7, 1941. Her crew manned deck guns during the attack and helped to shoot down two Japanese airplanes. She would go on to successfully complete fifteen war patrols and receive fifteen battle stars for her service, despite her tendency to leak oil in prodigious amounts, leaving a slick that was easily spotted from the air. Interestingly, *Narwhal* was one of the largest diesel submarines ever constructed to that point— about 350 feet long and displacing almost 2,800 tons—and thus was often called upon during the war to lay mines and deliver cargo and passengers into dangerous areas.

While Marvin Kennedy was still aboard *Hammann*, and Mush Morton was having kids and taking voyages aboard USS *Fairfax* and the "Nickel Boat," a new class of submarine was laid down (the formal beginning of construction) at Electric Boat Company in Groton, Connecticut. The USS *Gato* (SS-212) was the lead boat in the class, with construction under way in October 1940. (Her sister boat, USS *Drum* (SS-228) was actually laid down a month earlier than the so-called lead boat, and she was the only *Gato*-class boat in commission when the war started. *Gato* was formally placed into commission on New Year's Eve, 1941, more than three weeks after Pearl Harbor.)

The foresight of those in the Navy who recognized the need for this particular brand of submarine must be acknowledged. Visionaries realized that not only would submersibles be essential in a Pacific war, but they also knew those boats would have to be more advanced in every way than the S-boats. Even so, not all in the upper reaches of the Navy were yet convinced. For example, from the beginning, this new variation was dubbed the "fleet submarine," because some still assumed that they would be used to support the regular battle fleet. They were to be primarily defensive in mission, to observe, to attack only if the appropriate opportunity presented itself, and then only to soften up the enemy to prepare them for the ultimate attack by cruisers and battleships.

Certainly some strategic thinkers knew the submarine would eventually serve a broader purpose. Either way, though, everyone agreed that a vessel that had much greater surface speed, more reliability, much more range, and better armament would ultimately be required. Developing such a vessel would not be easy. However, with increased technology and advanced manufacturing capability, the Navy was finally able to begin building the new *Gato* boats in 1940 after a long time of preparation.

Gato was five feet longer than her predecessors (not including the *Narwhal* class, of course), 312 feet, which allowed for the engine room to be divided by watertight bulkheads into two sections for her four big diesel engines. She would be able to operate routinely at 300 feet in depth, 50 feet deeper than previous boats, and could go to about 450 feet deep in an emergency. She would also carry more fuel, allowing the luxury of a typical patrol of 75 days, or 20,000 miles. Again, those who foresaw the Pacific war knew this was enough gas to steam out of Pearl Harbor, operate in the waters around Japan, and return home without a pit stop.

Even though she was a relatively large vessel, *Gato* would eventually be able to submerge completely in less than forty-five seconds. This came after her designers did some experimenting, modified the design, and trained her initial crews on how to quickly pull the stopper and disappear. This was still not quite as quick as the British and German boats could submerge, but everyone agreed it was adequate.

Because of their original purpose—shadowing a fleet of ships—this class of submarine proved to be a better-than-tolerable surface vessel as well. In fact, they maneuvered much better on the surface than when submerged, which put them at odds with the way most submarine skippers were accustomed to operating. Some described them as actually being surface ships that were blessed with the added advantage of being able to disappear if things got too dicey up there.

These boats carried twenty-four torpedoes and could use one of ten torpedo tubes to fire them, six in the forward torpedo room and four aft. They were typically equipped with three deck guns, and the commissioning captain usually had the option—within reason—of what size he preferred from among those available. At the beginning of the war, the vessels most often were commissioned with a three-inch or four-inch fifty-caliber deck gun, but once the captains and their commanders came to more fully appreciate the possibilities of surface assaults, larger, more powerful weapons would be requested and installed. They also typically had one or two antiaircraft guns, and mounting points for additional thirty- or fifty-caliber weapons on their decks.

The *Gato* boats were capable of speeds just over 20 knots (just under 24 miles per hour) on the surface and 8.75 knots (just over 10 miles per hour) while submerged. They came equipped with four diesel engines/ generators and four electric motors that actually turned the submarine's two propellers and shoved them through the water.

Crew habitability for their six to ten officers and up to seventy enlisted men was also a consideration on the *Gato*-class boats. Not only was it assumed that the next war would be fought in great part in tropical climates, but, besides the comfort of the crew, there was another very practical reason for improved air-conditioning systems on these vessels.

Condensation in tropical humidity can wreak havoc on equipment, causing corrosion, shorting of electrical circuits, and even fires. Dehumidifiers that produced air-conditioning in the boat greatly improved the reliability of all systems.

In all, seventy-seven submarines in the *Gato* class—usually pronounced "gate-oh" instead of the Spanish "gah-to"—were built before and during the early months of the war. While eleven more boats were constructed at Electric Boat in Groton after *Gato*, the other sixty-six were built at other locations scattered around the country—Portsmouth, New Hampshire; Mare Island in California; and Manitowoc, Wisconsin. In fact, twenty-eight World War II submarines were built in the Midwest, on Lake Michigan. They were then floated to Chicago, down the Chicago River and the Illinois River to the Mississippi River and on to New Orleans. In order to get beneath the bridges on the way, their periscopes and most of the submarine above the conning tower were left off, shipped separately, and attached once they arrived in New Orleans.

Mare Island Naval Shipyard in Vallejo, California, just up the bay from San Francisco, was a bustling place just before and during the war. Submarines were first built there as far back as 1901. The "yardbirds" employed boats from there to help fight the fires that resulted from the 1906 San Francisco earthquake. The Marine Detachment football team from Mare Island beat a U.S. Army team in the 1918 Rose Bowl. By the first years of World War II, more than fifty thousand people worked at Mare Island, not just building new submarines—primarily all construction there during the war was of submarines and tenders—but repairing, maintaining, and overhauling many vessels in use by the United States and allied nations.

There, on June 28, 1941, construction began on a *Gato*-class submarine that would eventually be dubbed USS *Wahoo*. She would be named after a long blue fish common around Florida and into the Caribbean, prized by sport fishermen for its speed and fight. *Wahoo* would never be dampened by the same waters as her namesake.

Up and down the ways, where the Napa River spilled into San Francisco Bay, sister boats to *Wahoo* were in various stages of assembly under supertight security. Their names read like a roll call of more or less obscure fish. There was even an aquatic mammal thrown in for good measure.

Trigger, Whale, Sunfish, Tunney, Tinosa, Tullibee, Seahorse, Skate.

(Later in the war, the Navy had built so many submarines and would be so desperate for "fish" names for them that they resorted to some very murky designations, including some that are suspected to have been made up completely.)

As *Wahoo* was being built in California and her crew was coming together to get her ready to take her to war, Dudley Morton was still commanding the old *R-5* back on the East Coast, having that one less than spectacular encounter with the German U-boat.

Lieutenant Commander Marvin Kennedy was already in the midst of a much hotter war in the Pacific and—from its very beginnings—in the wardroom of *Narwhal*, second in command to Charles W. "Weary" Wilkins.

Then, in March 1942, Kennedy received orders to report to Mare Island as prospective commander of a new ship. That was indicative of how quickly someone could advance in wartime.

Wahoo would soon be completed, ready for sea trials, and she needed a qualified hand at the helm. With his four years of experience aboard the old S-boats, and now after a year in *Narwhal* and four months of it at war, both the Navy and Pinky Kennedy felt he was ready to have his own boat. He had already earned a reputation as a taut officer, a by-the-book kind of guy who believed in training, training, and more training. Some even described him as a "slave driver." But Kennedy was convinced that a crew had to be ready for anything that might happen out there in the storm of war. The only way to prepare was to drill the crew on every possible scenario. And then evaluate the results and drill on it again until it was perfect every time.

He was considered very technically astute, a solid engineer who understood every nuance of every system on his boat. He was excited about getting into his new submarine. He could not wait to see her piping, wiring, and propulsion systems, to study the manuals and diagrams until he knew it all backward and forward. And to drill his crew until they were just as informed about their vessel as their "old man" was. Their "old man" who was, by then, thirty-six years old.

Of course, Kennedy had no way of anticipating the group of strong personalities he would have in his wardroom once he got there. (The wardroom is the compartment on a vessel where officers gather to eat meals and socialize. "Wardroom" is the term typically used to refer to a ship's complement of officers.) Just as the enlisted men had no say in who their officers would be, few skippers had much input into choosing the men who would help them run a boat.

Later, some of the more powerful personalities would assume a more active role in handpicking the officers they wanted. Not at that point, though. Not Pinky Kennedy. And not with *Wahoo*. Most all of them were there when he showed up.

Nor did Kennedy know that the strongest personality of all would soon be taking a cruise on *Wahoo*. He would be there at the invitation of the U.S. Navy, joining Kennedy, his officers, and his crew for a tense, fateful ride during his new submarine's second run.

When that hitchhiker came aboard, everything would change.

CHAPTER 5

Ingredients in the Stew

"Four years together by the bay where Severn joins the tide,
Then by the service called away we're scattered far and wide.
Yet still when two or three shall meet and old tales be retold,
From low to highest in the Fleet, we'll pledge the Blue and Gold!"

—From the third verse of "Navy Blue and Gold,"
the U.S. Naval Academy alma mater

*T*he USS Argonaut (SS-166), like her sister V-boat, Pinky Kennedy's Narwhal, did not enjoy the benefit of adequate air-conditioning. That not only made life aboard her miserable for her crew members, but the nagging condensation caused almost continuous electrical shorts and ground faults. Often it seemed as if it were raining inside the hull of the massive submarine. Mold grew from every surface, laundry was musty, and sweat did not evaporate from clothes or skin. The men were perpetually in bad moods and suffering from colds and chills, even when the atmosphere inside her hull was hot and humid.

That was only one reason that "Dick" O'Kane was looking forward to relinquishing his spot on the old boat, even though he had just been moved up to become her executive officer, second in command. *Argonaut* was the first submarine Richard Hetherington O'Kane, a 1934 graduate of the U.S. Naval Academy, had served aboard. He had joined her in 1938 from duty in the surface Navy.

O'Kane was excited about going to submarines. He was of the opinion that this was where he wanted to spend the rest of his career. He was convinced, too, that the submarine could be used in a much different way than previously assumed and be far more effective in punching the enemy.

Besides, his interests were in navigation and tactics, and in his estimation, the smaller, more maneuverable submersibles offered better opportunity in those areas than did lumbering, big-crewed surface ships.

Argonaut was patrolling off Midway on December 7, 1941, when the crew received word of the Japanese attack on Pearl Harbor. Later that evening, they clearly heard two Japanese destroyers pounding the naval base on Midway Island with artillery.

With O'Kane serving as diving officer, *Argonaut* made what turned out to be the first submarine sonar approach on an enemy warship in World War II. Since she was not a true attack submarine, and was woefully ill equipped in just about every way to stalk, aim, and shoot at a target as nimble as a destroyer, she was not able to do much more than take a look. Then, when the Japanese got wind of their presence, they had no choice but to dive and run away to hide.

That night was the lowest point in Dick O'Kane's time in submarines to that point. He would carry the frustration with him the rest of his career, using it as a catalyst for how he would employ his better-equipped vessels in the future. And he would do so spectacularly.

O'Kane knew that the new boats they were building back home were far superior. Even though *Argonaut* was his first boat and had been built not far from where he was born and raised in New Hampshire, he was ready to move on to something that gave him at least a fighting chance. No more watching impotently as the enemy launched shells on an American facility. No more running and hiding without even firing a shot of his own.

Now, with the Midway debacle behind them, he had orders in hand to ride the old V-boat back to Mare Island. There she would get some much-needed refurbishing, including replacement diesel engines and one of the new torpedo data computers (TDC).

O'Kane would not be around, though. He was to ship over to new construction. To a *Gato*-class boat named *Wahoo*.

The biggest worry on the way from Pearl Harbor to San Francisco Bay was not the Japanese. It was friendly aircraft. Recognition codes were often not updated or were misunderstood. There were too many gun-happy pilots who were quick to fire on anything in the sea that looked like a submarine. *Argonaut* was up and down like a yo-yo, ducking from any aircraft they encountered, trying to avoid a potentially deadly friend-or-foe challenge. They bobbed all the way until they picked up a destroyer escort thirty miles out that took them safely into San Francisco Bay.

Then, midmorning on February 22, 1942, just after passing beneath the Golden Gate Bridge, Dick O'Kane was rewarded with a remarkable sight. They steamed right past USS *Wahoo*, out on one of her early trial runs.

She was a beautiful ship! O'Kane told one of his shipmates she was a "dandy-looking submarine." Soon he would be aboard her, taking her to war, and his opinion of her would not change.

With her XO in town, the legend of *Wahoo* was just beginning. Others who would be a major part of it all were gathering, too.

George Grider, who was to become *Wahoo*'s third officer, was another one who almost had his naval career derailed before it even began. He was on the verge of not qualifying academically to get into the Naval Academy. He was up for appointment on a technicality in the first place. Grider received his appointment because his father was killed in World War I. However, he had trouble passing the entrance exams. Like Dudley Morton, he had attended a prep school. That prepared him to retake the exams, and this time he squeaked by. No one gave him much of a chance in the challenging academic atmosphere of the academy, though.

Once at Annapolis, however, the Memphis, Tennessee, native made the most of the education he was offered there. He not only became captain of the water polo team and served as editor of the academy's humor magazine, the *Log*, but he was also class vice president, and received a letter of commendation from the academy's superintendent. The skinny, blond-haired Southerner had a sunny nature, enjoyed a joke, and was very popular with others in the "brotherhood of the blue and gold," the men who had attended the academy. And he managed to make himself a very good student as well.

Like Mush Morton, Pinky Kennedy, Dick O'Kane, and many others, Grider graduated from the academy and spent time on surface ships before coming to submarines. In Grider's case, that move to submersibles happened in 1939, when he volunteered for the Silent Service.

His first boat was USS *Skipjack* (SS-184), based on the West Coast. Again, despite his early academic challenges, Grider proved to be an exceptional engineering officer with a gift for using the sonar listening gear to its maximum effectiveness. The former mediocre student even taught at the Navy's West Coast Sound School in San Diego. The guy who had gotten into the academy on a technicality emerged to become one of the brighter young officers in the Navy.

Then came Pearl Harbor.

Though he was not even thirty years old yet, George Grider was pulled out of his assignment in the classroom at the sound school on March 2, 1942. He was ordered to travel up the coast to Mare Island to help get a new boat—USS *Wahoo*—ready for war. He was more than ready to go. Submarines and the reliance they necessarily had on sonar had already caught his fancy. He was fascinated by the slippery diving boats and the quickly emerging technology that was sure to make them a formidable weapon.

Once he knew what he would be doing in the war effort, the young officer made it a point to engage in conversation anyone he encountered along the way who had already been to war. He asked questions, grilling those who would talk for every detail they were willing to share about the boats. Some began avoiding him, crossing the street, sitting at the other end of the bar, so they would not have to answer questions about systems and equipment from the skinny, curious young officer with the Southern drawl.

But the ones who did take the time were prepping another of the men who would contribute so mightily to the legend of *Wahoo*.

Roger Paine was a Navy brat, the son of a rear admiral. He had been born in Texas but moved with his family at the whim of the military throughout his early years, attending high school in California and Washington, D.C. He received his appointment to the academy from the District of Columbia in 1935 and graduated from Annapolis in 1939.

His first ship out of school was a battleship, and one that would have an ominous place in history. It was the USS *Arizona* (BB-39), the best-known of the vessels that would be destroyed at Pearl Harbor a year and a half later, and with a loss of life of almost twelve hundred men. Paine had left her by then, though, headed for a new adventure. He had opted to go to Connecticut and sub school.

Paine's first submarine out of New London was USS *Pompano* (SS-181). Though relatively new compared to the first boats of the other *Wahoo* officers—her keel had been laid down in January 1936 and she was launched in March 1937—the *Dolphin*-class boat was hardly state-of-the-art.

Paine reported for duty in April 1941 as her communications, radar, and sound officer. He was aboard the *Pompano* as she steamed away on a routine run from Mare Island, bound for Pearl Harbor in early December. Along the way, the crew got the awful news about what had happened at their destination. Still, they were not ready for what they saw when they arrived in Hawaii shortly after the Japanese attack. Paine and the rest of the *Pompano* crew were stunned by the devastation all around them.

If there had been any doubts from the cryptic radio messages they had received, it was now all too clear: They and their boat were at war.

Pompano made hasty preparations and was readied for departure again only eleven days later. Her routine run to Hawaii was extended into her first war patrol.

The first action Paine and his submarine saw was almost catastrophic and came from an unexpected quarter. *Pompano* came under fire from friendly aircraft—or what should have been friendly, anyway—off the decks of the aircraft carrier USS *Enterprise* (CV-6). The carrier had been out of port when the Japanese attack occurred and was steaming back to Pearl Harbor at the time. The pilots, who were understandably keyed up, mistook *Pompano* for a Japanese I-boat and launched an attack. She was not damaged, but her crew was shaken.

Despite mechanical problems and continual trouble with their torpedoes inexplicably missing their targets or failing to explode if they hit, *Pompano* managed to claim sinking one enemy ship, estimated to be a sixteen-thousand-ton vessel. Postwar records would take that "kill" away for lack of or conflicting evidence.

When he returned to Pearl Harbor from the patrol at the end of January, Paine learned that his first run on *Pompano* would also be his last. The Navy was reassigning him "to new construction" that was almost complete, ready for sea trials. He was on his way back to Mare Island. The Navy had also promoted him to the rank of lieutenant (junior grade).

His orders were to leave Hawaii on March 4 to report to *Wahoo* as her first gunnery and torpedo officer. There was a minor distraction, though. His wife was due to deliver their first child on March 1. As much as he wanted to get to his new boat, Paine wanted nothing more than to be with his wife and to welcome his new child into the world.

To hurry things along, he and his wife, Bebe, took strenuous hikes up and down Hawaii's volcanic hills. It worked. Their son actually made his entrance early, born six days before Paine flew away toward the mainland and his new assignment. Not only did he get to visit with Roger Paine III for a few days before he left, but he also became the first of her new officers to actually set foot aboard *Wahoo*.

So several key members of the new vessel's crew were aboard at Mare Island, already at work getting her ready for battle. However, there was still the matter of who was going to skipper this new warship.

Dick O'Kane—who took time to resettle his wife, Ernestine, and kids in California after they had been whisked away from Hawaii—was the first senior officer to show up for duty on the new vessel, just after Paine arrived. He found plenty to do, getting her ready, welcoming the rest of the officers, getting to know the dispositions and specialties of new crew members as they came over from wherever they had been before.

It was always interesting when a crew came together on a new boat, more so than just when replacements relieved crew members when a seasoned boat came to port. This was an entirely new crew, not just ten or twenty men. The eventual personality and capability of the boat was formed by the forced mixture of ingredients that made up the stew.

Often the officers knew one another, or at least knew one another by reputation. That could lead to tension or to teamwork. The enlisted men might or might not have run across their new shipmates in previous duty or at sub school, or more likely in a bar somewhere. It was always a hoot when sailors who had brawled against one another were forced to share the same bunk space. Sometimes bygones were bygones. Sometimes old wounds festered.

With the help of one of the enlisted men, radioman James Buckley, Dick O'Kane went right to work, cobbling together a rough target-bearing transmitter (TBT), an instrument that had not yet been installed on the new boat. The TBT was a binocular device that allowed an officer on the submarine's bridge to sight a potential target and automatically relay bearing information to instruments in the boat's conning tower. This was invaluable when doing the complicated geometry necessary to align the submarine for an attack on a fast-moving target. It was especially useful at night, the time when a submarine was most likely to stalk a target on the surface.

There was a reason *Wahoo*'s new XO was so determined to create the TBT. O'Kane was still seething from his previous experience off Midway. He was certain that if *Argonaut* had been equipped with such a device— even a home brew one like the one he and his radioman had contrived— she might have been able to do some damage, to wreak some blessed revenge on those destroyers they encountered the night of the Pearl Harbor attack. That episode continued to stick in his craw, and he was determined to be prepared next time.

But even as he kept busy with his various duties, O'Kane had one big concern: Who would be the captain for whom he would be the right hand?

It seemed to be taking a long time, and there was considerable conjecture. Scuttlebutt was that Duncan MacMillan, the XO on *Argonaut*, would get the helm of *Wahoo*. Even the captain of the Navy Yard told O'Kane that would be the case when the new XO paid him a visit on his first day at Mare Island. It was a done deal. But official word was slow in coming.

Though older than many of the other officers, MacMillan was experienced and appeared to be a good leader of men. O'Kane and the other officers agreed they would be fine with him as their boss.

But as it turned out, MacMillan had unique abilities that were required elsewhere. He held an advanced degree in engineering, specializing in engine mechanics; instead of having him man the bridge of *Wahoo*, the Navy dispatched him to Beloit, Wisconsin, the home of the Fairbanks Morse company. The company was a longtime manufacturer of diesel engines for railroad locomotives, but they had come up with a solid engine design that fit very well the precise needs of the newer submarines. The Navy wanted MacMillan to go to Wisconsin and help win the war by supervising the manufacture of those big diesels for their submersible fleet.

Word finally came that the skipper would, instead, be Marvin Kennedy. Dick O'Kane told the other officers that he felt good about that choice. Though he heard Kennedy had spent time at the staff level—and such desk duty was a potential negative—O'Kane knew that Kennedy had also served as XO on *Narwhal*. She was an almost identical sister to O'Kane's previous boat, *Argonaut*.

Kennedy had something else going for him, too—he had already been to war aboard *Narwhal*. That meant that he was not strictly a desk jockey, like so many of the other new skippers. His reputation was that he was a tough guy who believed in training his crew well, and that he was about as knowledgeable in the technical aspects of his boat as any skipper around. All of that sounded positive to *Wahoo*'s XO.

Regardless, O'Kane, in his usual reconnoitering style, decided that he would do what he did in any situation. He would meet his new CO, gather data, assess the situation, and then do what he had to do to make the most of it.

O'Kane was already openly anticipating his own command. His plan was to not only be an asset to *Wahoo* but to learn all he could—from his captain, from the other officers with whom he served, and even from the chiefs and other enlisted men who brought their own experiences and talents to the boat—in preparation for the day when he had his own submarine beneath him.

Meanwhile, across the continent from Mare Island, Mush Morton was finishing up another turn at sub school in New London. Though he had done little to distinguish himself during his time as commander on *R-5*, and had even gotten negative marks for the aborted U-boat incident, he was in a group of officers obviously destined to lead the submarine squadrons to war in the Pacific. The Navy needed all of them it could get.

In June of 1942, Morton received orders to report to Pearl Harbor "for duty as prospective commanding officer and on board a submarine of Squadron Four." He knew better than anybody that he was ready for battle. Despite his limited wartime submarine experience, he was not lacking in confidence. He had been thinking a great deal about what it took to be successful in a submarine. He read, studied, and talked with other submariners and instructors at the school. He studied the patrol reports that were already being sent back, fresh off the boats that were actually fighting the war out there.

But something nagged at him. Much of what was written and taught and put into practice made little sense to him in the context of what the next generation of submarines would be capable of doing. Even in *R-5*, he got a little taste of it, and the thoughts had begun to coalesce in his head into a set of radical theories.

The books were too conservative. The old-line officers had the wrong ideas about how to run a submarine, how to aggressively attack and sink enemy ships. The submarine force would never be a major factor in the war by doing it the way it had always been done.

As the war geared up, Morton developed an even stronger hatred for the enemy. Those who knew him and served with him at the time were sometimes shocked by the vehemence of his comments about the Japs. He had actually fired at Germans already, but the full force of his hatred was clearly aimed at the Japanese.

The Japanese were almost always portrayed negatively and stereotypically in newspapers and movies of the time, drawn or written about in ways that would be considered patently racist today. The writers, cartoonists, and filmmakers usually rendered the enemy in a way that made them easier to dehumanize and hate: with buckteeth and eyes exaggeratedly slanted, short in stature, and with voices gratingly high-pitched and nasal. It was simply another way America focused its anger and dislike at someone most of them hardly knew. Japanese culture, the reasons for the attacks on American ships, the motivation for brutally initiating war against the United States—these were not easily understood by the average citizen.

To Morton, there was nothing to understand. It was cut-and-dried, and he had a very specific job to do. The U.S.A. was good. The Japanese empire and everyone in it were evil.

The Japanese had started a war against his country. They were, as of December 7 and his commander in chief's and Congress's declarations, the enemy. He was trained to wage war on the enemy, regardless of who it might be. It could have been the Germans, the Russians, even the Canadians. It just happened to be the Japanese.

He was supposed to kill the enemy if possible. If not, he was supposed to make him suffer, and deny him whatever he needed to wage war against America and Americans.

If that meant sinking freighters to deny the enemy raw materials, then so be it. Sinking fishing boats so soldiers would not have fish to eat, fine. The crews of those freighters and fishing boats were as much combatants as bomber pilots and battleship captains. They provided oil to fuel bombers, battleships, and submarines, food to feed soldiers who were sniping at American Marines. The enemy had a better chance of prolonging the war and winning it, and they would claim more American lives in the process, if that oil or those fish reached the Home Islands or enemy-held territory.

President Roosevelt had called for unrestricted naval warfare against the Japanese. While Morton tried to keep *R-5* afloat, he vowed that he would take the most literal definition of "unrestricted" when he had the opportunity, the crew, and the submarine to do it.

He was convinced that if he could get on the bridge of a *Balao* or *Gato* boat, he could strike a mighty blow against the "sonza bitches"—that was the tag he had hung on the Japanese—who had launched such a brutal and underhanded pair of lightning strikes at Pearl Harbor and Manila.

Mush Morton thought and talked often of the men who had died in Hawaii and in the Philippines. He continued to hear reports of atrocities the Japanese were committing in the Philippines, China, and around the Pacific. They were similar to the ones he'd heard from James Avent and his friends in Tsingtao while he was courting Harriet.

Those were places he associated with better, more pleasurable times, associated with his friends, his shipmates, his wife, his in-laws. His home near Manila, where he raised fighting cocks in the backyard and the bars he frequented near Cavite. Tsingtao, now in Japanese hands, where he had raised the American flag over the pretty harbor below the ancient city. Where he took his nieces and nephew to visit the ships on which he so proudly served with his shipmates. Where he spent enjoyable time with people who now had a Japanese boot on their throats.

But before he would get the opportunity to punish those who had stirred up this storm in the first place, before he would be given the helm of one of the new boats, Mush Morton had a date with a dirty, dangerously slow submarine. The result of that experience would come very close to derailing his submarine career completely, even as it galvanized his resolve to "kill the sonza bitches."

In the summer of 1942, the man who would eventually become the first submarine ace of World War II—the man who would rewrite the book on submarine warfare—would find himself only a fortuitous handshake away from getting bum-rushed off submarines for good.

CHAPTER 6

The Ineffective Fleet

"I like the way that Mush Morton shakes hands."

—Submarine squadron commander
John Herbert "Babe" Brown

A *merica's submarine war against Japan was going poorly.*
At the beginning of the war, the commander of the Pacific submarine force was Rear Admiral Thomas Withers Jr., who had assumed the position in January 1941. Withers had cut his teeth on submarines in World War I, and had commanded the old S- and K-boats during peacetime. So far, though, he had little experience with the fleet submarines.

Though he had been an early proponent of a slightly more aggressive style of submarine warfare, Withers was still an advocate of attacking enemy ships while submerged, as opposed to making surface approaches and using weapons mounted on the submarines' decks. Even though German U-boats were proving the value of surface attacks in the Atlantic—with distressing results, often within sight of the shoreline of the United States—neither Withers nor others in the submarine force saw the need for such tactics by U.S. boats.

He ordered all boats under his command to practice diving, and instructed captains to take their vessels to "test depth" at least once on every patrol. Test depth is considered to be the deepest point to which a submarine can safely dive before it risks being damaged or destroyed by the inevitable and relentless pressure of seawater. Withers maintained that submarines were made to submerge and should stay submerged as much as possible.

Withers's insistence on submerged attacks was partly due to a strong belief that enemy aircraft were by far the greatest threat to submarines. He made it a point to take his skippers up in an airplane and fly over a submerged vessel. In the clear waters of the Pacific, a submarine well over a hundred feet deep could typically be seen from the air. He even had aircraft drop practice bombs—called "firecracker bombs"—on boats to powerfully demonstrate the danger of sub-hunting aircraft.

Wolf packs, effectively employed by U-boats, were not considered prudent by the American submarine command, primarily because of the early success by Allied code breakers. Submarines operating in packs required extensive communication among themselves, both to coordinate attacks and to keep from shooting one another. Based on the success Allied code breakers were having already in deciphering the give-and-take among the German wolf packs, the Navy brass stubbornly refused to allow American submarines to operate that way. Boats should work alone and maintain radio silence.

Problems with the exploders on torpedoes also hindered American efforts. The exploder is the device on the nose of a torpedo that arms itself after being ejected from the submarine's torpedo tube, then causes the weapon to explode when it hits or runs near the desired target. The new Mark VI magnetic exploder was touted as the biggest technical advance in torpedoes yet. Though testing was minimal and few really understood the proper way to arm, repair, and use them against the enemy, they had replaced the older Mark V contact exploder on many torpedoes by the time the war started. Not only would they prove to be disastrously unreliable, but reports of their ineffectiveness tended to fall on deaf ears. Those submarine skippers who complained too much were relieved and sent to other duty. Submariners, and not their torpedoes, were blamed for all those misses.

In the early months of 1942, there appeared to be little effective submarine strategy in place. The operations of whatever boats were available seemed as scattered as the submarines themselves. Only seventeen war patrols departed Pearl Harbor during the first three months of the year. Boats tended to be sent to areas where enemy antisubmarine activity was most concentrated, all in the hopes that this indicated worthwhile activity. Commanders gave great credence to intercepted top-secret Japanese communications and sent boats off on what turned out to be fruitless missions. Skippers were already grousing about the dismal performance of the Mark VI exploders. However, even when they received reports that the Germans had abandoned their own magnetic exploders, the Navy brass still refused to acknowledge there was a problem.

Finally, Admiral Withers was relieved and sent back east, to command the naval yard at Portsmouth, New Hampshire. While it was portrayed as a normal change of command, most assumed it was because of the way the submarine war had started. The final straw revolved around the Japanese aircraft carrier *Shokaku*, which had been damaged in the Battle of the Coral Sea. Even though she had been spotted and reported by nine Pearl Harbor–based submarines, not one had even managed to get off a shot at the wounded vessel.

Withers's relief was Robert Henry English, but he, too, was a longtime staff officer and not all that popular with the submarine skippers he would lead. Like his predecessor, he, too, stubbornly maintained that there were no problems with the torpedoes.

Things did not get much better. Twenty-five submarines were sent to intercept the Japanese fleet near Midway, some of which were possibly damaged from one of the pivotal battles of the early war. However, orders about what to do when they got to the area were slow to come and often contradictory. Only two American submarines spotted elements of the fleet. One of them started but did not press an attack, getting off only two torpedoes, and neither one of them hit anything. Then she ran away and went deep. The second submarine did mount an aggressive assault and, even though they were under fire and came under a depth-charge pounding, still managed to get into position and fire off four torpedoes.

None of them did any damage. One never left the tube of the old tub when it was fired. One missed, running ahead of its target. Another also missed, passing just astern. The fourth torpedo was dead-on, striking the target vessel amidships.

It was a dud. Other than its making a resounding clunk, nothing happened.

Meanwhile, Pinky Kennedy was busy preparing *Wahoo* and its crew. True to his reputation, Kennedy pushed his men hard—officers and enlisted men alike. He was a perfectionist and would not tolerate any mistakes, making the crew perform the training over and over until they had it down pat. They had practiced scores of torpedo attacks, lining up against "enemy" vessels that zigged and zagged crazily, employing the complicated geometry necessary for a submarine to attack a surface ship, using the TDC to absolute perfection, and successfully shooting off dummy fish that would have sunk many of the targets had they been real. Throughout it all, Marvin Kennedy's tactics and test results were impressive.

Despite their later differences, each of the officers in Kennedy's wardroom would insist that the training they received and the drills they performed in those first weeks on *Wahoo* would stand the crew in good stead later, when it mattered most.

They would not be as appreciative of some of Kennedy's other methods and ideas. But they were finally on their way, leaving Mare Island on August 12, 1942, waving up at family members who had gathered on the Golden Gate Bridge to bid them farewell.

Mush Morton was also getting ready to take a submarine to war in the Pacific. But it was not to be a *Gato* boat. And there was not to be a PCO cruise after all. His next command would be as skipper of USS *Dolphin* (SS-169).

The *Dolphin* had been the result of early development efforts to concoct a better fleet submarine. She was considered a V-boat, like her predecessors, including *Narwhal* and *Argonaut*, but was actually an odd variant, not quite as large as those behemoths but with a new set of engines developed and manufactured by the Navy specifically for this type of submarine. She was launched with high expectations in 1932, but experienced nagging problems from the very beginning.

The specially designed engines, despite being much too big for the boat's cramped hull, had proved to be woefully inadequate, underpowered, and unreliable, leaving the *Dolphin* unable to keep up with the surface ships she was asked to protect. She spent so much time in various Navy yards undergoing repairs that she and her crew became the butt of many jokes.

Still, the Navy was adamant about getting the most from the investment. After spending most of her life based on the West Coast, *Dolphin* made Pearl Harbor her home port in 1937. That was where she was sitting on the morning of December 7, 1941. Despite her poor design, she struck an early blow in the war completely out of desperation, but not with her torpedoes.

As with her half sister boat *Narwhal*, *Dolphin*'s crew manned her deck guns during the attack, firing furiously at airplanes in the sky above Pearl Harbor. According to the official action report, they believed they shot down at least one Japanese aircraft and maybe a second.

When Mush Morton first laid eyes on his new boat, his stomach fell. True to his nature, he let everybody who would listen hear his complaints. She was rusty, dirty, smelled awful, and needed a long list of repairs. There was, to Morton's way of thinking, no chance that those fixes would be enough to make her good in battle.

He had already heard the stories from her first two wartime patrols. *Dolphin* had steamed thousands of miles, yet she had claimed possible damage to only a single ship. On her first patrol, her captain reported seventeen major mechanical failures and eighteen minor ones. The skipper had what was then termed "a nervous breakdown" and was relieved of duty and shipped back to the mainland to recover. He would ultimately spend time in a mental hospital.

The captain on the second patrol headed straight for the infirmary when *Dolphin* docked upon returning to Pearl Harbor, seriously ill with bronchial pneumonia. He blamed it on the damp, musty environment inside his submarine. Much of that patrol had been spent trying to work around a serious fuel leak, distracting the crew from their real goal out there in the middle of the war.

As Morton studied the work orders and visited the yard to see how repairs were coming along on *Dolphin*, he came to a firm conclusion. When his new executive officer, Carter Bennett, reported for duty, Mush looked him right in the eye and told him exactly how he saw things.

"This old bucket is a death trap," Morton said. "I'm going to do my damnedest to get off her and I advise you to do the same."

But Morton had no luck. His commander pointedly told him to stop grousing and get *Dolphin* and her crew ready for her next patrol. The Navy needed every submarine that would float.

Morton gritted his teeth and did as he was told. Then one day, when he brought the submarine in from drills, the division commander, John Haines, happened to get a look at her. The boss was hardly happy with what he saw. Already displeased with Morton's open and well-known desire to give up command of one of his boats—one of the few Haines had at his disposal to fight a brutal war—the commander called in the young officer and did all but fire him on the spot.

Mush Morton's career in submarines was dead in the water.

"Your boat is filthy, and frankly, I don't think you are capable of running her," he told Morton. "From what I see of *Dolphin* and your record on your previous boat, I do not believe you are cut out to be in submarines, Lieutenant."

Haines relieved Morton of his command of *Dolphin* and asked the yeoman to prepare the paperwork to ship him out of submarines and back to duty on a surface vessel.

There are differing reports on exactly what happened next. Several superior officers went to bat for Morton, but it was John Brady, Admiral English's operations officer, who apparently went to Haines's boss, John "Babe" Brown, to see if he could save Morton and keep him in submarines. Brown agreed to have a chat with the brash and brutally honest lieutenant commander and see if he could glean one good reason why he should counter his division commander's decision.

Apparently Brown and Morton hit it off immediately. When Morton bounded into Brown's office, a grin on his face, he grabbed the senior commander's hand in his own big mitt and gave it a solid shake. We can only assume that Morton knew this was his last and only chance to continue his career in submarines, and he apparently turned up the wattage on his famous charm. Brown was also a big, genial fellow, and the two of them had other interests in common. Brown was a former football star and coach at the Naval Academy and knew everything about the games during the time Morton was on the gridiron at Annapolis.

There was one defining thing that kept Mush Morton in the submarine service. At least according to Babe Brown.

"I liked the way Morton shook hands," Brown reported later.

Brown intervened on Morton's behalf, taking him out of *Dolphin* and putting him back in the PCO pool.

Dolphin, meanwhile, steamed off for frigid waters off Alaska, under the command of her previous skipper, the one who got pneumonia and put Mush Morton into his unfortunate and near-career-wrecking position. There, while approaching Dutch Harbor for still more repairs, she narrowly escaped a harrowing torpedo attack. Her skipper later reported, "I hit the bridge just in time to see two parallel torpedo tracks. We threadneedled them and got out fast." When she ultimately returned to Pearl Harbor after that northerly patrol, the Navy finally decided *Dolphin* would best contribute to the war effort in other ways. She became a training boat out of Pearl Harbor and later went back to New London for similar duty.

At about the same time Mush Morton was settling in Hawaii and preparing for command of a Pacific submarine—August 1942—USS *Wahoo* had also arrived in Pearl Harbor and had begun several days of refitting and sea trials, making final preparations for her first war patrol.

The crew of *Wahoo*, long since tired of drilling, practicing, and answering their captain's pointed questions about the tiniest details, were more than ready to get to war. Dive-bombers, depth charges, and enemy destroyers seemed a better option than all that rehearsing and practicing and interminable drilling.

On August 23, exactly five days before Mush Morton was ordered to assume command of *Dolphin*, *Wahoo* backed away from the pier at Pearl Harbor. As a final good-bye, once they were a safe distance from shore, Kennedy ordered the standard trim dive (a maneuver to test the various tanks on the boat and to check for leaks). During that dive, their escort gave them a little going-away present: two "indoctrinational depth charges"—practice depth charges.

Many of the crew had already experienced a similar event while conducting sea trials off San Diego, but this all-too-real demonstration was to give several new crew members who had joined *Wahoo* in Hawaii— including two officers—a taste of what they might get when they arrived out there in the real war. The "minor" explosions—well over a hundred yards away—still managed to rattle everyone's fillings.

Then Kennedy brought the submarine back to the surface, pointed her bow westward, and set off for their assigned patrol area, plying the beautiful green Pacific waters at a brisk fourteen knots. With foam bracketing her bow, *Wahoo* headed for the war.

CHAPTER 7

Opportunities to Attack

"We did not enjoy the captain's full confidence."

—Dick O'Kane, XO, USS *Wahoo*

Wahoo *had a lot going for her. The new boat had assembled what appeared to be a fine crew, including a relatively experienced war-time skipper who knew her systems and capabilities inside and out. George Grider was her engineering officer, based on his seniority and experience. Roger Paine, though younger than most of the other officers, had the most combat experience and had worked with the torpedo data computer on his previous boat,* Pompano, *so it was natural that he be the torpedo and gunnery officer. Lieutenant (JG) Chandler Jackson had come aboard as communication and commissary officer, and all who met the young University of Wisconsin graduate liked him. Dick O'Kane, the XO, was clearly a take-charge leader, destined for his own command soon, and seemed to inspire confidence among the officers and crew.*

The enlisted men consisted of the usual duke's mixture of experienced submariners and novices. Roger Paine knew exactly who he wanted to be chief of the boat (COB), the key enlisted man and an important member of the crew. The COB during Paine's stint on *Pompano* had been Chief Torpedoman's Mate Russell Rau, who was now aboard *Wahoo*. Even before he was named COB, Rau busied himself organizing crew assignments and watch stations. The crew had already nicknamed him "Pappy," and it stuck.

While awaiting the arrival of the new CO back at Mare Island, Dick O'Kane had personally greeted each crew member when he reported aboard. He visited with the men throughout the boat, learning all he could about each. He knew the chief petty officers (CPOs) were the real backbone of any naval vessel. They were the more experienced enlisted men and had undergone training and peer review as a precursor to being designated as chiefs.

He was especially impressed with Chief Electrician's Mate Norman Ware and Chief Machinist's Mate Andy Lennox. Ware would be responsible for the complicated control cubicle, located in the maneuvering room. This was the center from which all the power from the diesel generators was meted out to the electric motors and to the storage batteries. The equipment used an amazing array of levers and rheostats that were mounted on a console. The men working there manipulated those knobs and levers in a way that was truly a fascinating dance to watch.

O'Kane left from his visit with Ware assured the vital "heart" of the boat was in good hands.

He was equally reassured after spending time with Lennox. The machinist's mate had just returned from school at Fairbanks Morse, the manufacturer of the four big diesel engines that were installed on *Wahoo*. Lennox also had ten years of experience, and that was an exceedingly valuable commodity out there where they were going. There would be no nearby tender to take care of them if something went haywire in their propulsion system.

From what O'Kane was learning about the assembled crew, *Wahoo* was blessed with a good core group. They would have the new guys fresh out of sub school whipped into shape in no time.

But O'Kane and the other officers would soon begin to wonder about their new CO. They were a bit put off by Kennedy's demeanor from the very beginning. He seemed more formal, stiff, and aloof than some of the others they had met before. Quite often and for good reason, the submarine service dispensed with many of the trappings of military primness. Because of the close working conditions, the constant danger, and the relatively small size of the crews, things seemed to work far smoother if a little less spit and polish were applied. Discipline and attention to duty remained, of course, but when the hatch cover was closed and the boat made its first trim dive, much of the formality of the military was left topside.

It did not take long for O'Kane to have other doubts about their new leader, and it was more than just his being such a stickler for detail and his overblown and intense training methods.

After only a few days of working with his crew, Pinky Kennedy issued a series of odd commands that caused his officers to look at one another and shake their heads—behind the CO's back, of course.

First he ordered that the new Kleinschmidt stills, which O'Kane had admired and was anxious to test, were not to be used. Kennedy felt they required too much electricity, which took precious fuel to generate, and thus were a waste. These were a greatly improved version of devices designed to distill clean water from seawater, producing all that was needed for bathing and washing clothes. They could provide 750 gallons a day, more than enough water necessary for a typical patrol. The submarine came equipped with washing machines and showers, but without the water from the stills, they could not be used.

It would not have been proper protocol for the officers to question Kennedy about the decision. Instead, the crew got busy following the captain's directions, installing tanks to catch the water that evaporated from the air-conditioning units aboard. Buckets were placed in the officers' staterooms and in strategic spots in the crew quarters and were to be kept filled from the distillate tanks. No showers were to be taken. Only sponge baths. Clothes were to be worn dirty. They could be washed at the end of the patrol.

Next, Kennedy surprised them by ordering that all lights in the boat be replaced with red lightbulbs. He reasoned that red lighting would protect the night vision of the boat's lookouts or anyone else who had to go topside after dusk. Pappy Rau located a half dozen cases of bulbs and set about replacing the perfectly good white ones. The crew grumbled quietly about having to eat red mashed potatoes and red dinner rolls. They even had to craft some special playing cards to be able to tell the red suits from the black. But there were more serious ramifications.

"Captain, I see a little problem here," O'Kane finally told Kennedy.

"What's that, XO?"

"I'm sure you know that dangerous navigational areas are marked on our charts in red. We are not going to be able to see those with the red lighting."

Kennedy scratched his chin, thought awhile, and then reluctantly agreed to allow a single white bulb in the ship's office. But even then, he required a trip switch on the doorway so the white light went out anytime the door to the office was opened.

Another problem popped up, and it could have been quite serious. During a practice dive, the magazine flood valve—whose handle was painted red—was accidentally opened, partially flooding the compartment. Kennedy remained passive when told of the incident, but grudgingly agreed to allow a small white light in each compartment.

The captain also ordered that large, poster-size pictures of various Japanese ships be hung throughout the boat. His theory was that this would allow lookouts and others to learn to recognize enemy ships by class so they would be better able to report what they were seeing. The chance of anyone getting a view as close as the posters offered was minute, though, and the crew members snickered at the posters or drew rude pictures on them.

Sea trials had gone well, though, from San Francisco Bay to the California coast and on to Hawaii. The officers now tried to put their concerns aside as they began their first war patrol. The solemnness of the good-bye from Pearl Harbor, the pride of finally being able to head out to avenge the death and destruction that was all around them, and the excitement of finally going off to strike a blow against the enemy seemed to override any qualms anyone had about their skipper. He had done well in their sea trials, so they could live with his quirks if he led them to do enough damage out there.

As they proceeded toward their patrol area amid the Caroline Islands group in the South Pacific, Dick O'Kane had come to a realization that was more than a bit worrisome to him. Between the wars, the Navy had decided that submarine commanders needed a broader background and sent them off for surface or staff duty. Now, once the war had started, it often happened that skippers had less "bridge time" in submarines than did their XOs, who had started half a decade later and spent almost all their time in subs. While they may have been adept at tactics and understood all aspects of naval warfare, the commanders who were running the boats at the start of the war were not so familiar with the day-to-day operations of the modern submarines. Kennedy had already demonstrated symptoms of that ignorance with the red lightbulbs, his refusal to allow use of the distillers, and many other minor but puzzling pronouncements.

He had also irritated O'Kane with several decisions that seemed to undermine his XO, such as creating watch lists for the crew, a job normally handled by the executive officer. That included naming a totally inexperienced sailor as assistant navigator without even discussing the appointment with O'Kane, and then instructing his XO to train the young seaman. Kennedy also devised a truly crushing schedule for his second in command, one that allowed him only about four hours' sleep a day. Kennedy also was on the bridge or in the conning tower anytime they were on the surface, whether O'Kane was on watch or not. It was typical for the XO to share such responsibility with his skipper. Kennedy's reluctance to allow O'Kane to do what XOs usually did hinted to everyone that the skipper did not trust his "right hand" with these jobs.

It was soon obvious to everyone on the boat that their captain was reluctant to delegate much responsibility at all to his very capable group of officers. Even when he did, he tended to countermand a perfectly good order one of them had issued, effectively cutting the officer off at the knees.

During sea trials, Kennedy had ordered installed a substantial metal cot in the already cramped conning tower, right up against the TDC. It was common for surface ship captains to have an "emergency" cabin somewhere near the bridge for long nights in battle, but it made no sense at all on a submarine. The captain's stateroom was close enough, down a short ladder and a few steps forward.

Still, no one really expected him to use the cot once they were on war patrol, but he did. Often.

The thoughts of their skipper napping in the cramped conning tower unnerved O'Kane and the other officers. It was also disconcerting when watchstanders had to whisper to one another to keep from awakening their slumbering captain. But even worse, by showing that he felt the need to always be "on watch," Kennedy was effectively sending the message that he did not trust his officers to run the boat long enough for him to catch a nap down in his quarters.

Running mostly on the surface during the night but submerged during the day, *Wahoo* made her way toward her patrol area pretty much on schedule, past the international date line and into tomorrow. By then she was more than three thousand miles from Hawaii. Finally, on the distant horizon, they could see through the periscope the tops of the stunted palm trees on one of the small islands that made up Truk Atoll. This was the area in which they were to patrol, looking for ships running in and out of the islands that made up the atoll. Japanese ship captains were using the Piaanu Pass to reach relative safety. They were also protected by Japanese aircraft that were based there.

Dick O'Kane quickly found himself pulled in many directions by a recent dictum from the skipper that two officers always be on watch in the conning tower when they were under way. That practice was not typically the case in any submarine on which the *Wahoo* officers had served. It was assumed one officer was enough and others could and would be quickly summoned if help was needed.

Still, Dick O'Kane had been busy holding class with one particular pupil. He was working diligently with the young seaman and inexperienced assistant navigator Fertig Krause. O'Kane, an exceptional navigator in his own right, was trying to do all he could to get the youngster up to speed.

The XO was the perfect teacher, and Krause was an eager student. Now, as the appearance of land indicated they were where they were supposed to be, O'Kane took advantage of a rare opportunity to reward his pupil. The captain was not in the conning tower at the moment, so the XO allowed Krause to take a look through the periscope.

The young sailor grinned as he saw Tol Island illuminated in the first rays of the rising sun.

"That's it!" he shouted as he lowered the scope. "Three thousand one hundred and ten miles and we are exactly where we are supposed to be!"

"Assuming that really is Tol," O'Kane said with a wink. "When we see some bigger palm trees on the larger islands we'll know for sure. They're still over the horizon a bit."

Just then, the captain's head appeared in the hatch from below. He climbed up from the control room, casually raised the periscope, and took a look without saying anything to anyone in the conning tower. As he swung the scope in a broad circle, he suddenly stopped and moved back a few degrees in the other direction. He had obviously spotted the tiny spit of land Seaman Krause had just so proudly spied.

"You'll have us aground!" he shouted angrily, and quickly ordered a course redirection to the northwest.

O'Kane, distressed by the crestfallen look on his pupil's face, later wrote, "Krause and I gathered that we did not enjoy the captain's full confidence."

It had already dawned on O'Kane well before that incident that his skipper did not have much confidence in him. Others noticed it, too, and even began to have their own doubts, not only about Kennedy but about their XO, as well. George Grider later wrote, "Dick was a young man who seemed overly garrulous and even potentially a bit unstable."

True to the way he had been trained, Kennedy was extremely cautious in how he ran the submarine. Any chance of the detection of their presence by any enemy ship or aircraft was to be avoided. Anytime the periscope was to be raised, the boat was slowed to almost a standstill so it would not leave any wake on the surface. Even then, it was not to be raised any higher than about three feet, and that meant they could hardly see beyond six thousand yards, even in good weather. Since they rarely surfaced during the day—Kennedy shared his boss's abundant fear of aircraft sneaking up on them—the temperature inside the submarine was stifling, and the air so bad most of the men had severe headaches by the time the sun fell and the captain finally allowed them to go up to take on fresh air.

Now that they were in the part of the South Pacific where they were supposed to be, and as tired as they were from Kennedy's continuous training, the crew was ready to do some damage.

"We were on the fine edge of exhaustion, training all day and working all night," George Grider later wrote. In fact, they suspected they were now the best-trained submarine crew in the U.S. Navy, and they desperately wanted to prove it. A kill or two would settle everyone's nerves and effectively remove doubts about their skipper.

Finally, on September 6, two weeks into the patrol, just after five a.m. and the appearance of a bloodred sun, the mast of a freighter appeared in the eye of the periscope. There was no sign of an escort, and the ship was strolling leisurely *Wahoo*'s way. O'Kane put the boat on an intercepting course that would put them in prime attack position, ordered the crew to battle stations, and summoned the captain to the conning tower.

The dance commenced.

Aligning a submarine to the best possible position to fire torpedoes at a moving target requires a constant stream of data and continual recalculating. Much of that data is verbal, leading to corrections in speed and direction as the vessel is angled properly for the position that offers the highest probability of success. Other data is fed directly into the TDC, which in turn sets the complicated parameters for the torpedo tubes so they can send their weapons off at the proper depth and heading. Clues about the target's heading and speed contribute to deciding where ship and torpedoes intersect—clues such as the height of the ship's mast, based on recognition manuals, and the number of turns being made by the target's propellers. Still, there is much guesswork involved.

Kennedy peered through the periscope. O'Kane called out the headings displayed on the shaft of the scope. The captain ordered changes in their own speed and heading until they were beautifully aligned, less than a mile from the target.

She was not exactly a sitting duck, but she was damn close! The endless training was paying off beautifully!

"I have a good firing solution," Roger Paine, the torpedo officer, reported.

You did not shoot where the target was—you shot where it would be. Now, if they fired quickly, the torpedoes would arrive at a point in the Piaanu Pass at the exact time as the targeted freighter got to the same spot. Whatever vital cargo she was hauling would be at the bottom of the sea, and the ship itself would be of no further use to the Japanese empire.

"Stand by," Kennedy said. Then, quickly, "Fire one! Fire two! Fire three!"

Throughout the submarine, the men could feel each of the slight kicks—about six seconds apart—as each torpedo whooshed away out of its tube. They could hear the buzz of the propellers and even feel a noticeable pop in their ears with the change in air pressure as the tubes vented leftover compressed air back into the boat.

"All hot, straight, and normal," came the calm report from James Buckley, who was manning the sonar equipment. Now he was listening for the explosions that would let them know their torpedoes had hit home, and the creaking and groaning of the ship's superstructure as she sank and broke up. It would take about one minute for the first torpedo to reach the freighter.

Meanwhile, Pinky Kennedy gazed through the periscope, watching the wakes from their torpedoes and bracing for the explosions.

Seaman Deville Hunter kept the count, calling out loud the seconds. Everyone else held their breath.

"Forty-five. Fifty. Fifty-five. Sixty . . ."

And he kept counting. There was no boom.

"Take her to ninety feet," the captain suddenly ordered.

Paine and O'Kane glanced quickly at each other, eyes wide. They knew what their skipper was thinking. It was a calm sea, and they would be easily visible from the air. Aircraft were known to be based on the islands that flanked the area where their target continued to steam peacefully, seemingly unaware of how close to death she had been. Both men, though, would have liked to have seen—if possible—whether they had missed because the ship changed course or whether they had simply not set up and aimed correctly. They also felt that they could have certainly gotten quickly lined up for another shot.

Then, as the captain ordered the boat be turned and as they headed away from the target, they clearly heard two distant explosions. They had come well over two minutes after firing. If they had been at periscope depth, they could have taken a look and maybe determined what blew up—if maybe they had been wrong on the distance but right on the angle and they had struck the target after all.

Could they have been that far wrong on the distance? Kennedy estimated the range by assuming the mast of the freighter was fifty feet tall. It could have been much higher, based on later consideration of the recognition manual. During the approach, Kennedy had mentioned that he was afraid of someone hearing the pings from *Wahoo*'s sonar. At that time, he specifically ordered that they not employ sonar, a decision that kept them from getting a second confirmation of distance to the target.

Kennedy was concerned about anything that might offer even the slightest risk of their being detected. And everyone aboard *Wahoo* knew how he felt.

Maybe the speed of the target had been estimated incorrectly. Maybe two of the torpedoes detonated when they hit the wake of the target. Or maybe all three torpedoes had failed to explode and what they had heard were two of them striking enemy mines.

Kennedy did later take responsibility for possibly miscalculating the height of the ship's mast and thus the distance. He assumed all three torpedoes missed astern.

As for not staying around to take another shot, Kennedy wrote in the patrol report, "Because of sea conditions, proximity of the base, and the presence of an airplane screen, no periscope observations were made after the explosions. There is no visual evidence to warrant claim of damage to the enemy."

In retrospect, none of the officers wanted to argue with Kennedy's decision to run and hide. Another attack would have been risky. They had plenty more time and likely many more opportunities, and it would have been foolhardy to take ill-advised chances or waste precious torpedoes this early in the patrol.

However, the failure to bag the ship in their first attack had a devastating effect on the morale of the crew. The heat and humidity, the headaches, the constant red lighting, the shortage of freshwater, and the perpetual drilling had everyone on edge anyway. Now the best-trained crew in the Navy had failed miserably on their first attempt against a sitting-duck target. The disappointment was palpable in every compartment up and down the length of the boat. The officers noticed that when they entered a compartment, conversation among the enlisted men suddenly ceased. Their sudden silence in front of their officers spoke volumes.

It was more than a week later before they had their next opportunity. A long, frustrating week.

Midmorning on September 14, sound (the sonar operator) clearly heard a ship's screws. The vessel was sighted through the periscope shortly afterward. A small freighter was obviously headed for Truk as hard as she could go. She was screened by a single floatplane overhead. Sound reported very briefly hearing another set of screws that could have been a surface escort, but none was visible in any direction or as far as the periscope could see.

Kennedy included that bit of information in his patrol report anyway, and made his approach assuming there was a warship up there somewhere, just waiting to depth-charge *Wahoo*. The target freighter was twelve thousand yards away.

Kennedy also followed his prewar training and made his approach to the target entirely by sound, not by running on the surface or even at periscope depth. He even brought the submarine almost to a standstill at times to pause and listen again for the screws of the presumed patrol vessel that no one had heard since.

The officers in the conning tower again exchanged meaningful glances. If they had any hope of getting within range to shoot at the freighter, they needed to hurry, to make the best speed they could while submerged and quit worrying about some phantom destroyer.

After about a half hour of the stopping and starting and keeping their heads down, Kennedy finally brought *Wahoo* cautiously to periscope depth and took a quick look. The freighter and its slow-flying pontoon-plane escort were still better than four thousand yards away and presented an angle that was hopeless for them to shoot at.

There was no chance, and still no sign of any surface patrol vessel; nor had sound heard anything beyond the one short blip of the mystery ship's propellers.

Kennedy secured the crew from battle stations and abandoned the approach.

In his notes, O'Kane wrote, "An estimated 2,500-ton freighter with no visible surface escort went on her way."

George Grider had similar sentiments. "After exhausting months of drills, it was demoralizing to creep away submerged from the target," he later said.

In his patrol report, Kennedy maintained, "The surface escort was not observed through the periscope, but was plainly heard and tracked by our sound . . . there was no indication that we were detected."

The ship was so quiet, the crew so subdued after this second disappointing failure to bag a kill, that even the skipper seemed to notice. He ordered the cook to prepare steaks for everyone. That helped considerably.

Then later that evening, just past ten p.m., Dick O'Kane was in the ship's office, using the white light there to study the charts, when he felt a pronounced bump, as if *Wahoo* had run into something. He ran to the control room and ordered the boat be brought to a full stop. Roger Paine, the torpedo officer, quickly learned what had happened and sheepishly explained it to the XO.

With O'Kane busy, Paine had gone directly to Kennedy and asked the captain whether he could test the torpedo tube firing valves. He would do that by shooting water slugs out of tubes two, three, and four. Kennedy, ever in favor of a drill, and without even suggesting that Paine follow usual protocol and double-check with the XO, told him to go right ahead.

While on patrol in enemy waters, at least one tube—and sometimes two—at each end of the boat carried a torpedo, ready to fire at a moment's notice. All the crew had to do was open the outer torpedo tube doors and shoot. That night, the torpedo was in tube one.

Paine gave the command to fire the water slug in tube three. The torpedoman instead carelessly raised the firing interlock and accidentally fired number one instead. The live torpedo banged hard into the outer door, which was, of course, still closed against the sea. The torpedo jammed there, its motors still running full bore until the built-in safety device inside finally engaged and stopped them when the motors got too hot.

Wahoo had herself a "hot run," and the results could have been disastrous.

Now the question was, before O'Kane brought the boat to a stop, had the torpedo armed itself? Water rushing past the sprung outer door would look to the arming device just like seawater on the nose of the torpedo as it raced toward its target. Would the metal hull of *Wahoo* be enough to detonate the magnetic exploder and send them to the bottom?

It was a dark tropical night, but it was still dangerous to be on the surface with a live, armed torpedo possibly protruding from the ship's bow. Feeling guilty about the incident, Roger Paine volunteered to be first over the side to take a firsthand look. Using his light sparingly—it could be spotted from miles away in the darkness—he could see that the torpedo was still inside the tube, but the outer door was sprung open by better than an inch.

Since the number one tube was the topmost and thus, when on the surface, just below the waterline, they were able to flood the stern of the boat just a bit, putting the open door high enough that they could then open the inboard end of the tube without flooding the forward torpedo room. Crew members attached a big chain fall and began trying to pull the fish back down the tube far enough so they could completely disarm it and attempt to fix the outer door.

No luck. The big cylinder was hopelessly jammed in the far end of the tube and would not budge.

They had no choice. They would be forced to continue their first war patrol with the outer door shoved open and tube one out of commission. And with one less available torpedo.

Crewmen drove wooden chocks in around the torpedo to prevent it from shifting in rough seas and possibly arming the exploder. Paine could actually reach in and feel the spinner-activator, and he was reasonably sure that rushing water from the forward propulsion of the boat would not cause it to arm itself.

The big worry was the possibility of a depth-charge attack. The open outer torpedo tube door would leave them unable to dive deep, and they would be especially vulnerable to such an assault.

O'Kane later told Paine how he felt about his decision to test the firing valves. Not at sea during a war patrol. Not with any live torpedoes in any of the tubes.

O'Kane also later noted, "This would not have happened if *Wahoo* had a full-time XO. I was tied up so much of the time pulling unnecessary double watches in the conning tower with another competent officer also there. These details bypassed me."

But that was the way Captain Kennedy wanted it—always two officers on watch.

O'Kane, of course, could not say anything to his skipper or to anyone else about how he felt about that dictum. But he was certain such an unusual arrangement not only meant more than just warmed-over suppers for him and the other officers. It also kept him from taking care of other important matters aboard the submarine.

It was not lost on the crew, of course, that they had been on patrol for almost a month in prime hunting grounds with a great, well-trained crew and a new boat, yet they had come closer to blowing themselves up than they had to sinking any enemy ships.

Soon they would finally get that first "kill," but almost in spite of themselves. However, they would also miss out on a couple of other prime targets, too.

Those disappointments would ultimately seal the fate of their captain. It would also make way for someone else to take the helm of *Wahoo*.

And history would be made.

CHAPTER 8

Wahoo's Fiasco

"In studying [our approaches on enemy targets] I find that they
each conform to my normal method of attack, and confronted with
the same situations again the results would probably be identical."

—Lieutenant Commander Marvin Kennedy, captain, USS *Wahoo*,
in the report on his submarine's first war patrol

"*. . . the remainder of the patrol was a fiasco.*"

Those were not the words of O'Kane or Grider or Paine, the officers
aboard *Wahoo* who had already decided their skipper lacked the skills
and temperament to run a war patrol. Those were the words of the captain himself.

In the "remarks" section of the report on *Wahoo*'s first war patrol,
Marvin Kennedy pulled no punches and accepted much of the blame.
R. H. English, commander, Submarine Force, Pacific Fleet, agreed with
Kennedy's assessment of his performance in his own remarks attached to
the report. The squadron and division commander were even blunter in
their criticism of Kennedy.

Those comments were seen by many and, as embarrassing as they
were, the boat's officers were hoping that it would mean one thing: They
would have a new commanding officer when they began their second
patrol in early November.

Once they ended their first patrol back at Pearl Harbor, O'Kane and
the others had ample opportunity to replay the last month of their run
in their heads and among themselves. Kennedy was nowhere around,

choosing to stay with friends elsewhere in Honolulu rather than remain near where his crew was, at the Royal Hawaiian Hotel, the R & R site for submariners.

Kennedy's term—"fiasco"—had been an apt one.

After the disappointment of missing their first two targets and the real danger presented by the hot-run torpedo, the crew had every reason to believe that they had finally broken the jinx when they finally sank a freighter south of Namonuito Island late on the evening of September 20.

George Grider was standing watch on the bridge as they ran on the surface when a lookout spotted smoke in the moonlight. They turned and ran right at the promising sight, then submerged for a night periscope attack. It appeared to be a modern freighter, about 6,500 tons.

Kennedy noted that the ship ran along for a spell at about twelve knots, but then would come to almost a stop for a bit before resuming speed. Based on the starts and stops, the captain immediately surmised that the target was in the process of rendezvousing with an escort—a patrol boat or destroyer—that would take it on into port. The freighter's captain was looking and listening for his buddy.

"Sound, do you not hear the screws of the escort yet?" he asked.

The sonar operator reported he heard nothing.

Angrily, Kennedy ordered that George Grider come up from where he was serving as dive officer and take over on sonar. There had to be a destroyer out there, and this guy could not hear it!

Of course, that meant Dick O'Kane, who was busily plotting the attack approach, had to go down to the control room below and take over from Grider as diving officer.

This sudden and impulsive shifting of personnel left Kennedy with no approach officer, and he thoroughly botched the attack. They actually came within a couple of hundred yards of the target freighter before the captain realized they were so close. He quickly ordered the submarine spun around and managed to get off two torpedoes.

They were so close, the first torpedo did not have time to arm itself. If it even hit the freighter, it simply bounced off. The second one, due to the poor angle, ran down the side of the target, serving as a warning to the ship's captain that an enemy submarine was firing on him. He turned his ship hard to port and poured on the steam.

Kennedy hurriedly ordered another shot, trying to hit the target before the destroyer—if it existed—could arrive on the scene. Without his taking time to line up for a better angle, that one, too, missed.

Finally, with only one torpedo available in the stern tubes, the freighter's captain made an inopportune turn and showed his full side to the *Wahoo*. Kennedy fired his last fish from a range of two thousand yards. Grider fully expected it to miss, too, but he kept the headphones clamped to his head. The blast almost deafened him.

That last torpedo struck the freighter directly amidships, and the vessel immediately began to settle at the stern. Grider reported to the captain that he could hear the ship's engines slow to almost a stop.

With a small, proud grin, Kennedy invited Grider, Paine, and others in the conning tower to take a look at their first bagged target. The captain reported considerable "confusion" around the ship, billowing black smoke, and the sounds of small explosions and what could well be the death rattle of the ship's superstructure breaking up.

But just then, they heard several distinct, distant blasts. Kennedy told the crew that he had spotted an escort approaching quickly from beyond where the damaged freighter listed even farther and appeared to be on the way down. The explosions could have been depth charges, though nowhere within several thousand yards of where *Wahoo* sat. Or they could have been their own torpedoes reaching the end of their runs and blowing up.

Either way, they went to two hundred feet and turned away as the rumbles continued, still some distance away, being launched blindly if they were depth charges. Even if the damaged number one tube had not been on the men's minds, the explosions would have been unsettling nonetheless.

After they pulled away a few thousand more yards, the captain ordered the boat to the surface and they ran away at top speed, later to hide in a rain squall. Kennedy maintained all along—and in his patrol report—that they were being pursued by the patrol craft, but no one on the bridge ever saw anything or any indication that the enemy vessel had spotted them. They did get themselves lost with so many sudden course corrections, steering away from the supposed patrol vessel in the rain shower.

They never actually saw the freighter sink.

"There is no doubt in the minds of any of this crew but that we sank the freighter," Kennedy wrote in the official patrol report. *Wahoo* was initially credited with sinking a *Keiyo Maru*–class freighter, 6,500 tons. After the war, the commission that ultimately decided credit for vessels sunk by American warships took away any mention of this one, despite the eyewitnesses who heard and saw the blast and observed the resulting damage through *Wahoo*'s periscope.

The crew, though, was elated at the time. Whether they actually saw their objective disappear beneath the waves or not, they were sure that they had their first kill.

The men would now be able to wear a submarine combat pin when they returned from patrol, indicating they had destroyed an enemy ship. Though they had made a relatively easy attack much more difficult than it needed to be, and though the captain of the freighter essentially steered right into their final readied torpedo, their training had finally paid off. They had struck a blow against the enemy. Now, where was the next target?

It would come an agonizing ten days later—ten days of no sightings, of diving, surfacing, but mostly diving, of charging batteries, and continuing to drill, drill, drill—but when they spotted their next potential victim, it would offer them a truly wonderful opportunity. An opportunity to turn around this disappointing patrol and make it a huge success.

Just after the morning dive on September 20, they spotted the masts and distinctive bow of a warship coming at them at high speed. They quickly leafed through their recognition manual and determined the vessel was a *Chiyoda*-class seaplane tender. That made her a very attractive target. But with its speed and zigzagging course, the crew quickly realized they had no chance of catching up and mounting any kind of attack. They had simply spotted the ship too late to do anything about it.

Kennedy later reported, "Weather was ideal for submarine approach and we were able to watch target continuously except when making high speeds to close the range. There were no screens or escorts, and any planes [that] might have been overhead never came within the periscope field. The Japs were just begging someone to knock off this Tender, but it was not our lucky day. In 24 minutes, he zigged 95d [degrees] away from us."

This was part of the informal postmortem O'Kane, Grider, and Paine would later conduct over drinks back in Hawaii. Not to question their captain, of course. "Any layman armed with the postwar facts can make the general look foolish," O'Kane later wrote. But the officers talked. For men who would almost certainly be running their own boats shortly, such rehashing could not only make them more effective skippers, but it might even save their lives and the lives of their crews.

They decided that the main reason they were not able to at least make a run at the *Chiyoda* was because of Kennedy's refusal to allow no more than three feet of periscope to poke above the surface of the sea. That restricted their range so much that the tender was upon them much too quickly to do anything about it. As even Kennedy had noted in his report, it had been a perfect morning for a submarine approach.

High winds whipped the waves into whitecaps. Their periscope simply should have been extended much farther. Earlier detection of the warship would have given them a better chance to angle for an attack. Kennedy had also guessed wrong on where the ship might be heading and sent them on what turned out to be the incorrect course, one that left them watching as the seaplane tender went "over the hill."

But then, five days later, they had an even bigger prize in their sights, an even bigger opportunity to right the course of this inadequate run.

O'Kane was on the scope early on the morning of October 5, peering into the rising sun. Suddenly, on the horizon there appeared two destroyers. Something big was in the area. Sure enough, O'Kane quickly determined that the warships were escorting—one in front and one behind—an aircraft carrier.

O'Kane did not hesitate. He called the boat to battle stations and immediately ordered them toward an approach course. They were already feeding information to the TDC as they ramped up to their maximum underwater speed. They needed every turn they could muster if they had any hope of catching the carrier and putting into play the geometry necessary to sink her.

The captain, summoned from his quarters, arrived in the conning tower.

"Back to one-third speed," he commanded at once.

O'Kane almost opened his mouth to question his skipper but thought better of it. Maybe he was only quieting *Wahoo*'s screws to get a better sound bearing on the Japanese ship. Then they would go back to full. They would have to hurry, though, or the rabbit would be in the brambles.

But Kennedy took his time, taking a look through the periscope, deliberately considering all the bearing and range data that had been fed to the TDC, as if to confirm O'Kane's and Paine's work on the approach so far.

The XO could hold his tongue no longer.

"Captain, I suggest full speed if we are to catch her," O'Kane said.

Kennedy did not appear to hear him. He continued on at three knots, watching the target draw farther and farther away from them. After an agonizing several minutes, the captain finally secured from battle stations and, without comment, went below to his quarters.

O'Kane would not leave it alone, though. He grabbed a pad of paper and sketched out a plan that would have them on the surface, running at a good nineteen knots, enough to allow them to catch the carrier if the vessel was headed the way that was most likely. Once on the surface, they could also extend their periscope to full height and use it—towering over the sea—to extend their view of the horizon and track the three ships.

Half expecting Kennedy to explode at even the hint of a question of his tactics, O'Kane actually found his skipper head down, depressed, subdued. When he told him the plan, Kennedy simply nodded, massaging his temples.

"We have to do that," the captain said, and headed back to the conning tower to oversee this new chase.

But after waiting an hour to come to the surface, and then running on the surface for another hour, dashing into and out of thunderstorms, they were seemingly drawing no closer to the carrier and her escorts. When the sun suddenly broke through the overcast, O'Kane could not believe it. They were not on the course toward the warships at all, but on a parallel course, one that would have never intersected the target.

O'Kane suggested a turn toward the ships, but he could see his captain was not interested.

"We've been on the surface too long in daylight already," he told his XO.

O'Kane looked pointedly skyward, at the heavy overcast that protected them from most any aircraft observation.

Kennedy, though, gazed toward the distant horizon. He told O'Kane that they were now too close to the islands and their threatening air bases. Without even considering continuing the chase, he ordered them to abandon the hunt and to take the boat down.

Again, Kennedy eventually took the blame for the botched attempt.

"Made approach which, upon final analysis, lacked aggressiveness and skill, and closed range to 7,000 yards. Watched the best target we could ever hope to find go over the hill untouched," he later admitted in the patrol report narrative.

They were scheduled to leave their assigned patrol area on October 7, but Dick O'Kane was convinced that they could still catch either the seaplane tender or the aircraft carrier as the enemy ships made a return course from Truk. In his previous experience on *Argonaut*, the captain routinely had a completely open discourse with his officers. Even as fourth officer, O'Kane felt he had the skipper's ear and could ask or suggest anything.

Now he had seen a glimmer of willingness to listen in his current skipper. Kennedy had actually paid attention to his suggestion, had allowed him to present a plan for once without cutting him off, and had taken his advice about trying to catch the carrier two days before. Maybe he would take the latest suggestion he had come up with.

In the privacy of the cigarette deck (a small platform behind the bridge and conning tower) and with no one else around, O'Kane made his case.

"Captain, here are the likely courses those ships will follow when they leave here. And we are in perfect position—and nobody else is even close—to catch them. I'm suggesting we ask for permission to extend the patrol for a week. We have plenty of fuel and provisions. Plenty of freshwater, as you are aware. And Lord knows we have more than enough torpedoes."

He paused and waited for Kennedy to answer, to either explode in anger or give his okay. O'Kane was ready for either reaction. He was not ready for the one he got.

"Dick, I appreciate the thought, but we are not going to do that," the captain replied quietly, almost forlornly, gazing into the darkness. "We are going to take *Wahoo* home and get someone to command her who can sink ships. We will never win this damn war this way."

O'Kane was speechless. He had no comeback. He thanked his skipper and went back to work.

October 7—1200(K) Departed patrol area.

There was still one little matter: the torpedo stuck in tube number one. When they approached the dock at Pearl Harbor, Kennedy told the sailor manning the signal light to request port-side mooring so the weapon would be away from the dock. There on the pier a Navy band played, family members were gathered, staff officers awaited their arrival, all in a festive atmosphere, everyone happy to see a submarine returning safely to home port. Eight boats had already been lost by then.

But when the message was relayed to the admirals that *Wahoo* possibly had a live torpedo protruding to starboard, the crowd rushed away. The band set up again at a safe distance and resumed playing Hawaiian tunes from afar.

Once ashore, the crew rested and worked. Engines needed maintenance. The torpedo door had to be reworked and tested. Workers installed a new four-inch and two new twenty-millimeter deck guns. Some crew members left for assignments on other boats. New ones came aboard, including a young ensign with a pretty good pedigree. John B. "Jack" Griggs III was the son of Admiral English's chief of staff, John B. Griggs Jr.

Dick O'Kane spent a great deal of time rifling through stacks of paperwork, aided by his new yeoman, Forest Sterling, who joined *Wahoo* in Pearl Harbor. Marvin Kennedy was at the boat very little, and as they neared the beginning of their three-day "readiness period"—the final days of preparation before returning to patrol—O'Kane was convinced Kennedy had kept his word and had convinced Admiral English to allow him to serve his country in some manner other than as a submarine skipper. He avoided speculation among the crew about who the new captain might be.

"I want the new skipper to concentrate on getting us ready to sink Jap ships," he told Sterling. "Not have to worry about all this paperwork."

Meanwhile, George Grider brought back news about a new friend he had made. Grider was an expert swimmer, a former member of the academy water polo team, so anytime he was in port, he was in a pool somewhere. It was his preferred form of getting back into shape after a month in the belly of a submarine.

One day while *Wahoo* was in port, he was swimming brisk laps in the pool at the submarine base when he struck up a conversation with another Annapolis man, a big, friendly guy with a crushing handshake. A guy with the unusual name of Mush Morton.

"Hell, I'm lucky to still be in the submarine Navy," Morton told Grider as they splashed alongside each other. He told Grider about his recent experience with *Dolphin* and how he had somehow managed, by the skin of his teeth, to not get shipped over to be the commanding officer of some garbage scow. "I'm waiting for a 'makey-learn' assignment," he told Grider. That was the preferred sarcastic term for the prospective commanding officer cruise. Some saw the exercise as a good one, allowing a captain to get on-the-job experience at the elbow of an experienced skipper, and maybe even be a help to him along the way. Others found it awkward, putting the PCO in a position to second-guess every step the veteran man made, but giving the PCO no real power to do anything about it.

"Too bad you're not ready to take the helm of *Wahoo*," Grider told him. "We're getting a new skipper this run, and whoever he is, it has to be an improvement." He told Morton in detail why his former captain was being relieved.

Morton just pursed his lips and shook his head.

"Lots of that going around," he said, and swam away.

Back on *Wahoo*, with only a few days left in port, Dick O'Kane was starting to wonder why the new skipper had not shown up yet, and why the usual Navy scuttlebutt network had not yet supplied him and the wardroom with the name of somebody. He was in the crew's mess with his beloved charts spread out all over the table when he overheard news that sent him into a rage. He could hear two sailors in the control room talking.

"Hey, our new skipper just came aboard, and guess who it is."

"Yeah, who?"

"Lieutenant Commander Marvin Granville Kennedy."

A livid Dick O'Kane left the charts lying there and went straight up the ladder from the crew's mess topside. He ignored proper procedure, which called for him to formally welcome his captain back aboard the ship. Instead he double-timed ashore and angrily ran all the way to the office of Commander Joe Grenfell, his squadron commander.

O'Kane knew it was a terrible breach of protocol to do what he was doing, and a move that could wreck his own naval career. But he was infuriated and not a little bit afraid of what might happen if they again went out with Kennedy at the helm.

Grenfell had not seen the reports from *Wahoo*'s first war patrol, the reports in which Kennedy had admitted his own failures, but that he would do things exactly the same way if he were out there again. "Confronted with the same situations again the results would probably be identical," he had written in his report.

Nor, apparently, had Grenfell heard about Kennedy's own desire to leave submarines. The skipper must have had a change of heart on that matter.

O'Kane shared with his superior the details of how hesitant the captain had been when they had the opportunity to make significant kills, how he had such odd ideas about how to run a submarine and, most disturbing, appeared to not trust his officers and especially his XO. No matter the effect all this might have on his career, O'Kane did not hold back.

"Commander, you have to help us. *Wahoo*, the crew, and our captain. We need your help on this thing."

Grenfell could only shake his head.

"Dick, not ten minutes ago Admiral English had his arm around your captain's shoulder and was telling him that he and *Wahoo* had sunk one ship already and that this time out he and his crew would show everyone what you could do." Grenfell leaned in a bit closer and lowered his voice. "And you know Kennedy and the admiral are good friends, right? They served together."

O'Kane spread his hands in his lap.

"The truth is, I don't think he can make it through another patrol without someone closer to his age to lean on. He's five years older than we are. He thinks we are too young and inexperienced. He just does not have any faith in us. Any confidence in me."

Grenfell rubbed his chin. A thought seemed to have come to him. He pondered for a moment and then smiled slightly.

"I have an idea," he said. "We have a guy who has been to PCO school and commanded *Dolphin* for a bit. He's waiting on a PCO run. He has seniority comparable to your captain's. It might be a good thing for him as well as for your captain if he went along for the ride on *Wahoo*."

O'Kane knew about Morton already from talking with George Grider. Their new yeoman, Forest Sterling, had served with Morton in China, too, and told colorful stories about him.

As the XO arrived back at the boat—in a much better mood than when he'd left it—he had already decided that having a PCO aboard was the best solution to their problem. That was especially true if there was little likelihood Admiral English would allow Kennedy to leave *Wahoo*.

The night before the submarine was to depart on her second war patrol, Lieutenant Commander Kennedy acknowledged Dick O'Kane's report that the crew was all present and aboard the boat. Then he promptly informed his XO that he would not sleep aboard the boat that night. Instead he would spend it ashore with friends and would see them well before the scheduled 0900 under way the following morning.

At supper that night in the officers' mess, O'Kane made the announcement he had been sitting on since his meeting with the squadron commander.

"Fellows, it looks as if we will get a PCO for this run, either tonight or first thing tomorrow." He deliberately did not tell them who the hitchhiker was or how it came to be that he would be riding along with them. "I suggest we all keep quiet about any thoughts we might have about the problems on the last patrol. Let's give him the chance to help make this a good outing."

As if on cue, an hour later, Dudley "Mush" Morton came aboard with a flourish, carrying his seabag, a broad smile on his face. He shook every officer's hand with his own giant paw, slapped sailors on the back, and greeted Forest Sterling with a bear hug, as if they were long-lost brothers. Some crew members later said that it was as if a pall had been lifted, as if someone had turned on a bright light up and down the length of the submarine. And not a red-hued one either.

Mush Morton's personality was just that huge and dynamic.

Sterling was happy to see his old acquaintance but still had some reservations about him. He had heard stories about an officer who kept fighting cocks in his backyard in the Philippines and loved to wrestle with the enlisted men.

Jack Griggs was only an ensign, fresh out of the academy and on his first submarine duty, but he had been around the Navy his whole life. He knew enough about Navy politics to wonder how this oil-and-water arrangement on *Wahoo* might work. He had also heard that Morton's PCO assignment was likely the last chit the big Southerner had left to play. He would have to make the most of it if he hoped to stay in submarines. Would Morton push Kennedy to take undue risks just to ensure a good patrol to make him look good?

George Grider already considered Morton to be a friend, just from their casual conversations poolside at the sub base. Still, he knew little about him as a skipper and wondered what fireworks there might be between him and their captain. Heck, he was not sure about Dick O'Kane yet, either. The XO seemed quick to anger and too highly opinionated sometimes to be an effective right hand. With this addition to the mix of strong personalities aboard *Wahoo*, did they have the makings of a volatile stew?

Perhaps the one man on board who was most heartened by Morton's arrival on *Wahoo* was O'Kane.

"When I hit my bunk that night, I felt better," he later wrote. "Hope had replaced apprehension concerning our upcoming patrol."

CHAPTER 9

"If the Skipper Wakes Up . . ."

"When I first met Commander Morton it only took me one minute to realize that I would follow that man to the bottom of the ocean if necessary."

—USS *Wahoo* crewman Forest Sterling

W ith confirmation that the boat was "rigged for dive" and two blasts on Wahoo's klaxon, the submarine's bridge was cleared of men and she headed down, still only five miles out of Pearl Harbor. As prearranged, a waiting patrol boat maneuvered to within a few hundred yards and dropped depth charges to acclimate new crew members and remind old hands what it felt and sounded like to come under such an attack.

Then, with three blasts of *aahh-ooo-gah*, the crew brought her back to the surface, manned the new deck guns, and fired off several test rounds. With that finished, they turned to course 238 true and started the long ride to their new assigned patrol area, three thousand miles away near the island of Bougainville in the Solomon Islands.

The process of getting under way, just as with their arrival, had been an almost festive affair, with top brass dockside to wish them Godspeed. Admiral English had been aboard to see them off, and while Captain Kennedy went to the bridge to oversee their backing away from the pier, Dick O'Kane showed him ashore, across the brow. With a long blast from their air horn, they officially got under way at 0900, November 8, 1942.

As they made their way southwestward across the Pacific, zigzagging while on the surface during the daylight hours and running a straight line after dark, there were still plenty of things for the crew to do. Maybe most important to their future well-being was to continue to train the new men who'd joined the boat in Hawaii. Those who were not yet qualified in submarines—those who had not yet demonstrated their ability to successfully man any station on the boat—had to learn and be tested until they were.

It was dangerous out there. Even the common operations like surfacing and diving required a well-choreographed effort by all crew members. There was no way to anticipate what any one of them might have to do in the middle of battle, and a mistake by any one man could mean the end of all of them, and a long, long sleep on the bottom of the sea. That was (and still is) the basis of "qualifying in submarines": that any man on the vessel be able to do any chore required of him, and do it correctly. Only then is a sub sailor allowed to pin on the twin-dolphins insignia.

Besides its captain-in-waiting passenger, there were a couple of welcome changes on *Wahoo*'s second run. Since they had been issued a good supply of red-tinted goggles, Captain Kennedy relented and allowed white lighting in the crew's mess and wardroom, where the officers ate and played almost continuous games of cribbage. Everyone was happier without having to eat red mashed potatoes and play with specially marked cards. Men who were set to serve as lookouts put on the goggles a half hour before going topside and allowed their night vision to improve.

The captain also informed O'Kane that, due to the number of officers aboard—including their PCO ride-along—he would no longer be required to pull double watches.

"We were making progress," O'Kane jotted down in his notes.

Kennedy still stuck to his policy of staying submerged during daylight hours, popping up to periscope depth periodically to look around, going back down as quickly as possible. Then they could surface at night to charge batteries, take in clean air, put lookouts in the shears—the area above the bridge and sail of a submarine—and look for targets.

Once they were far from shore, the chance of aircraft sneaking up on them was small. The lookouts instead watched the horizon, looking for smoke, masts, or the periscope of an enemy submarine. Supply boats bound for the enemy troops on Guadalcanal would be passing through the area to which they had been assigned. That promised good hunting once they got there.

By the time *Wahoo* passed that point in the ocean where command shifted to ComSoPac, Admiral William Halsey, on November 14, Lieutenant Commander Morton was well along on his own personal mission of meeting and learning about every single member of the crew. He wandered from one end of the boat to the other, often wearing an ugly red bathrobe, chatting with anyone and everyone.

In keeping with O'Kane's pointed suggestion, and because it was not proper form for officers to criticize their captain, none of *Wahoo*'s officers shared any details about Pinky Kennedy or what had happened on their first run. Morton did not press the point. He understood the protocol and likely learned much simply from their reluctance to talk.

It was not unusual to find Morton in the engine room, washing his underwear in a bucket of suds, jawing with the sailors working there. Or to walk back to the aft torpedo room and see him sitting there in his skivvies, swapping sea stories as if he—an Annapolis-trained officer who would soon once again be a submarine skipper—were one of them, a "rag-hat" enlisted man.

The men quickly got over his lack of formality and accepted him as an enlisted men's officer, a guy they could talk to, regardless of his rank. They almost certainly did speak frankly, without the restrictions O'Kane had placed on the wardroom.

Morton made no attempt to go behind the captain's back when he visited with crew members. He could tell from the expression on Kennedy's face that the captain did not like it, whether he felt they were talking about him or thought it simply was unseemly for an officer to be so familiar and informal with enlisted men. Either way, Morton did not care.

November 20—Arrived in patrol area Dog (East) as directed by ComTaskFor 150805 of November. Sea condition 6, wind force 6, visibility low, and rains frequent.

Once they arrived off the banana-shaped island of Bougainville, *Wahoo* found herself in the midst of a full-blown gale. Lookouts had to wear foul-weather gear and could see little in the murk, not even with the brilliant lightning flashes illuminating a roiling sea. When they were submerged, the soundman could hear only the hissing of heavy rain on the surface and the distant deep-throated rumble of tropical thunder reverberating off the island.

Marvin Kennedy had reinstalled his cot in the conning tower and once again got most of his sleep there. One evening, Forest Sterling was on sound, trying to hear something helpful or promising in the midst of the storm above them. As usual, he and the others on watch there were whispering or using hand signals to keep from waking their skipper.

Suddenly Kennedy threw back the light blanket that covered him, leaped to his feet, and grabbed Sterling by the shoulders.

"Where?" he screamed, his eyes wide, wild. "Where? What bearing?"

But then, just as suddenly, the captain realized he had been dreaming. Without explanation or apology, Kennedy turned and took the ladder below. The men in the conning tower exchanged glances before lowering their heads and going back to work.

The weather finally got a bit better, though distant sheet lightning persisted, making surface running a nerve-racking experience, even in an otherwise dark night. They were near the northern part of Bougainville, watching a narrow strait between the island and a much smaller hunk of volcanic dirt named Buka. The strait was navigable and reportedly used by the Japanese as a relatively safe shortcut, but after a week they had not seen a single vessel in the area.

One evening, O'Kane came down the ladder from the bridge and conning tower into the control room. He dropped into the middle of a conversation between Morton and one of the chiefs. Mush paid him no mind and continued his questioning.

"How come you don't use your Kleinschmidt stills?" Morton was asking. That was one dictum Kennedy had flatly refused to reconsider for the second run. "Are they broke or something?"

"No, sir," the chief responded, watching O'Kane's face to make sure he did not disapprove of his answer. "They ain't broke. They take electricity and that means fuel, so the captain only uses them to make water for drinking, cooking, and the batteries."

Morton winked at O'Kane and turned back to the chief.

"Tell you what. The captain's asleep right now. I think I'm going to take myself a shower. If the skipper wakes up, send a messenger forward to let me know, on the double."

"Yes, sir."

Morton headed off for his shower. He would have taken it, too, but for the sudden chiming of bells that indicated the lookouts had spotted something of interest.

O'Kane bolted back up the ladder to the bridge with Morton in his red bathrobe right behind him, headed for the conning tower. O'Kane paused just long enough to check the time and their position: 2030; they were about fifteen miles east of Buka.

"We saw smoke on the horizon in the lightning flashes," one of the lookouts called down to the XO. O'Kane peered through his binoculars in the direction the young sailor pointed, even as he could feel the submarine turning beneath him. George Grider, on watch below, was already bringing the boat around to a bearing of 150 degrees.

O'Kane watched, waiting for more lightning as heavy raindrops began to pepper his face. Just as the captain arrived at his elbow and joined him in scanning the horizon, there was an almost continuous strobe of green-and-yellow lightning, effectively turning the night into flickering day.

Both men spotted the column of smoke. At its base, they could make out several blurry shapes that were almost certainly ships.

In the next flashes, they could see more. One ship had a high hull, clearly a vessel of some size. A freighter, and a big one at that. Then, in another blaze of lightning, both officers could tell another of the ships—one running off the port bow of the freighter—was a destroyer-type vessel. And there were other smudges on the lightning-lit horizon, too.

They had themselves a Japanese convoy!

Even better, they were only six thousand yards away, and O'Kane knew that they could almost certainly run on the surface, get closer, and line up an attack without the destroyers even knowing they were there, thanks to the wind and rough seas.

But just then, O'Kane heard his captain give a command.

"Take her to periscope depth. Dive!"

The Klaxon gave two quick blasts and every man on watch immediately moved from surface approach status to dive. Lookouts on the platform above the bridge scrambled down the ladders as the boat began to nose down into the choppy waves.

As he dropped down the ladder from the bridge into the conning tower, O'Kane thought to himself how similar this conservative move was to the captain's actions on their first run. They were about to give up an almost perfect surface-attack setup to try, instead, to catch a fast-moving convoy while submerged, using sound and periscope.

It was safer, of course, but their odds of sinking an enemy vessel had just plummeted faster than their submarine.

O'Kane and Morton had a chance to exchange only a quick glance, and there was no doubt both men had similar thoughts. But they were both busy for the next half hour as they followed their captain's orders, trying to hear the screws of the ships in the convoy well enough to get a good bearing and to line up a likely target through the periscope. They were still relying on the Lord's light show to reveal something to torpedo.

Finally, just before nine p.m., Kennedy got a surprise, a good look at a destroyer during a lightning strobe. The warship was only about three thousand yards away and presented a decent angle. But it would do so for only a few moments.

Kennedy chose not to fire at the warship. Convinced he could get a better shot, the captain said as much and ordered the boat be swung to the right. But the move was too slow.

Within minutes, there was no hint of the ships' screws in the sonar operator's earphones. The lightning flashes showed only black sky, white-capped water, and swirling rain.

In his patrol report, Kennedy wrote, "At 2100 all echo ranging stopped. Attack was essentially a sound approach. Attack position was lost by the time the first periscope information was obtained. Radar was not used because it failed originally to pick up target, and test off Pearl Harbor showed that even at short ranges the entire conning tower and bridge structure must be out of the water to obtain a contact. The approach was unsuccessful partly due to inaccurate, inadequate, and confused sound information and partly due to the failure to appreciate the true nature of the approach until too late, clinging to the hope that lightning flashes would provide data for a more accurate approach."

Dick O'Kane had trouble sleeping when he finished his watch. The excitement and disappointment of the attack left him wide-eyed. He sat down at the table in the wardroom with a mug of hot coffee, studying his ever-present charts but thinking more about the quick but disappointing half hour in pursuit of the convoy, the unconsummated attack.

Moments later, Mush Morton slid onto the bench across from him. He sat there sipping from his own steaming mug of strong, black coffee. He did not say a word as he studied the placement of the markers on the cribbage board on the table. Morton then began dealing the cards without even asking O'Kane whether he wanted to play.

In a few minutes, George Grider, just off watch and apparently not interested in sleeping either, joined them for a third hand.

Slowly, the conversation shifted to the topic on the minds of each of the officers. It was not cribbage.

None of them wanted to be disloyal to the skipper. That included Morton, even though his feelings about Kennedy were becoming obvious. That was based on glances and facial expressions, something the demonstrative Morton had always had trouble suppressing.

But again, each of the three knew he would soon helm a submarine on a war patrol—assuming they survived this one—and they should take every opportunity to learn from their failures, just as they would glean knowledge from their successes. Should there ever be any successes from which to glean, of course.

"I talked to one of the lookouts," Grider reported. "He said each of them saw different things in the lightning flashes, but that they were sure that was a convoy we had out there."

"I'm convinced it was," O'Kane said. "I saw the freighter and that was certainly a destroyer escort. And the captain was sure the ship he passed on at the end was a destroyer. The ship was not out here on a pleasure cruise. It was escorting something worth sinking."

Morton, who rarely lacked an opinion or hesitated sharing it, chimed in.

"We would have been best to have stayed on the surface and tried to run around the convoy. We could have gotten ahead of it by dawn, gone to periscope depth, and waited there to pick them off one at a time when they came past us. That is what we could have done. By damn, that is what we *should* have done!"

He slapped the metal table hard for emphasis. The cribbage board danced and coffee splashed over the edges of their mugs.

The officers silently studied their cards.

Each had the same thought: Morton's course was exactly what O'Kane was contemplating up on the bridge before the captain suddenly sent them down. It would have been a relatively bold maneuver for a single submarine, and it would not have been in keeping with the way skippers like Kennedy had been taught to run their boats, either. But it would have given them a good chance to sink something.

Submerge. Hide. Be quiet. Use sound and periscope sparingly to avoid detection. Await an opportunity that might pass nearby. Fire only when presented with a sure thing. Then run, go deep, and hide again before the escorts could locate them and counterpunch.

But the proof of the effectiveness of that strategy was there. During their first patrol and now, so far, on the second one as well. If they were going to sink enemy ships, cut off the supplies destined to help kill American boys, they could no longer simply wait for a target to come ambling by, right into the crosshairs of their periscope.

"Clinging to the hope," as Kennedy wrote in his report.

O'Kane was already gratified that Morton and he seemed to be on the same page, thinking the same way. He set about building a case that might be of use once they arrived in Brisbane, Australia, at the end of the patrol. He asked the COB, Pappy Rau, to poll the lookouts who had been topside during the initial sighting of the convoy and report back exactly what they had seen.

Shortly there would be another missed opportunity to salvage *Wahoo*'s second war patrol. Another anecdote for the dossier O'Kane was building against his captain. Another bit of fodder for the boat's gossip mill.

This one, though, would go a long way toward showing Marvin Kennedy exactly what several of his officers thought about him and his ability to fight a submarine war.

CHAPTER 10

Reciprocal!

"The only real training for leadership is leadership."

—Author Anthony Jay

*T*ime passed with no firm targets showing up. Not on radar, sonar, or the periscopes. Wahoo *heard what appeared to be a fleeing subma-rine on December 7, an anniversary not lost on the crew, but nothing they could confirm, let alone chase after.*

Then O'Kane was thrilled to see *Wahoo*'s radio call sign on the evening's Fox broadcast message, the regular official update from Pearl Harbor, notifying them that they were especially urged to be on the lookout for something important. Even better, within the message, a portion carried the "ultra" designation, signifying the contents contained intercepted enemy intelligence and had the highest operational priority.

This was the first time *Wahoo* had received such a high-priority missive and was only the second O'Kane had ever seen. When the message emerged from the decoding machine in the radio room, the XO was even more excited. A loaded tanker—eighteen thousand tons' worth—was scheduled to pass near them at midmorning, making eighteen knots. The ship was part of the storied "Tokyo Express," the stream of supply vessels taking crucial cargo to support the efforts against the U.S. Marines on

Guadalcanal. Stopping that tanker would be a big blow against that effort.

As O'Kane plotted their intercepting track, word spread up and down the length of the submarine. The message itself was top-secret, but it was impossible to keep every man on the boat from soon getting the gist of it, and the excitement was contagious.

Once again, *Wahoo* and her well-trained crew would have the opportunity to redeem themselves. To prove they were worthy.

Soon they reached the point where the tanker was expected to pass. They waited on the surface, batteries fully charged, radar sweeping, sound listening furiously, and lookouts in the shears with their binoculars sweeping the horizon. Torpedoes were loaded in their tubes, ready.

Surprisingly, sound picked up the first hint of the big target, even before it showed up on the radar scope. The enemy escort's echo-ranging gear could be heard, though its direction was fuzzy. Still, that was enough to give radar a better idea of where to look. At a range of eighteen thousand yards—about nine nautical miles—they could finally see the blip on radar.

They were on the right course, setting up for an attack, at a distance from the target of about twenty-five hundred yards. Soon they had visual contact, and the lookouts and officers on the bridge could see it was, indeed, a tanker, and judging from how low she rode in the water, she was loaded, zigzagging erratically, making just thirteen knots.

Perfect! This one would be hard to miss!

At 0305 range had closed to 6000 yards on a track and true bearing of 145d starboard when radar contacted the escort astern of tanker. At 0307 echo ranging stopped. The approach being over submerged to 40 feet and tracked by radar and sound. Kept radar contact on AO but lost it on escort at this depth.

Marvin Kennedy took them down to periscope depth, manning the attack scope in the conning tower. Dick O'Kane stood nearby, calling out bearings from the ring around the periscope housing so they could be entered into the torpedo data computer. Mush Morton stood over a small chart table, watching the constantly changing courses of the target and the submarine, plotting angles, waiting to advise if needed.

The sonar operator sat nearby at his console, confirming the bearing of the target, based on his own pinging, and ready to report the presence of any other ships in the area or the sudden appearance of torpedoes or depth charges in the water.

The loaded tanker was clearly making for the relative safety of the Bougainville Strait. Her skipper had no idea *Wahoo* was lining up to put an end to those plans. There was no reason to suspect there was any escort vessel with her, either.

Sound had heard nothing that sounded like another ship. Kennedy reported nothing else in the periscope.

Busy with their duties during the approach, Morton and O'Kane had no opportunity to even exchange glances. Already, the two men had reached a point where they seemed to be able to read each other's minds. Both men were wondering whether the captain would do what needed to be done. Even the old way—the stodgy, conservative way of conducting a submarine attack—should ensure they would be able to sink this easy mark.

"Echo ranging on our starboard quarter!" the sonar operator called out. Enemy sonar, searching. But that bearing was the exact opposite direction from the target and from where any potential destroyer would likely be.

Mush Morton realized immediately what had happened. The sonarman had called out the wrong position. In truth, what the sonarman heard was almost certainly the target.

"Reciprocal! Reciprocal!" Morton shouted at once, clearly stating exactly what had just happened. But it was too late.

"Flood negative! Take her deep!" Kennedy ordered at the same instant as Morton's correction as he rammed the scope into its housing.

Every man on the boat was obliged to follow the captain's command, to do everything possible to pull the plug and dive to escape the phantom destroyer. As they did, they clearly heard the grumbling of the tanker's screws as the target passed directly overhead and quickly disappeared into the distance.

Morton turned to Kennedy, his mouth open to let him know, in no uncertain terms, what he thought of his hasty decision to abandon the attack and run. But he thought better of it. Instead, before he said and did something that might once again threaten to end his naval career, and possibly get him court-martialed, Morton dropped down the ladder from the conning tower and went below.

Kennedy's own face had gone white. He certainly realized that his hasty decision had just cost them an almost certain kill. But now, with the negative tank blowing compressed air and taking on seawater, it was making too much noise for the sonar operator to hear anything useful. Kennedy also knew that it would take them way too long to stop the dive and return to periscope depth, locate the tanker once more, and try to pick up the attack again.

The skipper simply left the conn and headed for his cabin without a word, off "to read one of his beloved Western novels," as O'Kane put it.

Dick O'Kane fought to keep his own anger off his face, but he could not erase it from his voice.

"Secure from battle stations!" he announced over the boat's public-address system. The rage behind his words was clear to every man who heard it. That was every man aboard *Wahoo*, including Mush Morton and Marvin Kennedy.

Kennedy would later write in his patrol report, "The two night contacts . . . should have resulted in attacks but we muffed the chances. Anyhow, we did learn something about night fighting, we hope."

Again a frustrated Dick O'Kane was unable to sleep. Instead, he studied his copy of *Navy Regulations*, and specifically the section on the circumstances under which an officer could assume command of a vessel, relieving the captain. The rules were specific about taking over if necessary to avoid running the ship aground. There was little, though, about what to do with a skipper not mounting a proper attack against an enemy vessel.

Just before dawn, it was time for O'Kane to go up to the bridge and "take the stars," or accurately determine their whereabouts based on the positions of objects in the sky. It was the usual time, just before the sun's rising erased the stars. He left the copy of *Navy Regulations* atop the cabinet that housed the SJ radar equipment in the conning tower. The book was opened to the section he had been studying.

When O'Kane came back down the ladder, he was surprised to see the captain standing there in the conning tower, inspecting the attack periscope. The scope had been leaking seawater into its optics ever since the beginning of the patrol, and it had been more than a considerable nuisance. But it was unlike Kennedy to be in the conning tower at that time of day. It was about the only time they could count on his being asleep in his quarters instead of napping on the cot on the conn.

The captain acknowledged his XO as he dropped down into the cramped compartment. Then Kennedy spotted the manual lying open atop the SJ radar. He reached and picked it up.

O'Kane's stomach fell.

Apparently assuming the book was the submarine's construction and repair manual, Kennedy waved the book at his XO, using his thumb to mark the place where O'Kane had left it open.

"Well, I see you have finally decided to break out the manual to learn how to properly pack a periscope," he told his XO. The captain then opened the book and began to read. For several minutes, Marvin Kennedy studied the section, not on packing a leaky periscope but on the conditions under which an officer could take over from a ship's captain.

O'Kane could only stand there, unable to do anything, waiting for Kennedy's reaction.

He later wrote, "It was one of life's touchy moments. No words were exchanged but now each of us knew exactly where he stood with the other."

Kennedy set the book back on top of the radar, looked once more at the scope, and headed back down the ladder.

A few nights later, Mush Morton had the conn and, except for the sonarman—who wore headphones—and another sailor who had the wheel, he was alone in the conning tower with O'Kane. Out of the blue, and speaking quietly enough so the sailor at the wheel would not hear him, Morton asked, "Dick, of all the boats in the U.S. Navy, why did I draw *Wahoo* for my PCO run?"

O'Kane smiled but said nothing. He could not tell Mush about how he had lobbied to have Kennedy tossed off the boat, or how, when he was made aware that the captain's political connections made that unlikely, he managed to convince the squadron commander to put Morton on board to try to give them a chance of a better second patrol. Or to decrease the chances of their all getting blown to hell.

Morton read O'Kane's sly grin perfectly. He poked the XO in the chest and flashed his own trademark smile.

"You son of a bitch!"

A couple of days later, Roger Grider was in the control room serving as diving officer, practicing their daytime search procedures. Dick O'Kane had the conn.

At the urging of O'Kane and Morton, Kennedy had finally relented and allowed periscope observations as often as every fifteen minutes, though he still groused about how reckless it was to expose the scope that often in daylight. O'Kane wanted to have the scope up continuously, but Kennedy still feared a sudden aircraft or patrol boat might spot it and attack them before they realized what was happening.

The new method required a lot of bobbing up and down, from sixty-four feet of depth to going deep for a while and then back up to sixty-four feet—periscope depth—to take a look for something to shoot at. Grider wanted to make sure everyone in the conning tower and control room could accomplish all that up-and-down efficiently. Accidentally broaching the boat, bobbing to the surface, would not be a good thing if the enemy was up there.

They had just come to periscope depth yet again and raised the scope when the crew member manning it quietly reported, "Heavy smoke, bearing two-nine-three true."

O'Kane sent word to alert the captain and then gave him a few seconds' head start before sounding the bells for battle stations. Shortly after Kennedy took over the scope, he saw the masts of two ships, and then, moments later, two more. There were three cargo vessels, running in a column, escorted by a destroyer.

The captain, peering at the approaching targets, began calling out a rapid string of bearings for each ship. It was far too many for the torpedo officer, Roger Paine, to keep track of and feed to the TDC.

O'Kane could see Paine was not able to get the data into the TDC before he got a new set of numbers. He did not hesitate or even consider how it might sound to the others in the conning tower.

"Captain, I suggest you give us angles and ranges on just one of the ships so we can concentrate on that one," he said, half expecting Kennedy to bristle, to remind him who was skipper of *Wahoo*.

He did not. He settled on one target, a freighter that ran low in the water, clearly loaded with cargo. He also used the identification manual to point out a picture of the escort. His finger fell on an *Asashio*-class destroyer. Though most of them were eight years old by that time, they were formidable antisubmarine vessels. The freighter would be an easy first target, and her two sisters on each side would have quickly become second and third, had it not been for the very capable escort that ran along, cutting back and forth in front of the ships to protect them from exactly the kind of attack for which *Wahoo* was maneuvering. It was a tougher problem to solve but they could do it. They would just have to time their shots perfectly and worry about the destroyer later.

Out loud, and to Mush Morton's amazement, Kennedy actually mulled the possibility of trying to torpedo the destroyer first, but quickly decided against that low-odds move. It was too fast, its course too random.

Instead, with O'Kane providing the data, they lined up for a shot on the heavily loaded freighter, their intention being to fire the torpedoes when the destroyer was at the far end of its zig and headed away from them.

O'Kane, Morton, and Grider were all pleasantly surprised at their skipper's unusually aggressive attitude. He actually seemed ready and willing to launch an attack, even though he could—this time—see and hear the *Asashio* destroyer up there. So far, he had tended to run and hide from shadows, faint echoes, and phantom warships. Even now, each man still expected a sudden duck-and-run.

They were positively amazed at what Kennedy did next.

The captain took a quick look around and then swung the scope to the direction of the target. All ranges and bearings and their resulting calculations were double-checked. They were seven hundred yards away.

"Final bearing and shoot!" Kennedy barked with excitement.

It was exactly what every man on the boat had been waiting to hear for the past two frustrating weeks. Four torpedoes zoomed away from *Wahoo*'s bow tubes, aimed in a spread calculated to pound into the big cargo ship from one end to the other.

"All hot, straight, and normal!"

"Twenty. Ten. Five. Whack!"

The explosion shook *Wahoo* hard enough to create a fine sift of dust from above, but it was a good feeling. Three torpedoes had hit the freighter.

"Target smoking. Listing to starboard," Kennedy reported, and, despite their differences, he even allowed Dick O'Kane a quick look through the periscope to see what a blow they had struck together.

It was almost as if Kennedy were saying, "Okay, XO. See. I can do it."

Instead, he said, "Take her deep! Rig for depth charge and silent running!"

The destroyer was now headed their way. It would have little trouble determining from where and what the torpedoes had been launched. They could simply follow all four trails left by the propellers to the point where they converged at their origination.

Sure enough, as they passed 120 feet headed down, the first depth charge rattled them hard, bursting lightbulbs and stirring dust up in the still air. A few bolt heads popped and zinged across compartments. Paint chips and bits of cork looked like snowfall drifting down, and a couple of smaller pipes sprang hissing leaks.

When they tried to level off at 250 feet, they realized they were taking on water from somewhere faster than they could pump it out. They sank to over 350 feet before they could once again gain control of the dive and take *Wahoo* back up a bit. The submarine had slipped below her test depth, the point at which she supposedly could dive safely. The gasket on a vent had given way from the force of the blast. The flood valve had to be closed by hand, which fortunately stopped most of the inrushing seawater.

The crew counted more than forty depth-charge blasts over the next hour and a half, many of them potent enough to throw a strong man to the deck if he were not braced against something solid. Eventually they drew farther away from the explosions as *Wahoo* followed the reverse of the convoy's course, making quick alterations to keep the Japanese from guessing their whereabouts.

The noise finally stopped altogether. The enemy had given up. All the while, the crew worked mightily to repair minor damage from the charges.

Finally, at about five thirty p.m., *Wahoo* came back to periscope depth and, from a reasonably safe distance, took a look. There was much activity in the area of the damaged freighter as boats worked to rescue survivors. The torpedoed ship settled lower and lower into the water, and the sonarman soon reported the inevitable sounds of her superstructure breaking up from the unrelenting pressure of seawater as she slipped beneath the waves.

Marvin Kennedy ordered that the entire crew receive a half ounce of what the patrol report called "medicinal rum" (actually Lejon brandy).

Neither Morton nor O'Kane could find fault with the way Kennedy ran this first truly successful attack. There had been an opportunity to press the assault when they came up for the look-see, to try to sink the other ships in the convoy. One of them sat still in the water, taking on victims from the sinking vessel, and she would have presented an easy target. But the destroyer was still there, along with other ships. It would have been risky.

Kennedy went straight to his cabin after the attack. Morton noticed that he looked exhausted, as if the incident had taken a lot out of him. Forest Sterling overhead one sailor say, "I never saw the old man act so brave."

Dick O'Kane wondered whether the incident with the *Navy Regulations* might have had something to do with the way Kennedy pressed the assault.

"Maybe [the captain] said to himself, 'I'll show that whippersnapper!' " the XO later said.

However, Marvin Kennedy's newfound bravado would not last long. And there would be an angry confrontation on the bridge of *Wahoo* that would finally set the stage for Mush Morton to show the world how to conduct submarine warfare.

CHAPTER 11

The Wrong Ball

"Our weakness in night fighting was clearly brought out by this patrol. The experience gained should make us more adept at this type of attack on future patrols."

—From Lieutenant Commander Marvin Kennedy's remarks in the patrol report for *Wahoo*'s second war patrol

A t 2340 received SUBS 42 NR 75A concerning probable ship movements in our area. Assumed this to be the convoy already contacted and continued moving to northeast. Decided to move in slowly to give the crew a chance to recover from effects of depth charging.

It was still the same day as the successful sinking of the cargo vessel, estimated to have been better than 5,600 tons. Radio received and decoded a couple of messages. One alerted *Wahoo* to a convoy—the same one they had just attacked, but headquarters did not yet know that—and the other extended their operation area so they could intercept a large freighter that was heading that way.

Before waking the skipper, and perhaps made even bolder by Mush Morton at his elbow, Dick O'Kane turned toward the heading that would take them in the direction where the freighter would be. It would require the better part of twenty-four hours to get there, since about twelve hours would, by the skipper's policy, be spent submerged and making much less speed. They really needed to get moving if they wanted to get there well enough ahead of the freighter to wait on it.

When Kennedy came to the conn, though, he casually studied the charts and advised the crew to proceed at one-engine speed.

"The crew has had a tough day," he told O'Kane and Morton. "We can get there in plenty of time without wearing anybody out."

Neither officer argued. In truth, they should have had enough time to get there, though it would have been to their advantage to arrive in the new area a bit early.

Kennedy asked that he be awakened at 0200. O'Kane told the duty officer to wake him an hour before he did the captain. That put the XO on the bridge in the middle of a beautiful, calm tropical night, sipping from his ever-present mug of coffee, using a sextant to look at the stars blinking at him from a clear sky, showing them precisely where *Wahoo* was. Bits of phosphorescence danced in their wake, as if the sea had captured some of the stars from the canopy overhead. The breeze was fresh with a hint of the fragrance of earth and foliage from the distant islands.

But just as O'Kane was enjoying the rare calm, sound reported hearing something suspicious. It was either a ship echo-ranging—using sonar—or employing a fathometer to sweep the seafloor, trying to keep them out of shallow water. Either way, the vessel was announcing its approach, and in this part of the world, it could only be flying the Japanese sunrise flag.

Just after 0130, there was no doubt. The lookouts could see her, and radar confirmed it. It was a big cargo vessel, and there was no sign of an escort.

Now, with the captain on the bridge, they would surely go to battle stations, put all four engines online, and give chase. With the ship's speed—and she was fast—it would take a while, but they could catch her well before dawn. Besides, the target was zigzagging drunkenly, as if her skipper had a premonition that *Wahoo* was about to try to line up and shoot at her.

The submarine needed only speed and a bit of imagination to angle for a prime attack position.

Marvin Kennedy denied them both.

Dick O'Kane gripped the bridge railing so tightly his knuckles turned white. The target was pulling away! He shocked himself, not just by the tone of his voice when he finally spoke up, but by the open challenge he made to his superior officer.

"Captain, she's getting away! We have to go after her!"

Two other crew members on the bridge and the pair of lookouts in their perch overhead all went wide-eyed, and their jaws dropped. None had ever heard anyone speak to a boat's skipper in that tone, not even an XO.

When the captain responded, his voice was just as angry as his XO's had been.

"Don't be stupid!" he spat, glaring in the darkness at his second in command. "There is no way you can attack a ship from here!"

O'Kane bit his tongue and kept the binoculars to his eyes, watching the target grow smaller with each second that passed.

"For a long moment, I considered pressing the point, but realized that in his agitated situation, he would most likely send me to my stateroom. That would do neither me nor *Wahoo* any good."

O'Kane later told Morton that he and Kennedy "were simply not on the same wavelength, and tactically, we were in different wars."

Marvin Kennedy had shown up at a ball game with the wrong ball.

The crew soon heard about the verbal confrontation on the bridge. They had already noticed that their XO had grown irritable, hard to figure. The strain of his interfacing with the captain was telling on him. Within minutes, he could be friendly, easygoing, and then suddenly lash out at a seaman or one of his junior officers. Such mood swings did not give the crew much confidence. Were the pressure and frustration getting to the XO?

In contrast, Mush Morton's bright-light personality did not seem to ever dim, regardless of the situation on the bridge or in the conn. But the tension between the skipper and his exec made Morton's own presence on the boat even more awkward. Though he had not tried to hide his own questions about Kennedy's style and tactics, he did not dwell on them. Instead, he told sea stories, wrestled, played cribbage, and soaked up as much knowledge as he could about not only *Wahoo* but the men who made up her crew. Some of the men openly wondered what they might have to do to get themselves assigned to whatever boat Morton got when they arrived in Australia.

Later that morning, about breakfast time, Marvin Kennedy surprised them again with another uncharacteristically aggressive tack. A mast of a ship suddenly appeared on the horizon. He ordered them immediately to battle stations and struck off to intercept the vessel.

Morton and O'Kane once again exchanged quizzical looks. This "good captain/bad captain" routine was vexing! Still, both men enthusiastically set to doing what they had to do to help initiate an attack.

"She's not a freighter," Kennedy announced as he gazed through his binoculars, bracing himself against the metal railing of the bridge. "She's a transport of some kind."

Troop transport? Not likely down here, but if so, she was a good target.

She did not seem to be zigzagging, and there was no visible or audible escort, either. That was curious. Whatever and whoever she was, she seemed fearless.

Wahoo continued the chase, though, until they found a perfect attack position. When *Wahoo* was submerged and waiting, the captain raised the attack scope, ready to deliver the final range and bearing and to give the order to open the outer torpedo tube doors.

"Secure from battle stations," Kennedy suddenly announced. Morton and O'Kane bristled. What was he doing now? "She's marked as a hospital ship."

In the better light of the new sun, it was obvious now. The vessel was clearly a hospital ship, was following a steady course, and had no air cover, all in conformity with international law.

They chalked the chase up as good practice.

The crew soon had another chance to put that practice to use. It was also further evidence that *Wahoo*'s luck had changed for the better.

Forest Sterling was getting some training on the sonar gear when he heard what sounded like a raging rainstorm. George Grider was on the periscope watch and asked Sterling to put the sound on the loudspeakers in the conning tower.

"That's not rain," Grider noted. "Hail, maybe? But I've never heard hail that sounded like that. It's rhythmic, almost like some kind of odd propeller."

It was not yet time for their regular periscope search, but Grider was curious enough that he decided to bend the skipper's rules just a bit and go up for a look. When the scope popped out of the water, his mouth fell open and he dropped the periscope back into its housing.

"Submarine! Battle stations! Open the forward outer torpedo doors!"

They were already within firing range of a Japanese submarine—an I-boat—running on the surface. But they had to hurry if they had any hope of shooting this wonderful target. She was only twelve hundred yards away, and Grider had swung the boat's bow ninety degrees to be ready to shoot.

Marvin Kennedy showed up in the conn wearing nothing but a towel, still covered with soap. The men paused only a moment to wonder why the captain could take a shower when no one else was allowed.

As Kennedy grabbed the handles of the periscope and made a 360-degree sweep, the towel fell down the hatch into the control room. *Wahoo*'s captain stood there, stark naked, calling out range and bearing on an enemy submarine until a mess attendant climbed up with pants and a shirt.

In less than seven minutes after first sighting, torpedoes were on their way toward the 356-foot-long warship. But as the count was called, there was a solid explosion a full ten seconds before the first torpedo was due to hit.

The captain reported a direct hit, a geyser of water forward of the conning tower, and men leaping off the bridge into the water. With his headphones firmly pressed to his ears, Forest Sterling was certain that the torpedo had exploded early—a "premature." And there was no sound of the other two fish hitting anything.

More than two minutes later, there was a deep-throated detonation that O'Kane described as "greater than the explosion of a warhead."

Sterling noted "breaking-up sounds." Grider heard "crunching noise, the sound of metal collapsing inwardly."

Combined with the captain's report of what he had seen in the periscope and all the noise they heard, they were convinced they had sunk a Japanese submarine. Grider said he had seen "*I-2*" painted on the vessel's conning tower.

There was a different feeling up and down the length of *Wahoo* after sinking the submarine as compared to destroying the freighter. It was not lost on the crew that they had apparently taken the lives of brother submariners, and only submariners can understand how strong that brotherhood is. Still, they reasoned, *I-2* could easily have been looking for them, and would certainly have sunk *Wahoo* if the situation had been reversed. Bagging a warship and a freighter, though, had salvaged the second patrol, and spirits were high as they prepared for their final few days on patrol.

It is now generally agreed that *Wahoo* did not sink *I-2* that day. That submarine was actually sunk by a destroyer in April 1944. The Joint Army-Navy Assessment Committee (JANAC), the commission that made final determination about number and tonnage of vessels destroyed during the war and by whom, decided that no Japanese submarine was sunk in that place and at that time. Some speculate that Grider was right, that one of the torpedoes exploded prematurely, and the other two simply missed. The watch on the I-boat's bridge spotted the approaching torpedoes and diverted course while doing an emergency dive. Though rattled by the premature explosion, she likely got away to fight another day.

But what of Captain Kennedy's report of seeing the boat hit, of observing her listing, of men diving off the bridge to escape the doomed vessel? No one else had looked through the periscope that day. The captain had ordered them quickly to two hundred feet to get away from any possible patrol craft that might have been summoned by the sinking submarine.

The noises of a submarine being crushed by the sea? There is no explanation for that.

Kennedy was clearly pleased with the effort and results, though. He even praised his officers in his patrol report.

"This attack was brought to a successful end largely through the splendid coordination of four officers, whose performance was outstanding. They were: Lieut. G. W. Grider—O.O.D. and Diving Officer; Lieut. R. H. O'Kane—A.A.O.; Lieut. R. W. Paine—T.D.C. Operator; Lt. Cmdr. D. W. Morton—A.A.O."

Still, this emotional yo-yo of a war patrol was about to have a couple more downward spins, another heated exchange over tactics between *Wahoo*'s skipper and XO, and yet another potential blowup that would be quelled with a simple signal from the PCO.

In good spirits from their two sinkings, the crew was anxious to get one more kill, but they had less than a week left before they would strike out for Brisbane, Australia, and the end of the run. They were steaming along close enough to Bougainville that they could easily see tall radio towers on the island in the first light of dawn. But suddenly, in the pink hue of the rising sun, there was something far more interesting on the horizon—a sizable ship's masts and no sign of an escort.

O'Kane was on the bridge and he immediately set a speedy course to meet up with the ship and get into position so they could sit submerged and wait on her to pass into their sights. But when O'Kane told his captain that he wanted to run on the surface for an hour, in daylight, only miles off a Japanese-occupied island, the old, conservative Marvin Kennedy reverted to his typical nature.

"Absolutely not, Dick!" he said, his jaw jutted out. "Why, the Japanese would have planes on us in minutes."

The tone in his voice and the smirk on his captain's face enraged O'Kane, but again he held his tongue and allowed the crimson color rising up from beneath his collar and across his face to let the captain know his feelings.

"One more week," he told himself. "One more week."

Hell, the nearest Japanese air base was two hundred miles away! Even if a plane could be sent from one of the nearer islands, they could have pulled the plug and been deep long before the aircraft could have shown up and done any damage. And they would have almost certainly left a sinking target in their wake.

Then, as they made their way toward the Australian coast, they had occasion to cross a major shipping lane for the Japanese empire. Sure enough, they spotted puffs of smoke and knew they had a ship trapped between *Wahoo* and Bougainville. This time, they would even have the advantage of remaining submerged as they brought the boat to a prime firing point, arriving there just after dark.

O'Kane ordered that the captain be alerted. When Kennedy arrived in the conn, he slowed the boat so he could take a look of his own through the periscope. O'Kane was not worried. They still had plenty of time to head off the small ship they were stalking. Not even the captain's reluctance could get in the way this time.

Kennedy lowered the scope, resumed speed, and did not change direction. O'Kane was heartened. Maybe they would get that one more kill after all!

December 21—At 1650(K) sighted smoke bearing 048dT. Closed on normal approach course until dark but never sighted any ships. At dark we were about ten miles into GROUPERS area. Broke off the approach and resumed assigned track.

It was a small ship but worth the effort. The XO glanced at Mush Morton and grinned. Morton flashed back his own smile, winked, crossed his arms, and casually leaned back against a piece of equipment in the conning tower with an odd look on his face.

O'Kane knew the look. It was almost as if Morton knew Kennedy would blow this one, too, and he was just going to sit back and see how the captain would go about it.

Kennedy took no note of the wordless communication between O'Kane and Morton. He stepped to the chart table and began studying the map in depth. He picked up the dividers and leisurely measured distances and bearings, as if working out complicated courses. Time passed. They were quickly drawing near the spot where they would need to stop, set up, and wait for the target to come idling past them. The spot where they would have the ship dead to rights.

Kennedy suddenly stood up straight, the dividers still in his hand, and turned to face his XO.

"Secure from battle stations."

"Captain?" O'Kane asked, wide-eyed, the disbelief obvious in his voice.

"Secure from battle stations. We will be in *Grouper*'s operation area by the time it gets dark."

Grouper (SS-214) was a sister American submarine. It was true that they would soon be in the patch of ocean assigned to that boat. Still, that arbitrary line in the sea was no reason to avoid attacking a perfectly good enemy vessel they had been stalking already.

Mush Morton still leaned against the radar unit, only feet away from Dick O'Kane but behind the captain. Kennedy had bent back down to once again busy himself by intently studying the chart.

Morton took quick note of the look on O'Kane's face. He did not need to read the XO's mind. He was about to explode. He seemed to radiate white heat as he stood there, eyes squinted, clenching and unclenching his fists. It would not have surprised Morton if O'Kane had suddenly thrown a punch at his skipper. He was clearly that angry.

The weeks of frustration, of avoiding what O'Kane was convinced were solid opportunities to attack, of putting up with his captain's odd way of running a submarine, were all about to culminate in an incident that would not only likely end Dick O'Kane's Navy career but would certainly put a black mark on *Wahoo* for the rest of the war.

Morton's innate sense of the situation told him he had better do something. But what?

He caught O'Kane's steely gaze and shook his head from side to side. Then he looked down at his own hand, nodding, directing O'Kane to look there, too.

Morton was making a sign with his palm and fingers. The "OK, cool it" sign.

Dick O'Kane immediately knew what Morton was telling him. *It's not worth it. Not for a little freighter like this one. Calm down, XO. Calm down. We'll fix this in a few days.*

O'Kane gritted his teeth; his face was still beet red, but his anger was under control.

Kennedy soon dropped down the ladder out of the conn, and the men working there breathed again. That simple moment or two would eventually be the talk of the bars in Brisbane. O'Kane and Morton would also later acknowledge it as the defining moment that ended Kennedy's command and set the stage for *Wahoo*'s next chapter.

If there had been any hesitation in Mush Morton's mind about what he was to do when they arrived in port, it was decided when Kennedy allowed that little freighter to steam away from them untouched.

CHAPTER 12

Relieved

"You know, Dick, you would probably make a good submarine captain."

—Marvin Kennedy to Dick O'Kane, on the bridge of *Wahoo*

*T*he sailors on *Wahoo noticed a subtle change in Mush Morton's demeanor. In the last week of Wahoo's second patrol, he was no longer the joker he had been when he first came aboard. He still had the quick, broad smile, and he sometimes surprised a crewman with a sudden head-lock, but he was clearly more serious now.*

It may have been the brewing tension in the conn between the skipper and his executive officer. Morton was clearly just as frustrated, but in his odd position of PCO, there was little he could do in the face of Kennedy's timid style. On the contrary, if he had followed his gut and challenged the captain, it could have ended his hope of getting his own boat. Now if he could just hold his own temper, keep Dick O'Kane in check, and get to Brisbane without a fistfight on the bridge, he had a plan that would change the fortunes of *Wahoo*.

One thing was for sure. He wanted *Wahoo*.

He had already shared his hope with O'Kane and some of the others he trusted to keep quiet about it. She was a good boat with a fine crew, and if he could hold most of the wardroom and chiefs together, he was confident they could do some real damage against the Japanese. He already knew exactly how he would run the boat, and it was 180 degrees removed from the course Kennedy had taken with her in his first two patrols at the helm.

But there was one problem. On paper, the patrol appeared to be moderately successful. Surely the squadron commander would know what had really happened out there in the Solomons. But Kennedy could put a positive spin on just about everything that happened, and everyone knew he had a sympathetic ear back at the highest level in Pearl.

After the incident in the conning tower, O'Kane retired to his quarters to start working on the mass of paperwork that would form the patrol report. He was also mulling over what might happen when they got to port. He wanted to remain with *Wahoo*. But if it meant making a third patrol with Kennedy, he would not go back to sea with him. He would not have Mush Morton there to calm him down the next time he wanted to put out the captain's lights.

Later in the evening, the XO headed for the wardroom for a bite to eat. He found Mush Morton and several other officers there, drinking coffee, playing cribbage. The captain, as usual about this time, was asleep on the cot in the conning tower, getting in the way of the men working there.

Morton leaned back and stretched.

"Fellows, we'll be in Brisbane soon, and I have a plan," he announced. Morton had shared only a thought or two about Kennedy, his style and his capabilities, but had so far remained mostly silent on the subject. By implication, O'Kane had let him know that his hope was that Morton would become their skipper after this patrol, though it was not standard practice for a PCO to relieve the captain of the boat on which he made his "makey-learn" run.

Every officer aboard knew O'Kane's opinion of Kennedy. The enlisted men did not have to guess about it either.

"A plan?" the XO asked.

"I am going to report the captain for cowardice when we get to Australia," Morton told them, not sugarcoating it one bit.

The men around the table were quiet. Cowardice was a truly serious charge during wartime.

Even Dick O'Kane, who had as low an opinion of his captain as anyone around the table, thought it was a rather radical thing to do. Hesitant, not properly trained, unfamiliar with proper protocol on a submarine—all true of Kennedy. But cowardice?

A few days later, O'Kane went to the bridge early and found himself alone on the cigarette deck with the captain. Kennedy seemed to be in a foul mood. Before he could even give a "good morning," Kennedy started in on him.

"O'Kane, I don't know what I am going to do with you." The captain did not even give the XO an opportunity to ask to what he was referring. There were several things. His red face, angry announcements on the boat PA, the regulations manual. "I have been looking at the ship and aircraft reports in the patrol report. You left out that airplane that buzzed us the other night. The one with the running lights."

Several nights before, they had dived the boat in response to a report from the bridge that an airplane—landing lights blazing—was coming at them at a high rate of speed. Radar was not manned at the time, so there was no other confirmation of the sighting. From the bearing and time of night of the sighting, and because there had been no other aircraft seen in the area, O'Kane was certain the lookouts had spotted the planet Jupiter, not an approaching Japanese aircraft.

It had happened too many times before. Planets or the moon on a clear tropical night can take on many forms. He had decided to leave it out of the official report and had not thought it a big deal.

"I didn't think it was a bona fide contact, sir. If you think it was, I'll include it."

Kennedy stared for a moment at the point where the sun was dropping into the sea to end the day.

"Please do," he said, and watched the sun a bit longer. O'Kane did not know whether that was all the skipper wanted to say to him. He kept his own binoculars to his eyes, scanning the horizon. Suddenly Kennedy glanced sideways at his XO. "You know, Dick, you would probably make a good submarine captain."

O'Kane did not know how to respond. He just nodded, mumbled a "thanks," and began taking his sun sights, confirming where they were in the South Pacific and that they were on the proper course that would bring this tedious patrol to a close with some welcome R & R.

History would eventually prove Kennedy correct on his prediction.

They officially arrived at the sub base in Brisbane, Australia, the day after Christmas, 1942, entering Moreton Bay and winding carefully up the Brisbane River to the submarine base. Ironically—and certainly symbolically, as it turned out—Pinky Kennedy went below to prepare for the official greeting party and left Mush Morton on the bridge. It was Morton who guided *Wahoo* the last few miles upstream to the inland port and maneuvered the boat alongside other submarines at the pier.

George Grider noted that the crew was still quite discouraged, even more so than at the end of the first patrol, which was not nearly so successful as this one had been.

"The *Wahoo* was not making much of a record," he later wrote. "And we all knew it. For much of the run, we had been waiting in the wrong places at the wrong time like unlucky fishermen. We all felt thoroughly discouraged."

Admiral James Fife, the head man in Brisbane, met them at the dock and came aboard to formally welcome *Wahoo* to Australia. Because of the two claimed sinkings, Kennedy received the Silver Star. At the same time, the captain recommended that four of his officers—O'Kane, Grider, Paine, and Morton—receive special commendations for their efforts in sinking the enemy submarine. Fife agreed and made the presentations.

Fife was generous in his praise of *Wahoo*, her captain, and her crew. As it turned out, hers had been the most successful patrol in the area for a while. Morton and O'Kane could only wonder how all this acclaim would affect their plans to have their skipper run off the boat.

Fife's official endorsement to the patrol report was complimentary, but included a backhanded bit of criticism.

"Eight contacts were made, of which only two were developed into attacks, both of which resulted in sinkings. However, it is believed that at least three of the other contacts should have been developed into attacks . . . the radar functioned exceptionally well and it appears that this information was not used to best advantage to develop these contacts."

The crewmen were happy when the formal welcome was finally over and the big brass had left *Wahoo*. They finally acknowledged that they were too tired to know how tired they were.

Everyone went different directions according to rank. The enlisted crew would spend time in port at the Hotel Canberra on a floor reserved just for them, complete with room service. Captain Kennedy was off to a house, which included a cook and steward, in a neighborhood where other skippers had similar lodging. The officers had quarters in an apartment house that had been rented for their use.

O'Kane was still not sure where Mush Morton was going when he left the boat that day, during their three weeks in Brisbane or afterward. He could end up at the helm of another boat in Brisbane. He could get sent to some other sub base to await assignment to a boat. Or he could be the new skipper of *Wahoo*. O'Kane still hoped, based on his meeting with Commander Grenfell back in Pearl Harbor, that Morton would replace Kennedy on *Wahoo*, but he was far from certain at this point. Judging from the tired look on the captain's face as his car pulled away at the pier, he could not imagine Kennedy returning to the helm of the boat. But he had heard of other captains continuing to helm submarines, even after strongly requesting reassignment and despite dismal records.

Therein was the problem. The latest patrol by *Wahoo* was hardly dismal, unless someone realized how great it could have been had Kennedy been more aggressive. Despite Morton's less than stellar record so far, it was clear that he had the favor of some in the higher command of the submarine service and would get a boat soon. If Kennedy stayed on the bridge of *Wahoo* for even one more patrol, Mush Morton would be off to some other vessel.

Roger Paine had reported an offhand statement by Kennedy that gave hope that someone new would be at the helm of *Wahoo* on the next run.

"I've had enough," Kennedy told him directly, pulling no punches. "Morton and O'Kane are both against me. I'm going to turn in my suit."

O'Kane's best hope—and Mush Morton's, too—was that the difference in who their bosses were now that they were in this part of the world would lead to the personnel moves on the boat that both men sought. Here, in Australia, they were now under the command of Admiral Charles Lockwood, not Kennedy's friend and protector, Admiral English. Lockwood was a no-nonsense guy who favored flamboyant and gutsy boat commanders, so long as they got the job done and brought their vessels back home with "kill" pennants flying from the sail. Lockwood's second in command was James Fife. Charles "Gin" Styer—one of Lockwood's best friends—was the direct commander of Squadron Ten, in which *Wahoo* now fit.

Ensign Jack Griggs, son of Admiral English's chief of staff and in a position to hear such scuttlebutt, told of a tense meeting in Gin Styer's office the day *Wahoo* arrived in port. Kennedy was there, but so was his shadow, Mush Morton.

Kennedy gave a positive wrap-up of the patrol and was debriefed by Styer and his staff. The captain had an answer for all their questions about why they had not at least tried to launch attacks on some of the other contacts.

Then, more as a courtesy than anything else, Styer turned to Morton for his thoughts on the patrol.

"Mush, what do you think of the run?"

True to his nature, Morton did not hesitate to offer his opinion.

"Well, Commodore, this man is a yellow-bellied son of a bitch and should be relieved of his command," Morton reportedly answered. "If you doubt it, ask the XO."

That blunt answer to Styer's question is not confirmed. However, the tone and substance of the meeting was almost certainly in that vein. This was likely the closest Morton would come to bringing up Kennedy on charges of cowardice, as he had pointedly promised the officers of *Wahoo* that he would do. The results of the meeting certainly indicate that Morton's account of what happened on the patrol and his assessment of Kennedy's command were accepted. A change at the helm of *Wahoo* would be prudent.

When O'Kane and others arrived at the apartment house and were unpacking their seabags, they heard a familiar voice at the door.

"Hey, you guys got room for one more?"

It was Mush, seabag over his shoulder and his trademark broad grin shining. Though the quarters would be cramped with one more body, nobody complained, and they welcomed him in. Although he and O'Kane had hit it off already, it gave the other officers the opportunity to get to know the man, not just his friendly—almost playful—veneer. He instantly bonded even more with Paine, Grider, Griggs, and Chandler Jackson.

Whether it was preordained from O'Kane's face-to-face with Grenfell before the run, or Morton's harsh words in Styer's office after the patrol had sealed the deal, the Kentuckian was named the captain of *Wahoo* on New Year's Eve, 1942. There was no ceremony, no special announcement. Morton just showed up back at the apartment with the good word.

Marvin Kennedy was reassigned to staff duty, later served as repair officer on the new submarine tender USS *Bushnell* (AS-15), and even later became skipper of USS *Guest* (DD-472), a destroyer. There he earned a second Silver Star for heroic action in the Battle of the Philippine Sea.

After the war, he was commander of Destroyer Division 122 and served at high staff levels in the office of Chief of Naval Operations and in the Pacific Coast Section in San Francisco. There he eventually advanced to the rank of rear admiral. As with some other commanding officers who were not successful in submarines, Kennedy went on to serve his country with distinction in other ways, contributing to the successful conclusion of the war and to maintaining peace afterward.

Kennedy later commented that he was actually thankful for the change of command, in agreement that a more aggressive skipper should replace him, though he was not able to admit it—even to himself—at the time it all came down.

"[Admiral Fife] told me that a more aggressive conduct of the first two patrols would have resulted in more enemy sinkings," he said. "In retrospect, I can see he was right, but I was not so philosophical about it at the time."

Marvin Kennedy died in February 1997 at the age of ninety-one.

There was absolutely no doubt in the minds of the crew that things would be changing dramatically aboard *Wahoo* under their new skipper. They had no idea!

On his very first day aboard the boat as her captain, Morton gave several key directives that won the crew over immediately. They were simple, mostly cosmetic directives, but ones that showed the men aboard SS-238 that they would soon be operating with a new, fresh outlook.

And that the damn Japanese had better watch out!

CHAPTER 13

Pinups and "Sonza Bitches"

"We must fight, we must shoot to kill, for our enemies have pointed the way to swifter surer crueler killing."

—General Lesley McNair

*D*espite his being the executive officer aboard Wahoo, and theoreti- cally the first to hear what was happening with his boat, Dick O'Kane got the news about the new skipper almost nonchalantly, and directly from the horse's mouth. He was relaxing back at the apartment house, resting up for the night's celebration to welcome in the year 1943.

Morton came back to the room, flopped down in the chair opposite him, and told O'Kane the news. The XO tried not to show too much glee, but he immediately felt as if an anchor had been lifted from his shoul- ders. He truly liked Morton, but he did not really know what caliber of skipper he would be. Still, he had to be better than the one they had had for *Wahoo*'s first two runs.

Morton took a big swig from a bottle of beer, studied the label for a moment, and then glanced over at what was now his XO.

"Dick, did I ever tell you about the big idea I got at PCO school?"

Morton and he had talked so much—and especially since arriving in Brisbane—he frankly could not remember. Mush seemed to always be coming up with "big ideas."

"Don't think so," he replied.

"Well, sir, at the school, we would be practicing attack procedures, me on the scope and my underway instructors standing there taking notes on everything I did and said. You know how it goes. You're calling angles on the bow of the target, reading the telemeter scale for the range, yelling out orders for the helmsman for rudder and speed, checking the plot for whatever course you can come up with to try to catch up with the son of a bitch somewhere where you have some hope in hell of getting off a good spread of torpedoes." Mush paused for another big draw from the ale bottle. "Hell, there's a lot going on! Well, I noticed that the instructors are standing there with their notebooks with nothing better to do than second-guess—with a lot more time to think about it—every move I was making. Afterward, when we looked at their notes and compared them and considered their suggestions against what I accomplished with everything going on there at the scope, it was clear that they almost always had a better idea of what to do than I did."

O'Kane looked at his new boss sideways, but before he could ask what he was getting at, Morton told him.

"Dick, you are going to be my co–approach officer, not my assistant. You'll be on the scope, not me. You'll be the one calling out the approaches and observations. If we are on the surface, I want you on the TBTs. Either way, I'll conn the boat to our best position and then you'll fire the torpedoes."

Mush sat back, grinning broadly, as O'Kane sat there, mouth open. What his captain was telling him was about the most radical idea he had ever heard when it came to who did what during a submarine attack. It was the captain who always manned the scope if he was in the conn or had his eye on the target-bearing transmitters. Few skippers would have even considered sharing such responsibility with their XOs, either out of protocol, ego, or because that was just not the way it always had been done.

O'Kane quickly regained his composure.

"Captain, I appreciate your confidence in me," was all he could think of to say.

But Morton's unorthodox move was not coming from out of the blue, and it did have a lot to do with the confidence he had in his XO. He had already had the opportunity to watch how O'Kane handled himself in an assault situation. The man had a mathematical mind and was able to do intricate calculations coolly in his head and quickly apply them to the maneuvering necessary to bring their submarine into prime attack position. Except for allowing his anger at his former captain to get in his way a time or two, O'Kane was the perfect choice for co–approach officer. There was nobody Morton would trust more with this new job—or to prove its merit—than Dick O'Kane.

Admittedly, there would be other officers aboard *Wahoo* who wondered whether O'Kane had the temperament to do the job. However, the captain had made his decision, and that was the way it would be when they were once again plying dangerous waters.

The New Year's partying that night by *Wahoo*'s crew was especially spirited. But for the senior officers aboard the boat, the next two weeks were hardly leisurely. They were scheduled to depart Brisbane on or about January 16, and there was much to do.

Dick O'Kane was improvising again, asking a carpenter's mate on the submarine tender USS *Sperry* (AS-12) to help him rig a circle sawed from wood as the base for a platform. He would use wood dowels to attach some small ship models he had acquired. This device was to be used during times when they were maneuvering for attacks on targets. He hoped it would allow them a better visual idea of angles presented by ships on the surface in relation to the submarine.

Morton had told O'Kane to practice for at least an hour a day, using flash cards with photos of ships of all types and in various positions, and try to instantly call out the angle on the bow. Ensign Griggs and other junior officers helped with this chore, and the practice was good for them as well.

As soon as Marvin Kennedy had left the boat, Mush Morton began to put his own mark on *Wahoo*. He grabbed the first sailor he met when he came aboard as her skipper and gave him the task of removing the big posters of Japanese ships that the former skipper had hung in every compartment. Those close-up pictures of enemy vessels had been the source of a great deal of muted ridicule. The men figured that if they were close enough to compare the real ship with these pictures, it was too late.

Next, he had a couple of sailors go from one end of the boat to the other, hanging in the place of the ship posters something much more to the liking of the men. Pinups. Girlie pictures. All from the captain's own personal stash. He even had one special poster he specifically asked to be hung in the crew's mess. It was a picture of actress Olivia de Havilland, personally autographed, and wishing all the best to the crew of USS *Wahoo*. No one ever knew where he got the autographed poster, but while stationed in California, the skipper had developed many friendships in Hollywood, long before there was a *Wahoo*. Some suspected it was a forgery, but the sentiment was certainly welcomed.

Morton had other wall hangings he wanted posted. In many of the compartments, he placed a sign that could be read from one end of the room to the other that contained a statement by Lesley McNair, a brigadier general serving under General George Patton—a quote that had been quite controversial when it hit the newspapers just after the start of the war:

"We must fight, we must shoot to kill, for our enemies have pointed the way to swifter surer crueler killing."

There was a reason for Morton's choice of that particular quote. Ever since he had arrived in Australia aboard *Wahoo*, he had heard stories of Japanese atrocities in the South Pacific. The Australians shared stories of the viciousness of the air attacks on Darwin on the country's northern coast. The first of those, in February 1942, has been called "the Pearl Harbor of Australia," and even more bombs were dropped in that assault than in the December 7, 1941, attack on Hawaii.

Morton had seen for himself the results of the Pearl Harbor sneak attack, and he continued to get letters from the Avents that relayed stories about what the enemy had been doing in China.

Mush Morton was convinced that he, his submarine, and his country were fighting an enemy radically different from any they had ever encountered before, an enemy who fought without regard to the accepted standards of warfare. An enemy even more vicious and radical than the armies of Hitler's Nazi Germany or Mussolini's Italy.

That also explains why Morton later asked Forest Sterling to hang an even more explicit placard in the smaller cardholders in each compartment on *Wahoo*. In bold red letters, they stated quite plainly what the new captain expected his crew to do:

KILL THE SONZA BITCHES

Dick O'Kane might have been a little taken aback by this radical signage, even though he, too, had seen the damage at Pearl Harbor. But some unsettling news he received only a few days before their departure quickly put him in a fighting mood as well. His old boat, *Argonaut*, had been lost with all hands. An American bomber actually witnessed the attack. The plane's crew—with no way to do anything about it—watched as the bow of the huge old submarine broke the surface, forced up top by a vicious depth-charge attack. A couple of Japanese destroyers fired on the boat with deck guns and sank her. A hundred and five men died.

O'Kane knew some of those men very well. They were his former shipmates from not so long before.

But O'Kane was almost as upset with his own Navy over the loss of his old boat as he was with the Japanese. Admiral Thomas Withers had understood that the old, slow, balky V-boat could best be used as a mine-layer and, in operations with her other big sisters, could lob ordnance onto fixed targets from offshore. But Withers lost his job over other issues and was sent back to New Hampshire to oversee the Portsmouth shipyard.

Admiral English decided *Argonaut*'s mine-laying gear was too noisy, despite what some considered compelling demonstrations that newly installed equipment worked much better and quieter. He decided she should be a troop carrier. That turned out to be a good niche. With her size, she was able to stealthily deliver a sizable group of Marines to where they needed to be, though admittedly not very comfortably.

But Admiral Fife was adamant in his views. Any submarine he had in his group needed to be out there on patrol, trying to launch torpedoes to sink enemy ships.

It was finally decided to base *Argonaut* in Brisbane. She had left from there on antiship patrol—one of the jobs for which she was particularly unsuited, in Dick O'Kane's view—only a few days before *Wahoo* arrived there from her second run.

O'Kane kept busy, trying not to think about those brave men with whom he had sailed. He spent hour after hour practicing the new, unorthodox methods that his captain had laid out for the way they would conduct attacks under his command. He used vessels coming up the Brisbane River as "targets," and employed his new wood platter with its ship models to simulate assaults on them. None of those ships could have guessed they were being tracked and "shot" by *Wahoo*.

Early on, Mush Morton called the officers together for an informal meal, meeting with them in the boat's wardroom. It was a meeting that would never have happened under Pinky Kennedy.

Morton laughed and joked and made a point of involving each of the junior officers in the conversation. By the time the meal was complete, every one of them understood that there was a new way of doing things on *Wahoo*. Junior officers were not only allowed to comment or make suggestions, they were encouraged to do so. The captain trusted them, cared about their opinions.

They were instantly energized. It was as if Morton had given each of them a shot of adrenaline.

He had already told the officers—and even Yeoman Sterling—to call him "Mush." He quoted the old submariners' adage, "You leave your rank on the dock." O'Kane, however, was just old-school enough that he could never quite manage that level of informality with his captain. He continued to address him as "Captain" or "Dudley" instead.

Meals in the wardroom dramatically changed tone, even before they left port.

"They were more like parties," George Grider noted. "Instead of staring at our plates and fretting as we had once done, we found ourselves led along by a captain who was constantly joking, laughing, or planning outrageous exploits."

There were other obvious changes, too.

Pinky Kennedy's cot was unceremoniously ripped out of the conning tower. The compartment's interior space seemed to grow dramatically with it no longer there.

The holding tanks Kennedy had installed to capture condensation from the air-conditioning units were torn out, replaced with lockers to be used by the crew to store personal items. The crew also understood that the Kleinschmidt stills would now be employed as intended to provide enough water for them to use the ship's washing machine to clean their clothes and—within reasonable limits—the showers to wash their bodies. They could now wear clean dungarees and T-shirts.

Morton instructed Sterling to "somehow get the Captain's Mast book lost. We won't be needing the damn thing on my boat." The book was a record of each man's transgressions, on board and ashore, and the punishment meted out by the captain. Morton's message was clear: The captain expected the men to behave themselves, but he wanted them to do so because they wanted to go out there and kill the enemy, not because their skipper was trying to be a hard-ass.

As they made final preparations for patrol, the new captain roamed the length of his boat day and night. He never seemed to sleep, and admitted he had trouble doing so when he was aboard the submarine. The officers could not help but notice how much the men liked him, how much they respected him, even when he did things none of them had ever seen a skipper do before. Things like often wearing nothing but skivvies, roaming the boat in that ratty old red bathrobe, or sitting down among them and gleefully taking part in their bull sessions and sea-story marathons.

George Grider noted, "He seemed to understand their anxieties. He was as relaxed as a baby. The men were not just ready to follow him. They were eager to."

Forest Sterling later wrote, "There was a feeling [among the men] of being free, of being trusted. He seemed to have a high degree of confidence in the capabilities of our ship. We became a bit cocky. It was a feeling that *Wahoo* was not only the best damn submarine [in the force] but that she was capable of performing miracles."

Morton made it clear that he expected each of his officers to follow his lead and purchase his full ration of alcohol from the officers' club prior to departure. That seemed odd, since Morton rarely drank anything stronger than beer. But then he suggested that the booze go into the ship's safe. After an attack, he explained, the whiskey would be rationed out to the entire crew to help settle their nerves. Word of this, of course, instantly spread among the crew and only added to the loyalty they were gaining for their new "old man."

A series of directives from the captain had some of the crew members shaking their heads. Shaking their heads but smiling.

No longer were two officers at a time required to stand watch, as Kennedy had dictated. The officer of the deck was in charge, trusted, totally in command of the boat, unless he specifically asked for help. No longer would the skipper show his distrust of his officers and lack of confidence in their abilities by insisting on sleeping in the conning tower. Mush Morton made it clear he would be in his quarters asleep if they needed him for something. Whoever had the conn had the conn.

Going forward, all administrative reports went through the XO. With that simple pronouncement, Morton reestablished the authority of his executive officer. If the captain had confidence in the XO, so should everyone else.

Once they were under way, Morton ordered, watch standers would rotate every hour. A reduced number of lookouts would be in the shears at any given time so they could more quickly clear the decks and dive if need be. Also, they would be topside for only an hour at a time, not for four grueling hours, as was the previous policy. Then they would rotate to radar or sonar or some other station. It was Morton's opinion that long, monotonous duty stations led to boredom and a loss of alertness. He also promised that if any lookout was the first to spot an enemy vessel, and that ship was ultimately sunk, the lookout would be promoted immediately to the next highest grade.

And Mush Morton, who happened to be handy with a needle and thread and openly admitted to anyone how much he enjoyed sewing, would personally stitch the new patch on the sailor's sleeve.

Morton made it known to everyone from his senior officers to the stewards in the crew's mess that he encouraged new ideas and suggestions, regardless of their origin. Someone suggested—and the captain enthusiastically jumped on the idea—that a spare Mae West life vest should be attached to the periscope housing. Then, if someone accidentally got trapped topside when they made a hasty dive, that man would at least have the opportunity to grab the flotation device, greatly increasing his chances of survival.

On the day before they were to depart Australia and return to war, Morton called the crew to quarters early. Reveille still echoed across the wharf, and a thick morning mist hung over the harbor.

Mush Morton may have called on some of the pep talks he had heard before Naval Academy football games as he spoke a few words to *Wahoo*'s crew that morning. Or he may have been thinking for a long time about what he would tell the men with whom he would serve on his first real warship command. He wanted to inspire, but he also wanted to make a strong point about how things were about to change aboard the boat.

His voice was so quiet the men had to strain to hear him.

"Men, I want you to understand one thing. *Wahoo* is expendable. Our job is to sink enemy shipping. We are going out there . . ." He pointed to the east, where the Brisbane River snaked its way toward the Pacific. ". . . we are going out there to search for Japs. Every smoke trace on the horizon, every contact on watch will be investigated. If it turns out to be the enemy, we *will* hunt him down and we *will* kill him."

His voice grew louder as he went. Morton paused for only a moment. There was not a sound on the deck of the submarine, where the men stood listening to their new skipper. Only the distant chatter of seagulls broke the quiet, though it would not have surprised a man standing there in ranks if there had been a punctuating bolt of lightning and an instant clap of thunder. Their captain's simple, direct words were just that powerful.

"Now, if there is anyone on this boat who does not want to go along on this run under these conditions, just see the yeoman." He pointed to Forest Sterling, just to make sure everyone knew whom he was talking about. "I am giving him verbal authority here and now to transfer anyone who is not a volunteer, and there will be no questions asked and no repercussions against him. You have my word that nothing will ever be said about anyone who remains behind. You have thirty minutes to see the yeoman."

Sterling had no idea what to expect as he waited in the ship's office, smoking one cigarette after another and draining several cups of coffee. He really needed to hit the head, but what if someone came to unvolunteer while he was gone? What if half the crew showed up and wanted out? What if that part about *Wahoo* being expendable spooked some of the best sailors aboard?

No need to worry. Nobody showed up to opt out.

Exactly thirty minutes after Morton had finished his stirring speech and dismissed the crew, he stuck his head into the yeoman's office.

"Any customers, Yeo?" he asked happily, as if he knew the answer already.

"No, sir. Not a soul."

Morton slapped the bulkhead with an open hand.

"That's the kind of men I like in a crew," he exclaimed. "That just tells me that we are going to sink some Jap ships on this trip."

Sterling nodded.

It must also be reported that the captain's speech on the deck that morning had, indeed, unnerved a few of the crew. One of the chiefs, Ralph Pruett, was career Navy, and he had seen all types of sub sailors—officers and enlisted men—in his day.

"I've always been wary of men like the captain," he later said. "I just did not think he had a postwar plan. I did. I planned on coming back from the war alive. Morton? I don't believe he thought that far ahead."

Several of the chiefs asked Sterling to meet with them in the CPO quarters—a part of the submarine usually called the "goat locker." They knew Sterling had served with Morton in China, and they hoped he could give them a bit of an idea of what kind of man they were about to follow into battle. Sterling had no special insight, telling them the captain was pretty much what they saw.

Grider and Paine talked about Morton's style after the speech, too.

The tone of it, along with some of Morton's comments on the previous patrol when he was shadowing Kennedy, left both officers just a tad uneasy.

"There had been times on that second patrol when his opinions suggested the absence of any reasonable degree of caution. It's one thing to be aggressive and another to be foolhardy. It would be a mistake to think an average man never thinks about his own hide. Most of us, in calculating the risk, threw in a mental note that we were worth more to the Navy alive than dead. Worth more to our wives and children as well. But when Mush expressed himself on tactics, the only risk he recognized was the risk of not sinking enemy ships."

But Grider and the other officers were even more worried about their XO. They watched as O'Kane almost fanatically practiced his new role in the conning tower and on the bridge.

"Dick talked a great deal," Grider later wrote. "It was reckless, aggressive talk, and it was natural to wonder how much of it was no more than talk. During the second patrol, Dick had grown harder to live with. He was friendly and easygoing one minute, and then he was pulling his rank on his junior officers the next. One day he would be a martinet, and the next he would display an overlenient, what-the-hell attitude. That was not reassuring."

And that, of course, left the big question several men in the crew of *Wahoo* were asking as they made final preparations for the boat's third war patrol. George Grider stated it quite succinctly.

"With Mush and Dick in the saddle, how would the *Wahoo* fare?"

CHAPTER 14

The Definition of "Reconnaissance"

"Just sight, track, shoot, and sink!"

—Mush Morton, quoted in *Newsweek*,
May 3, 1943

"*All hands aboard and* Wahoo *ready for patrol, sir!*"

With those words from Dick O'Kane, Mush Morton knew that everything was set for departure. On the morning of January 16, 1943, officially pronounced ready for sea, they sat at the pier, nestled among other submarines. With the river's current, it would be a bit tricky backing away and getting turned to head for the sea, out there beyond Moreton Bay—renamed already by the crew as "Morton" Bay—without risking a fender bender with the other submarines and the tender *Sperry*.

But the skipper showed his inclinations from the very first maneuver with him occupying *Wahoo*'s bridge.

"Cast off all lines," he ordered. And once they were untethered, he said without hesitation, "All back full."

Mush did nothing slowly or cautiously, and crew members—approving or not—took note of his demeanor from the very beginning.

Anytime they were on the surface, he ran the boat at full speed, about twenty-one knots. He had everyone practice quicker dives, and even routine trim dives were treated as emergency ones. They quickly shaved three or four seconds off their best record to date, but not without some bumps and bruises when lookouts literally came down the ladder from the bridge into the conn without touching the rungs, landing on top of one another.

"Boys, we want to be able to stay on the surface as long as we can," he told them. "That's where the hunting is. But we have to be able to pull the plug in a hurry if we do."

Wahoo also practiced quick surfacing, bobbing to the surface, opening the after hatch from the conning tower for the gun crew to man the four-inch deck gun as soon as the hatch was above the surface of the sea.

From Moreton Bay and for the first two hundred miles, *Wahoo* performed practice operations with USS *Patterson* (DD-392), already a hero of Guadalcanal, mostly simulating attacks and avoiding detection while giving the crew of the destroyer the chance to stalk a submarine by sound and sight. Along the way, Morton told the destroyer's skipper that anytime he spotted *Wahoo*'s periscope, he was to stop anything else he might be doing and charge toward the submarine as fast as he could. Morton wanted to practice the dreaded "down-the-throat" shot—firing on a rapidly approaching vessel that presented the slimmest of profiles, only her bow and the width of the ship.

Some of the officers looked at one another with worried eyes. Surely he wouldn't! Not if the vessel steaming straight toward them was Japanese, intent on ramming them or dropping depth charges on them or both. The gleeful look on Mush Morton's face the one time he had the chance to practice the down-the-throat shot with *Patterson* did little to make them feel better. Roger Paine had actually experienced such an attempt back aboard *Pompano,* and it had nearly resulted in disaster. He never wanted the experience again.

Before they realized it, because of all the full-speed running on the surface, they had left their practice partner behind and were four hundred miles farther along than expected. According to their operational orders, they were on the way back to the vicinity of Truk, an area even busier with enemy shipping by then. But there was also a rather vague look-see scheduled for them along the way.

The crew knew exactly where they were headed this time. That was unusual, though it was always difficult to keep much of anything secret aboard a submarine. Once the navigational charts had been taken from the ship's office, most everyone could deduce their destination. But there was a good reason why everyone aboard *Wahoo* was now so well-informed. As they made their way through the South Pacific and Coral Sea back toward the Solomons, the captain had decreed that the top-secret operational orders be posted so every crew member could read them.

The XO bristled. He was still a fan of Morton, and even of some of his relaxed and commonsense methods, but this was simply not done. Enlisted men were not let in on top-secret orders. He decided to say so to his captain when he got the chance.

Morton just grinned and slapped him hard on the back.

"Hell, Dick, last time I checked, we are all in the same boat. Why not let them take a look?"

O'Kane shrugged. He had never thought of it that way.

One afternoon, George Grider had the watch as they ran on the surface. He was nervous, running along in enemy waters, up there where everybody could see them, leaving a long, visible wake. But the captain was in a hurry.

Just then, Morton popped up the ladder next to him, in a talkative mood.

"Nice day!" he told Grider. "Hard to believe there is a war going—"

"Aircraft! Starboard bow!" one of the lookouts called. Radar saw the plane at the same instant, with the news that it was eight miles away and approaching.

Grider turned to head down the hatch to the conn, fully expecting the captain to give the "Dive!" command. Instead, Morton grabbed Grider by the collar with one of those big hands and literally dragged him back to the bridge.

"Hang on. Let's wait until he gets in to six miles. We'll still have time to get down."

At just over six miles, Grider was on the verge of giving the order himself. He gripped the bridge railing with both hands, ready to jump down the hatch and deal with the wrath of his skipper later. Morton calmly watched through his binoculars the speck in the bright sky that was the deadly enemy aircraft.

"It's turning. Opening distance. He doesn't see us," radar reported.

Morton continued to scan the sky. *Wahoo* plowed on.

Grider later wrote, "I knew then we were under the command of a madman."

There was one portion of the operational orders that left everyone scratching their heads: "Adjust speed, if possible, to permit daylight reconnaissance vicinity Wewak Harbor, New Guinea, Lat4 (degrees) S, Long144 (degrees) E."

There were reports from aircraft that an unusual amount of shipping had been spotted in the area of a tiny glob of sand and shallow water called Wewak, on the northern shore of New Guinea. The orders were fuzzy on the exact location of the harbor, describing a point that was actually a square that was sixty miles long on each side. The charts aboard *Wahoo* did not even mention Wewak. The ship's copy of *Sailing Directions*, usually a reliable listing of bays and harbors, did not offer a clue either.

Well, the orders did say "if possible." They could simply steam on past and go to where they were eventually supposed to be.

But the captain was not willing to give up so easily. The aircraft reports said there were Jap ships there. He wanted to do all they could to find Wewak and the Jap ships.

"Pappy" Rau, the COB, stuck his head into the wardroom where Morton, O'Kane, and the XO's assistant navigator, Fertig Krause, were poring over the charts, looking for the unmarked harbor.

"Captain, we may have some help for you," he announced, and ushered in one of the enlisted men, Chief Motor Machinist's Mate Dalton Keeter.

Keeter, who bore the nickname "Bird Dog," had purchased a cheap grade-school atlas while in Australia with the intent of sending it to his children back home when they got to port. Since he had been privy to the operational orders hanging there for all to see, he had looked up Wewak in the book. Sure enough, there it was, shown in surprising detail, including the islands that protected it.

After doing some comparisons, O'Kane noticed that the map was drawn at the wrong scale to match it up with their real charts. George Grider, an amateur photographer, had the answer. He pulled out his father's camera and used a lamp as a projector to cast an image of the kid's atlas on top of the ship's charts. Krause traced the squiggly lines that were Wewak and its surrounding barrier islands right on top of the official chart.

"Look at that, boys," Morton said as he compared the overlay with the details on their usual chart. "Plenty of landmarks and deep water in the harbor. We could get in there and get out easy."

Each man hearing the skipper had the same thought: What was the captain's definition of "daylight reconnaissance"?

"George, what does reconnaissance mean to you?" Morton asked Grider, sensing the misgivings.

Without hesitation, Grider quoted the textbook definition: "We are cautious and avoid detection. We look at the area from as far out at sea as possible, through the periscope, while submerged."

Morton shook his head.

"Wrong! The only way to really reconnoiter a harbor is to go right in there with some daylight and take a close look at what's there."

Such a thing had been done before. Done and reported by at least one U-boat skipper. However, that had been at night and with a submarine that had proper charts.

On the way, too, they had to pass through the narrow Vitiaz Strait, and there was the added danger from a Japanese airfield on the island of New Britain, only thirty miles to their starboard. Normal procedure would have been to make the run through the strait while submerged, but Morton was intrigued by the possibilities at Wewak and wanted plenty of time to play there.

He doggedly kept them on the surface, plowing ahead at just better than twenty knots.

He did order two additional lookouts, each equipped with specially equipped binoculars that allowed him to look close to the sun. He did not want to be surprised by enemy aircraft zooming down at them from that blind spot in the sky.

As they drew even closer to the island where the air base was—as close as twenty miles at one point—it was George Grider who once again had the bridge watch in a dicey situation.

"What the hell," he decided, and sent for his sunglasses. Morton, standing at his elbow, grinned.

Later, still certain the skipper had no intention of hiding unless they actually saw an approaching aircraft, Grider sent someone to bring him a bottle of suntan lotion.

Morton laughed out loud, from his toenails.

Then, fifteen minutes later, the captain checked the chart, considered the distance yet to go to Wewak, looked up into the blazing tropical sun, and, while appreciating Grider's bravado but noticing his discomfort as well, said, "All right, George, you can take her down now."

They arrived in the vicinity of Wewak just before dawn on January 24, eight days out of Brisbane. Morton proclaimed to all that he was ready for a fight. With the periscope poking up through the wave tops, they almost ran smack into a couple of torpedo boats. *Wahoo* scooted away to maneuver around and get a look past the several small islands that blocked their view of the harbor's anchorage.

Several of the officers were still concerned about what Morton might do in the name of "reconnaissance." They were about to find out.

At 1318 an object was sighted in the bight of MUSHU ISLAND, about five miles farther into the harbor, much resembling the bridge structure of a ship. Commenced approach at three knots. As the range closed the aspect of the target changed from that of a tender with several small ships along-side to that of a destroyer with RO-class submarines nested, the latter identified by the canvas hatch hoods and awnings . . . it was our intention to fire high-speed shots from about 3,000 yards, which would permit us to remain in deep water and facilitate an exit.

No, he wasn't!

Mush Morton was going to enter Wewak harbor and fire torpedoes at a destroyer! And the sun was about to show up on the horizon within the hour!

Everyone in the conn was busy charting and confirming islands, the beach, shallow spots—all in the name of plotting a course of escape after this mad intrusion into an enemy harbor inevitably blew up in their faces. But Morton seemed calm, at ease, in control.

Once, the boat began to rock noticeably, side to side. They were so close to a reef that the swells were actually moving the submarine.

Dick O'Kane, who had been calling out every bit of land and shallow he could see through the periscope, suddenly shouted, "Captain, we're too close to land! All I can see is one coconut tree!"

"Aw, Dick," the captain responded calmly. "You're just in low power."

O'Kane, his mouth little more than a thin line, flipped the scope handle to increase the device's magnification and took another peek.

"Down periscope! All back emergency!"

Men grabbed anything solid they could find as the boat reversed direction.

"What's the matter, Dick?"

"All I could see was one coconut!"

Grider later reported, "The captain was in his element. He was in danger but he was hot on the trail of the enemy, so he was happy. The atmosphere in the conning tower would have been more appropriate to a fraternity raiding party. Mush even joked when we almost ran the boat aground."

On the next observation, when the generated range was 3,750, our target, a FUBUKI-class destroyer, was under way.

"George, we can take that son of a bitch by complete surprise," Morton told Grider. "He'd never suspect a submarine would be in here shooting at him."

No shit! No one on *Wahoo* would have suspected it either.

The water in the bay was dead calm, and even a small portion of their periscope sticking up would be easily spotted. O'Kane raised it every few minutes, took a quick look, and dropped it back into its housing.

It was beginning to get uncomfortable up and down the length of the boat. With the boat rigged for silent running, the humidity and temperature inside had gone up dramatically, and tension only added to the discomfort. Men wiped sweat from their eyes as they studied gauges and listened on headsets.

In retrospect, even the most aggressive skippers would have probably let the destroyer go, backed away, and reported what they had found at Wewak. And would have done it from a safe distance while proceeding on to their primary hunting grounds. Pinky Kennedy and others who commanded submarines at the beginning of the war, trained in totally different methods of running their boats, would never even have been there to begin with.

However, Mush Morton was not backing away from anything. It was clear that he had every intention of shooting at the enemy warship. Forget the shallow water, the tight escape route, and the likelihood that even if they hit this quick and agile target with a good enough shot to cripple or sink her, there were likely other ships up there that could do them harm. Hell, they had already seen and driven away from two patrol boats.

At 1441 fired spread of three torpedoes on 110-degree starboard track, range 1,800 yards, using target speed fifteen, since there had been insufficient time to determine speed by tracking.

Oh, there was that, too. The destroyer—determined now to be the *Harusame*—was moving rapidly, following an erratic course. With only quick peeks through the scope and by listening to the noise she made, even O'Kane, who was a master at such calculations, found it difficult to determine where to fire torpedoes.

"Anytime, Dick," Morton said, his voice cool, unruffled.

Three torpedoes were away on O'Kane's command of "Fire!" Three torpedoes, fired from the forward tubes, eleven and twelve seconds apart, set to run only two feet deep to ensure that they would punch holes in the ship at the waterline, not run beneath her.

O'Kane boldly left the periscope up and watched all three torpedoes miss astern. The destroyer was moving quite a bit faster than they had hurriedly calculated. They got off another torpedo, based on a new estimated speed, but the Japanese captain had seen the first three fish swimming his way and past him. He easily dodged the fourth.

O'Kane's eyes at the scope suddenly grew large.

"He's turned and he is coming straight at us!" he reported, fighting to keep his voice calm, cool. "Down scope!"

The men in the forward torpedo room were moving as quickly as they could, getting ready to reload their empty tubes. The men in the maneuvering room stood ready to move the array of rheostats and levers to get the power they would need to run.

Back in the crew's mess, Forest Sterling felt "an almost uncontrollable urge to urinate."

"To hell with that!" Mush Morton shouted. "Leave the damn scope up, by God! We'll give the son of a bitch a point of aim if he wants one!"

Jesus, he was really going to do it! Mush was going to try a down-the-throat shot on a charging enemy warship in a tiny armpit of a harbor.

They were all about to die.

As O'Kane raised the periscope back up, he dreaded what he would see. But he also quickly did the math in his head. If they shot before the destroyer was any closer than a thousand to twelve hundred yards away, the Japanese captain could easily dodge out of the torpedo's path and keep coming. If he got any closer than seven hundred yards, a torpedo would not have time to arm itself. That meant that even if it struck the tiny sliver of a target presented by the destroyer's bow, it would only clank against its hull harmlessly.

There would be a range of three to four hundred yards of glassy harbor in which they had any hope of doing damage. Everything had to work perfectly. Otherwise, they would have an angry hornet buzzing directly overhead, dropping TNT on them and with little room to flee its wrath.

Watched him come and kept bow pointed at him. Delayed firing our fifth torpedo until the destroyer had closed to about 1,200 yards, angle on the bow 10 degrees starboard.

O'Kane blinked away sweat. The wake off each side of the destroyer's bow looked like a white mustache, reaching almost to the ship's anchors. She was plowing directly at them at high speed.

"She's yours, Dick," Morton said, his words barely audible in the din of the conn.

"Right a hair," O'Kane said, his voice surprisingly calm and measured, almost a whisper in the conning tower, influenced by the contagious composure of his skipper. "Left a hair. Range twelve hundred yards."

O'Kane was waiting for any sign that the destroyer might vary its course enough to give him a view of anything besides her sharp knife blade of a bow. Or that he could maneuver *Wahoo* left or right enough to give them a broader target. But at the speed the target was approaching, there simply was no more time to wait, to hope.

"Anytime, Dick."

Morton might just as well have been asking his XO to pass the salt.

A few seconds later, after calling a couple more course corrections and with the ship lined up as best it could be, O'Kane shouted, "Fire!"

Their fifth torpedo was away. Only one was left loaded and ready in the forward room, and there would be no time to get more ready or to swirl the boat around and shoot from the aft tubes.

O'Kane's face now showed no emotion at all as he watched the destroyer easily skirt away from the latest war shot.

"Missed to her port. Range nine hundred and fifty yards," O'Kane reported, as if announcing the menu in the officers' mess.

"Fire when she fills four divisions," Morton told him. Fire when the destroyer covered four of the range markings in the periscope's optics, the captain was telling his XO.

"Captain, she's filling eight already."

For the first time, there was a fleeting look on the captain's face that hinted he might be questioning the decision to steam into the harbor and make a mess of things. Only a couple of men in the conn who glanced his way saw it. But just as quickly, his face went stony once more.

"Anytime, Dick."

To ensure maximum likelihood of hitting with our last torpedo on the forward tubes, withheld fire until range was about 800 yards.

It was probably closer to 750 yards when the final torpedo whooshed away.

Forest Sterling remembers, "I was calm. There was the firm certainty that I was going to die."

George Grider was mentally congratulating himself for remembering to leave his last will and testament behind when they left on the patrol.

God help them if they had miscalculated the range—the torpedo would not be armed—or the target's speed as it closed on them. Or if the destroyer veered. Or if the torpedo was one of the duds. Or if one of a hundred other possible things had gone wrong.

Varrrooommm! Booommmm!

"This last one . . . clipped him amidships in twenty-five seconds and broke his back. The explosion was terrific!" was the description in the patrol log.

Men bounced off bulkheads and some hit the floor as the blast gave *Wahoo* a hard shove. O'Kane later described "a mighty roar and cracking, as if we were caught in the midst of a lightning storm. The cracking became crackling, like steam heating a bucket of water, but amplified a million times."

The destroyer was coming apart, and her boilers had erupted in a staggering blast.

George Grider had exited the conn to the control room below as soon as the last torpedo available in the forward tubes was fired. His job was to take them down as deep as they dared go as they escaped in unfamiliar and treacherous water. They did not want to ram the bottom of the harbor after successfully destroying one of its occupants.

Ninety feet. That was as far down as he could take her without expecting the sharp jolt of their bottoming out. Even then, he half expected to find the floor.

They had been there only a moment when the captain called down to Grider to bring them back to periscope depth. His order came amid the shouts and cheers that rang out up and down the length of *Wahoo* in response to the thunderous explosion.

"We hit the son of a bitch!" Roger Paine said, wide-eyed, sweat streaming down his face.

Mush Morton shrugged.

"By God, maybe we did."

Dick O'Kane looked through the scope and reported the destroyer literally broken in half. They were so close he could see crew members diving off the wreckage and others—many in their dress white uniforms—climbing the masts, trying to postpone the inevitable swim they were about to take.

Grider was back up the ladder. This time he brought his camera and was busy shooting pictures through the scope, describing "a ship broken in two like a matchstick, her bow already settling into the water. Her crew swarmed all over her, hundreds of them, in the rigging, all over the deck."

Fubuki-class destroyers typically carried a crew of more than two hundred men.

The topside was covered with Japs on turret tops and in the rigging. Over 100 members of the crew must have been acting as lookouts.

The captain sent out a call to the crew. Anyone who could safely break away from his duty station could come to the conn and take a look at the damage they had done.

"Come on up, boys," he told the quickly forming line. "Come on up and look what a great crew and a great ship can do. Look at the slant-eyed devils in the rigging about to get their asses wet."

We took several pictures, and as her bow was settling fast we went to 150 feet and commenced the nine-mile trip out of WEWAK. Heard her boilers go in between the noise of continuous shelling from somewhere, plus a couple of aerial bombs. They were evidently trying to make us lie on the bottom until their patrol boats could return.

A quick ping of the fathometer—all they dared risk—showed 150 feet of depth, but Grider kept them at 100 feet anyway, just to be safe. He and the crew used mostly the noise of waves hitting the beach and reefs to guide them out of the place.

After fourteen hours of running submerged, *Wahoo* finally surfaced just after five p.m. The fresh sea air smelled especially sweet as it whistled down the open hatches.

The captain ordered the dispensing by the pharmacist's mate of the rations of "medicinal alcohol" to every crew member. That, too, tasted especially good that afternoon.

Dick O'Kane tried to stay awake to enjoy the afterglow of their experience. Morton would have none of it. His XO had been on his feet—mostly in the conning tower dancing with the periscope—for the better part of thirty-six hours.

"Dick, get to bed," the skipper told him. "I may need you to man the scope again here in the next little while." And then Morton went to the crew's mess to thank them again for their stellar performance in the face of a harrowing attack. "Boys, this is one sea story you can tell the rest of your lives."

Nobody doubted it. Assuming they had a "rest of their lives," if this was any indication of how their new skipper was going to run the patrol.

In addition to Mush Morton, the one man whose reputation benefited greatest from the Wewak assault was Dick O'Kane. Forest Sterling remembers, "He was cool as a cucumber. He stayed right on the periscope and looked right down their throats with that destroyer coming in plenty fast and shooting right at us. I had never seen anything like it."

George Grider was impressed, too. He later wrote, "I marveled at the change that came over Dick O'Kane since the attack began. It was as if during all the talkative, boastful months before, he had been lost, seeking his true element, and now it was found. He was calm, terse, and utterly cool. My opinion of him underwent a permanent change. It was not the first time I had observed that the conduct of men under fire cannot be predicted accurately from their everyday actions, but it was the most dramatic example I was ever to see of a man transformed under pressure from what seemed almost adolescent petulance to a prime fighting machine."

Someone later asked Mush Morton how he had kept so calm in the face of a charging enemy warship and during such a risky assault.

"Hell, why do you think I had Dick on the periscope? He's the bravest man I know."

Morton took his praise of O'Kane one step farther in his summation in the official patrol report.

"The conduct and discipline of the officers and men of this ship while under fire were superb. They enjoyed nothing better than a good fight. I commend them all for a job well-done, especially Lieutenant R. H. O'KANE the Executive Officer, who is cool and deliberate under fire. O'KANE is the fightingest naval officer I have ever seen and is worthy of the highest of praise. I commend Lieutenant O'KANE for being an inspiration to the ship."

Those words went a long way toward O'Kane's eventually getting his own command, and toward his eventually becoming the top skipper of World War II, based on number of enemy ships sunk.

As the men savored their brandy and pushed ahead to the waters off Truk to continue their hunting, they had no idea that this was only the opening act in what would turn out to be one of the most historic submarine patrols ever, one that would inspire not only the Navy but the entire USA.

Their success would not be credited only to such a "superb" crew, a fine ship, and "the fightingest naval officer" who served as her XO. It would be because their skipper was a man who was doing exactly what he had been placed on the planet to do.

To kill the sonza bitches.

CHAPTER 15

Like Ants Off a Hot Plate

"Prisoners of war . . . must at all times be humanely treated and protected, particularly against acts of violence, insults and public curiosity. Measures of reprisal against them are prohibited."

—Article 2, the Geneva Convention accords

*T*hey were in a war zone, enemy-controlled waters. For that reason, no one really expected any special marking of their crossing of the equator, certainly not the traditional shellback-and-polliwog ceremony, a long-established nautical rite of passage. Captain Kennedy had hardly even mentioned it on the way down. That meant those who were on the first patrol and crossed the equator for the first time had not been through the initiation yet.

Once again, Morton showed he was of a different mind-set than Pinky Kennedy.

He insisted that everyone take part in the festivities—Japanese-controlled waters or not—and that all polliwogs be properly indoctrinated as new shellbacks. King Neptune made an appearance, greased bellies were kissed, rear ends were paddled, and vile substances were ingested.

There was no mention of the fun in the patrol report, only that they dived at 1645 and "held various drills." And while submerged, they "passed under the equator." Everyone had a rollicking good time, even the ones who caught the worst of the ceremony.

Just after 0800 the next morning, Morton was called to the bridge. A sampan had been spotted far from land, and its crew was rowing as hard as it could to get away from *Wahoo*. Gunnery Mate Bill Carr fired a few quick bursts from his tommy gun across the little boat's bow and it stopped immediately. Morton brought the submarine closer, moving cautiously, fully expecting gunfire.

But *Wahoo* quickly determined the sampan's "crew" consisted of a half dozen haggard men, all in bad shape. There were also the bodies of three more men aboard the pitiful little craft. The survivors were skinny, covered with sores, and so weak they could hardly raise their arms in surrender. It appeared they had now lost the will to live.

Using crude sign language, Morton learned that one of the survivors was blind. He and the others were quite sick and on the verge of starvation.

Morton called the mess boys to the bridge. Though they had a long patrol ahead of them and would require all the stores they had packed away aboard *Wahoo*, Morton felt sorry for the pitiable men on the little death trap of a boat.

"Boys, give them all the fruit, canned goods, and bread you can spare," he told the mess boys. "And some cigarettes and water, too."

Meanwhile, Dick O'Kane got busy and marked up a spare chart, showing the course to the nearest land, and handed it over to the men.

The last they saw of the sampan, the men were waving at them, grinning weakly, chewing on the food the crew and kind captain of *Wahoo* had provided them.

George Grider was three minutes away from going off watch the morning of January 26 when he spotted something unmistakable on the horizon.

Smoke!

"Smoke on the horizon, broad on the port bow!" he called down to the control room on the communicator. Still on the surface, Grider brought the submarine around to make a run to try to get ahead of whatever was making all that smoke out there.

Within an hour, they were in position to see two ships' masts just coming into view, and then there was a third. There was still no sign of anything smaller that might be an escort. A convoy without an escort.

Two of the targets were freighters. A closer look through the periscope shortly after would confirm it. The type of the third vessel was still not clear, but it was too big to be a cruiser or patrol craft.

"Battle stations! Dive to periscope depth!" Morton ordered. Two blasts on the dive klaxon sent them down quickly.

They were soon in prime position to attack using the bow tubes, but a quick look through the periscope showed O'Kane that the ships had zigged and were now so close to them that the torpedoes might not have time to arm if they fired them. Morton ordered a sharp turn.

"We'll shoot from the after tubes," he announced. "Show 'em our ass!"

A crew member called out their speed even as O'Kane kept up a litany of bearings and ranges.

"Bearing mark!" One of the freighters—the leading one—was lined up in *Wahoo*'s crosshairs.

"Anytime, Dick," Mush Morton calmly said.

O'Kane waited a beat and then shouted, "Fire!"

Two torpedoes whooshed away from the stern tubes, but even before the submarine had settled down from the jolt of the torpedoes' launch, *Wahoo* had turned slightly and O'Kane had the second freighter in the sights.

The "Fire!" command sent two more torpedoes away, a mere seventeen seconds after the first two.

"All hot, straight, and normal."

But the ships were moving quickly and could just as easily make another quick course correction. They never had a chance to do that. Both torpedoes aimed at the first freighter struck home with a pair of mammoth explosions.

Only one fish struck the second ship, though. The TDC simply had not had time to input the last of the data that had been fed into it before the fourth torpedo was away. It missed.

Morton was not interested in taking time to inspect their damage, though. He was busy swinging *Wahoo* around so he could use the forward tubes on the other ship if need be. They now had six more fish loaded and ready to fire up there. O'Kane walked in a circle, trying to swing around to keep the targets in the scope as the submarine reversed direction beneath him.

"The first freighter is listing badly, sinking," he reported when he found it again, and then he started looking for the second one.

Something big suddenly filled his periscope and he stopped.

"You're on the wrong bearing if you are looking for the second target, Dick," Morton pointed out. "By now, it'll be—"

"That may be, but I've got a big one coming right at us," the XO said. "Zero angle on the bow."

Morton's face split into a broad grin.

"All right then," he said. "Shoot the SOB down the throat."

"There's the other target, too. Coming our way but she's limping, not close. The big one . . . she's a transport of some kind," O'Kane reported. "Still coming right at us."

Sound confirmed the XO's observation. The transport's screws were loud in his headset.

Sometimes it is just as good to be lucky as it is to be good.

But then, before the big ship was lined up properly, someone's hand hit the firing plunger prior to the command to fire being given. A torpedo was away. It would clearly miss, so O'Kane and Morton—ignoring the crewman's mistake for the moment—were quickly trying to get all information into the TDC so they could manage their second down-the-throat shot in three days. But then the transport's captain, who had obviously seen the errant torpedo headed his way, made a quick course move. He was trying to not only avoid the shot but to dodge any others that might be following that one out of the bowels of the American submarine. Once he made the feint, he would try to race away from the submerged vessel that was shooting at him.

In the process, he presented *Wahoo* a full broadside view of his ship.

Within seconds, two more torpedoes were away with a kick. Both struck the transport with earsplitting thunder. The roar of the hellish blast reverberated up and down the length of *Wahoo*.

But there was no time for Morton and his gang to enjoy the thrill of the kill. The other wounded vessel was still heading straight for them, their periscope possibly visible to the ship's captain by now. It was clearly the ship's intent to ram them, and she drew more than enough water to do a damn good job of it.

Swinging the boat that way, Morton got off two torpedoes. One exploded but did not slow the charging hulk. Probably a "premature," blowing up harmlessly short of the target. The other one hit the ship with a solid clang, according to the soundman. It did not explode.

Damn premature! Damn dud!

"Damn bad torpedoes are going to get us all killed," Morton muttered, red-faced.

The limping target charged on toward them, maybe aware of its mighty luck, maybe not.

The nerve of the enemy ship's captain was not lost on *Wahoo*'s crew. George Grider later noted, "I had a higher regard for the captain of that freighter than for any other enemy skipper we ever fought."

Whether the Japanese warship's commander was brave, stubborn, dumb, or whatever, Morton knew he had to duck the guy, and do it quickly, before the son of a bitch gave them one big headache. There was always the chance the wounded ship carried depth charges, too, and would be salting the sea with them shortly.

He quickly had *Wahoo* at top submerged speed. Grider took them down below a hundred feet as briskly as he could do it.

"That was Morton," O'Kane later wrote. "Be on the offensive or the defensive but never in between."

As they made their quick dodge, Morton and the rest of the crew could hear what sounded like a thunderstorm raging outside their hull.

There followed so many explosions that it was impossible to tell just what was taking place.

Much of the cacophony was the first freighter—the one that had taken two torpedoes—sinking, breaking up. The din was more than enough to render the submarine's sonar virtually deaf. They had to wait until the death throes of the target had subsided before sound could pick out the other two vessels and try to figure out where they were. Only then would it be safe to come back to periscope depth and look around. They certainly did not want to come up and bump their heads on one of the two damaged ships.

When they did come up for a look the transport ship sat there, dead in the water. Morton made the quick decision to finish her off, the easy target, and then they would chase the freighter down. That ship—the one with the tenacious skipper—was now hobbling away, steaming as fast as she could manage with her damaged engines.

As O'Kane gazed through the periscope, he noticed splashes in the sea all around them. The transport's crew was firing desperately at them, likely aiming for the scope that pricked the water's surface.

Headed for transport and maneuvered for a killer shot.

"Anytime," Morton said coolly, nodding at Dick O'Kane.

Two torpedoes were quickly away, headed for the transport. The fire control party cheered heartily, knowing it would be difficult to miss this sitting duck. O'Kane had already made the assumption that their target was a troop transport, and, judging from all the activity on her deck, she carried many enemy soldiers. Enemy soldiers on the way to kill Americans on some godforsaken volcanic island.

"The crew was cheering as if the torpedoes were racehorses and they had money on them," he recalled later. "But it was more than that. American lives could be riding on our assault on that troopship."

One torpedo struck and failed to explode. Another dud! But the second one hit home, just beneath the ship's smokestack.

The explosion blew her midships section higher than a kite. Troops commenced jumping over the side like ants off a hot plate. Her stern went up and she headed for the bottom. Took several pictures.

O'Kane was at the attack scope, and COB Pappy Rau watched through the search scope. Both could see a massive hole opened in the ship's side, but it soon disappeared as the vessel listed toward them and began to quickly sink.

Morton had already turned his attention to chasing down the wounded duck that was getting away. But then he grimaced and swore under his breath. They had a problem.

Their batteries were getting dangerously low after all the submerged maneuvering they had been doing. *Wahoo* could now only manage about three knots on battery power alone, and that would not last long. The Japanese freighter's engineers must have been able to work miracles and get another boiler online, because they were now making a good ten knots as they headed desperately for the horizon.

Frustrated, Morton pounded the chart table with the heel of his hand.

"Damn! Okay, come to the surface, get a charge going, and let's let the crew get fed and rested. We'll chase down the bastard on the surface when we can. If that's all the speed he can make . . ."

The disappointment was obvious in the captain's face and voice. He had likely just sunk two ships and severely damaged another. That one was a wounded duck waddling away, but it would be catchable. Still, their captain was angry that all three enemy ships were not already on the bottom.

Morton and O'Kane remained in the conning tower, eating supper but not tasting the sandwiches and hot, black coffee that had been brought up to them from the galley. Suddenly, out of the blue, another option appeared on the horizon. At first, O'Kane thought it might be a cruiser come to rescue the troops who were now either being pulled out of the water by a flotilla of lifeboats, clinging to debris, or trying to swim without attracting the attention of hungry sharks. This newcomer could also be a destroyer hurrying over to find and destroy the American submarine that had just sunk one of their troop transport ships.

Soon, though, they could see it was a tanker, another perfectly worthwhile target. On its present course, it would most likely steam right past the mess in the water that *Wahoo* had just made. Some of the officers were surprised when Morton made the snap decision to leave the tanker alone, allowing it to steam on unmolested.

"Aw, we'll let her go for now," he told the men in the conning tower. "She's on the same course as the freighter. We'll chase them down and sink 'em when we get a good battery charge."

The captain had just made a fateful decision, the results of which would become the most controversial and debated event in Mush Morton's tenure.

Decided to let these two ships get over the horizon while we surfaced to

*charge batteries and destroy the estimated twenty troop boats now in the
water. These boats were of many types, scows, motor launches, cabin cruisers, and nondescript varieties.*

Indeed, the sea seemed suddenly to be teeming with vessels of various
sizes, including some lifeboats from the transport itself. Others appeared
to be fishing boats or other small craft that had shown up to help the
survivors of the troopship. That ship, by the way, had now been positively
identified as the *Buyo Maru*.

Dick O'Kane later recalled Morton's reasoning for returning to the site
of the transport's sinking rather than pursuing the other two freighters.

"Dick, the Army bombards strategic areas and the Air Corps uses
area bombing so the ground forces can advance," Morton explained to
his XO when he noticed the questioning look in his number two's eyes.
"Now, with little risk of casualties among our crew, I will prevent these
soldiers from getting ashore. You see, for every one that doesn't make it,
it could mean an American life."

O'Kane had no objections. The XO understood perfectly what his
captain was saying. They both considered that if they did not go back to
destroy the "troop boats"—the scows and fishing boats picking up
survivors—it would be tantamount to aiding and abetting the enemy.

George Grider remembers it a bit differently. He saw what he described
as an almost "fierce joy" on Morton's face when he ordered, "Let's go finish them off."

At 1135 made battle surface and manned all guns.

With the gun crews ready to pop through the hatches as soon as they
were on the surface, the captain made his intentions quite clear to everyone who would man a deck gun or be up there carrying a weapon.

"I will order a single four-inch round at the largest craft," he told
them. "We will continue on into the midst of them, so be sure to keep
your crews in a protected area. If we draw any fire, I will give the command to commence return fire. Machine guns, you are to chase them out
of the boats. Chief Carr, use the four-inch to smash up the boats."

Men poured out of the hatches and onto the deck as soon as they
broke the surface. Morton and O'Kane took their positions on the bridge,

while Roger Paine watched over the gun crews carefully working their way across the slippery, wet deck. Paine later reported that he clearly heard the sound of bullets hitting the submarine's superstructure and others whistling overhead as soon as they surfaced and were topside.

Forest Sterling was on the starboard platform just above the bridge, stuffing cotton into his ears.

"Adrenaline was pouring into my bloodstream," he later recalled. "I felt a primitive instinct to do battle."

When the big diesel engines were started so they could begin charging the batteries, it must have sounded to the survivors in the water like the thunder of a rising storm on the horizon. They likely could not have seen the submarine yet. The ones in the boats could.

Fired 4" gun at largest scow loaded with troops. Although all troops in this boat apparently jumped in the water our fire was returned by small-caliber machine guns. We then opened fire with everything we had. Then set course 085 degrees at flank speed to overtake the cripple and tanker.

That was the complete entry—Morton's and O'Kane's entire official narrative in the patrol report—concerning the attack on the survivors of the *Buyo Maru*.

O'Kane later described the incident succinctly. When the scow returned fire after the single shot from the four-inch deck gun, Morton shouted, "Commence fire!" The XO likened the resulting assault to "fire hoses cleaning a street" and described enemy troops in their khaki shorts—all wearing life jackets—diving into the water as their boats were chewed to pieces by *Wahoo*'s guns.

Suddenly there was a sharp explosion right there on the deck of *Wahoo*. Some on the deck thought the Japanese must be firing at them with a bigger weapon. Bigger than what they should have had in those lifeboats.

From his spot on the lookout platform, Forest Sterling could see two men sprawled on the deck, writhing in pain. Later he learned that a shell had jammed in the barrel of the twenty-millimeter gun. A new barrel was quickly installed and the bad one was cast aside, left lying there on the deck. A minute later, the jammed shell exploded, sending shards of the gun's barrel flying. Two men were injured. Crew members helped them below for medical attention, and two more men took their spots on the gun.

At one point, Bill Carr spotted a Japanese soldier in the water, drifting closer and closer to *Wahoo*. It appeared to Carr that he was about to toss at them what the chief assumed was a hand grenade. He turned his .45 pistol in his direction and fired several rounds.

"Knock it off, Carr," Morton ordered, according to O'Kane.

The XO calculated that the entire operation—from surfacing to steaming away—took less than eighteen minutes. He also maintained that, although some troops were undoubtedly hit, no person was deliberately shot. Their goal, he stated, was to destroy the boats themselves and leave the enemy soldiers in the water.

Other crew members remembered it differently. Chief Engineman Ralph Pruett reported that the captain threatened to court-martial any man who did not come up on deck and help load the guns. And that those guns were definitely aimed at men floundering helplessly in the water.

George Grider was diving officer, but with almost half the crew on deck, he knew they were not going to do any sudden submersion. He came up the ladder to take a look at what was going on up there.

He later described "a sea of Japanese," men holding on to "every piece of flotsam, every broken stick, in lifeboats," looking at the submariners on *Wahoo*'s deck "with expressions beyond description." He would later characterize what he saw as "nightmarish moments."

At one point, another survivor floated near the submarine and appeared to be playing possum. A crewman called up to his captain and asked if he wanted him to attempt to take the man prisoner.

"I don't want the son of a bitch! Do you?" was reportedly Morton's answer.

And the swimmer was shot, according to reports.

There were other witnesses to the incident that day in addition to the crew of the American submarine besides the Japanese who were aboard *Buyo Maru* when she went down. Also on the troopship—and ultimately in the water—were almost five hundred prisoners of war, mostly Indians but a few British as well. These pitiful souls had already been held captive for a year and were being transported to the islands in the South Pacific to serve as slave labor.

As the American submarine appeared on the horizon, many of those POWs saw this, at long last, as their chance to be rescued. They yelled, "POW! POW!" and waved anything that they could find in the water that might be interpreted as a white flag, hoping the Americans would realize they were not enemy troops at all. But with the rumble of the submarine's engines and the clamor of all the gunfire, it is doubtful that anyone on *Wahoo* heard their shouts.

From his perch, Forest Sterling did notice one of the men waving a white piece of canvas, and it struck him that the swimmer might be trying to give up.

"I didn't think the Japs ever surrendered," he remarked to the lookouts above him, and pointed to the man. But his ears were still plugged with cotton, and he could not have heard what the man in the water was yelling.

Mush Morton was convinced by the uniforms he was seeing that the Japanese in the water were Marines. He had seen plenty of them during his time in China prior to the war in the pictures James Avent had shown him of the Japs casting an ominous pall over events they monitored.

That conviction made it even more important to Morton that these crack enemy troops not be allowed to survive to fight another day.

"For every one that doesn't make it, it could mean an American life," he had told his XO.

Then, just as suddenly as he had ordered the U-turn to deal with the troops who had survived their torpedoes, Morton decided it was time to go wreak havoc elsewhere.

At 1530 sighted smoke of the fleeing ships a point on the port bow. Changed course to intercept.

"Forest, can y'all still see the other two ships?" he asked Sterling, yelling to be heard over the continuing gunfire.

"Yes, Captain, I can still see their smoke," the yeoman answered.

"Let's go after those bastards as soon as we get a good charge on the batteries," Morton said. Then, shortly after, "Secure from battle stations surface."

Just that quickly, one of the most controversial combat operations of World War II was over.

At one point, Roger Paine estimated that there were "close to ten thousand of them in the water." Morton responded with his own guess, saying, "I figure about nine thousand five hundred of the sons a bitches."

Morton also later proudly reported that *Wahoo* had killed most of them. And he did not try to hide or deny the incident. On the contrary, he and most of the crew were pleased with themselves, convinced that they had struck a mighty blow, and that what they did that day would prevent American soldiers from "digging [those same Japanese] out of foxholes and shooting them out of palm trees."

Recent research—much of it based on the testimony of the surviving Indian POWs—indicates that in reality, the ship carried only about eleven hundred men, including the almost five hundred POWs who had been locked in her holds. Accounts show that about ninety Japanese were lost and almost two hundred POWs died, either in the initial sinking, in the gunfire from *Wahoo*, or in the water before additional rescue ships eventually showed up.

It is also likely that the assault lasted closer to an hour than O'Kane's estimate of about eighteen minutes.

Even though *Wahoo*'s third patrol—her first with Mush Morton at the helm—would become front-page news across America, there would be no details of the *Buyo Maru* sinking listed among her accomplishments. As we will see, the actions of Morton and his boat on this patrol would earn glowing praise from his superiors. Morton would not only receive the Navy Cross, but General Douglas MacArthur would award him the Army Distinguished Service Cross for his leadership in "his attack on a hostile convoy proceeding to reinforce the enemy forces in New Guinea." *Wahoo* would also receive the Presidential Unit Citation for, among other things, "destroying one transport and their personnel."

In retrospect, we know that even though Morton's actions that day were brutal—and within today's parameters certainly excessive and possibly criminal—he was operating in a different place and time, and against a different kind of enemy than his country had ever faced before. And it is also clear that he was completely within the command parameters prescribed by his superiors.

Perhaps the best indication of this is that no action was ever considered against Morton for his and his crew's assault on the survivors of *Buyo Maru*. Instead, he, his men, and his boat were praised and honored by his superiors for that assault as well as the rest of *Wahoo*'s third war patrol.

Other observers have attempted to portray Morton as racist, citing his white Southern upbringing. Those who knew him scoffed at such a pronouncement. Yes, he hated the Japanese, but that was because they were the enemy. And Mush Morton hated the enemy, whoever he was or whatever his race might be.

Forest Sterling later wrote, "You have to remember how badly we hated the Japs and how far we were behind in the war then."

After the third patrol, Morton was interviewed by a reporter who asked about the brutality of war and how it felt to take the life of an enemy soldier. The skipper did not sugarcoat his answer.

"That's the only way we'll ever lick 'em," the skipper explained. "The Japs fight hard and use all the tricks. We have to shoot, shoot, shoot."

That was exactly what Morton and *Wahoo* had done that day off New Guinea.

They "shot, shot, shot" at the enemy until it was time to chase down those other targets and try to take them down, too.

CHAPTER 16

"New Epic of Submarine Warfare"

"When Mush Morton expressed himself on tactics, the only risk he recognized was the risk of not sinking enemy ships."

—Lieutenant George Grider, junior officer, USS *Wahoo*

*W*ith *their smoke marking their position, the two fleeing ships—the damaged freighter and the tanker—were relatively easy to track. Morton brought* Wahoo *on a course to intercept them as they zigged and zagged, trying to line up while there was still enough daylight to attack. Still, they remained just over their horizon so the ships would not see the submarine coming after them.*

When he was close enough to make the decision, Morton chose to shoot at the tanker first, since she was as yet undamaged and more maneuverable. Just as it grew too dark to take the range through the periscope, *Wahoo* sent off a spread of three torpedoes.

One hit her hard with a deep-throated blast. Surprisingly, she continued plowing along. Morton swung the boat around to use the torpedoes in the stern tubes, this time aiming at the freighter. They had only four torpedoes left, and they were all aft. But the freighter's captain had seen enough and had turned away. The officers on *Wahoo* once again expressed their admiration for the vessel's skipper.

It was a moonless, dark tropical night, and fortunately the two wounded ships persisted in running close together. It took a while, but

Morton and O'Kane eventually solved the puzzle of what type of maneuvering the vessels were employing to try to get away from them. At one point, Morton had *Wahoo* running backward at full speed, but during the unusual maneuver, the force of the seawater on their rudder skewed the boat around into an unintended sharp turn, sending crewmen tumbling.

Finally, the word came from Morton: "Anytime, Dick."

With a quick check of his TBT, O'Kane gave the order and sent half of their remaining precious torpedoes spinning off toward the tanker, leaving only two for the other ship. A minute and twelve seconds later, they were rewarded with a brilliant flash that tore wide open the darkness of the night. And a second later, the force of the blast actually rocked the submarine beneath their feet, and the men topside could feel the concussion, much like the freshening winds from a gathering storm.

At 2025 fired two torpedoes at tanker, the second hitting him just abaft of his midships, breaking his back. He went down in the middle almost instantly.

"All ahead full!" Morton barked. "Let's go get that other bastard!"

There was good reason to hurry. The moon would be rising shortly, and as good as the freighter's captain and crew were, that little bit of light might be enough for the ship to evade *Wahoo* one more time. And this time, it might either get away or meet up with some help.

They passed close to the damaged tanker—now identified as *Ukishima Maru*—and saw the results of their shooting. Only the bow of the vessel was still afloat, and it was going down quickly.

As they drew closer to the limping freighter, desperately fired shells from the ship's guns pocked the sea. Nothing came close at first, but as the submarine ran on a parallel course, a well-placed shell suddenly landed in the water just ahead of them, its explosion splashing the bridge with water and forcing them down.

Morton was angry.

"Damn, Dick, how did they see us well enough to get a range on us?" he asked.

O'Kane could only shrug. "Those guys are damn good."

Now, with the solid thumps of shells landing in the water ninety feet above their heads, it appeared they would have to wait until morning and maybe try a dawn attack. But Morton would have none of that.

We tracked the freighter by sound until the noise of shell splashes let up, then surfaced at 2058, fifteen minutes after diving, and went after him. Two minutes later a large searchlight commenced sweeping sharp on our port bow, its rays seemingly just clearing our periscope shears.

The lookouts had just settled in the shears, water still dripping from their perch, when one of them excitedly called out, "Searchlight broad on our port bow!"

"Probably a destroyer," the captain said to no one in particular. "We gotta hurry. Figure the destroyer is making twenty knots and the freighter's doing ten. Give me a plot as quick as you can."

Morton figured the freighter would make a direct line for the approaching man-of-war, seeking its protection. In seconds, the fire control party had a position from which they could launch their last two torpedoes at the elusive freighter and still give *Wahoo* the best chance of running and hiding from the assumed destroyer.

Many on *Wahoo* had the same thought: The instant that searchlight was spotted, their former skipper would have been deep and gone.

At 2110, when the range was 2,900 yards by radar, twisted to the left for a straight stern shot, stopped and steadied. Three minutes later, with angle on the bow 135 degrees port by radar tracking, fired our last two torpedoes without spread.

"Anytime, Dick."

They were still a relatively long way out, but it was now or never. Dick O'Kane had a happy thought: If they hit the target, they would be out of torpedoes and on their way back to Pearl Harbor. But if they only damaged it more without sinking it, who knew what their captain might do to finish her off? Destroyer approaching or not?

"Constant bearing . . . mark!"

"Set."

"Fire!"

The first torpedo was away, and then, fifteen seconds afterward, the second whooshed off, both of their paths marked in the water by painfully bright phosphorescence. From that range, it would take the fish about three minutes to swim to their target. It was an agonizingly long time.

George Grider, studying the plots, had his doubts. He looked at Roger Paine and made him a bet, one that even the men on the bridge clearly heard over the 1MC announcing system.

"Roger, if either one of those torpedoes hits the target, I will kiss your royal ass."

As if on cue, first one and then a second detonation blew the night wide open. Both of them were powerful enough to shake *Wahoo*, even though she was over a mile and a half away.

Paine resisted the urge to drop his pants right there in the submarine's conning tower, but he grinned mightily at his fellow officer as shouts and cheers rang out up and down the length of the boat.

From his position topside, Forest Sterling could easily see the stubborn target turn over slowly, then split into two distinct sections, with one tilting up and sliding out of sight, all illuminated by the escort's light. He did not have a chance to see the second half disappear into the deep. The captain had them scrambling now to escape whatever kind of escort vessel was approaching, still advertising its presence with the sweeping searchlight.

As the belated escort was now coming over the horizon, silhouetting the freighter in her searchlight, we headed away to the east and then five minutes later to the north. Fifteen minutes after firing, the freighter sank, leaving only the destroyer's searchlight sweeping a clear horizon. It had required four hits from three separate attacks to sink this ship.

They would later learn that the tardy escort was *Choko Maru 2*, an armed merchant cruiser. She could have done serious damage to *Wahoo* if she had only shown up a few minutes earlier.

Later, as the officers gathered in the wardroom to discuss the day's fierce action, Mush Morton expressed his disappointment that they did not have any torpedoes left to go after the cruiser, too. He was especially miffed that several of their weapons had proven to be duds. He also once again expressed his admiration for the skipper and crew of the freighter—now determined to be the *Pacific Maru*—which had eaten up four of their torpedoes.

Morton praised his officers and especially his XO.

"Tenacity, Dick," he told him. "Stay with them until they are on the bottom!"

It was a philosophy O'Kane had adopted already from his captain, and one that would stand him in good stead for the rest of the war.

Morton had already gone up and down the boat, personally slapping men on the back, shaking their hands, thanking them for their effort, skill, and bravery so far on this amazing patrol. Everyone was of the same mind. They knew they were a good crew, that they were well trained. It had taken Mush Morton on the bridge to bring it all together. Headquarters would be under the assumption that *Wahoo* would be just now getting to its assigned patrol area, near Truk. Because of radio silence, they had no way of knowing that Morton and his crew had never even gotten there, that she had expended her full complement of torpedoes before she could get on station, and that she had sunk an enemy warship and a full convoy in the process.

No one aboard had ever heard of a submarine sinking its first target before arriving in the area where she was supposed to patrol. And they had sunk what they were certain was a total of five ships, which would have easily made this the most successful war patrol in U.S. Navy history. (They would claim five ships sunk for a total of 31,900 tons, but JANAC would reduce it to three ships and 11,300 tons.)

But now it was time to let the brass back in Pearl know what they had been up to and ask for permission to cut the patrol short and come home. Knowing other submarines would hear it, Morton wanted the radio message to strike the perfect tone. He wrote up several drafts on lined paper, crossing out words and starting over completely. He ultimately decided to keep it simple and to the point, allowing the results to speak for themselves.

Morton smiled and handed it to the radio operator for coding and transmission.

SANK DESTROYER IN WEWAK SUNDAY AND IN A
FOURTEEN-HOUR RUNNING GUN AND TORPEDO BATTLE
TODAY SANK CONVOY OF ONE TANKER TWO FREIGHT-
ERS AND ONE TRANSPORT DESTROYING HER BOATS.
TORPEDOES EXPENDED. PROCEEDING PEARL HARBOR
VIA FAIS ISLAND.

They could only suspect the impact the message would have on every-one at submarine command headquarters. Indeed, on the entire fleet command. It was exactly the kind of positive news the country needed to hear. There had been precious little so far.

Preparations started immediately for a stellar reception for *Wahoo* and her crew. The Navy's public relations machinery was set in motion, too, ready to get the most mileage from the submarine's exploits.

Mush Morton was not satisfied, though.

As usual, they were running on the surface to make the most speed. George Grider had the watch when he spotted smoke on the horizon. Though the torpedo rooms were empty, and despite the fact that they could do nothing about any potential targets using their best weapons, Grider knew he was obligated to let the captain know.

Morton actually licked his lips and grinned as he took them down and approached the smoke submerged. What he saw through the scope was maddeningly frustrating: a six-ship convoy with no escorts any-where to be seen.

Morton, at the scope for one of the few times on the patrol, ran the list of potential targets, and then concentrated on the last one, a small freighter that trailed the other five by several ship lengths.

The captain's face was flushed when he turned from the scope and, his eyes flashing, looked at his XO.

"You know what, Dick? We are the only ones who know we are out of torpedoes. The Japs don't know it."

Then he outlined his plan. O'Kane liked it. The other officers in the conn were not so sure.

They would surface—in plain sight—and make a full-speed run toward the convoy, being certain to stay just out of reach of the guns they had spied on the decks of the bigger ships. The smaller, trailing freighter did not appear to have any weapons. Morton figured the other ships would try to run away, further isolating the straggler. Then *Wahoo* could swoop in, deck guns blazing, and take down the target.

The convoy sighted us in about ten minutes, commenced smoking like a Winston and headed for a lone rain squall. Only two of the larger freighters opened fire, and their splashes were several thousand yards short. Their maneuver left the tanker trailing, just where we wanted him.

Morton could hardly contain his glee. The plan was working just as he and O'Kane had hoped.

But as they drew closer, Forest Sterling spotted something unsettling: a smaller mast emerging from behind the fleeing ships. It was clearly an escort craft of some kind. Morton thought it was a smaller corvette, something they could easily outrun. Others were convinced it was a destroyer, and escape from such a craft would not be nearly so easy.

Either way, the surface deck gun attack was over and the gun crew was sent below, abandoning all the ammunition left on the deck in their haste to duck for cover.

Though Morton did not realize it at the time, they were actually in deep trouble. Still under the impression the escort was a slower craft, he ordered top speed, and they did seem to be opening up distance from their pursuer. But Morton later described the sudden turn of events in the patrol report, using his typical colorful style.

Found that our engineers could add close to another knot to our speed when they knew we were being pursued. We actually made about 20 knots, opening the range to thirteen or fourteen thousand yards in the first twenty minutes of the chase. In fact he was smoking so profusely that we called him an "Antiquated Coal-burning Corvette." He was just lighting off more boilers evidently, for seventeen minutes later he changed our tune by boiling over the horizon, swinging left, and letting fly a broadside at estimated range of 7,000 yards. There was no doubt about his identity then, especially

Perhaps the most famous portrait of Dudley "Mush" Morton, this picture was used by Warner Brothers Pictures in promoting the movie *Destination Tokyo*, for which Morton served as technical adviser.   US NAVY

Morton's roadster, which he kept in Tsingtao, China. While he was courting his future wife, he enjoyed riding around with her nieces and nephew in the rumble seat.

Morton wedding, Tsingtao, China, 1936: (*back row, left to right*): Morton's brother-in-law James Avent, unknown, Dudley "Mush" Morton, Harriet Nelson Morton, Morton's sister-in-law Jeanette Nelson Avent, unknown; (*front row, left to right*): Morton's nephew, James Avent Jr., and nieces Mayna and Jacqueline Avent.

Morton and new bride leave the Community Church in Tsingtao after their wedding ceremony.

USS *Wahoo* (SS-238) on the day of her christening and launch, February 14, 1942, at Mare Island Naval Shipyard, California.

USS *Wahoo* moments after the launch ceremony.

Wahoo executive officer, Richard "Dick" O'Kane, and her captain, Dudley "Mush" Morton, on the bridge of the historic submarine.

US NAVY

USS *Wahoo* in San Francisco Bay while conducting initial sea trials, 1942.   US NAVY

XO Dick O'Kane and skipper Mush Morton aboard USS *Wahoo*, early 1943.

US NAVY

Destroyer *Harusame* sinking in Wewak Harbor, New Guinea, January 24, 1943, photographed through *Wahoo*'s periscope. Morton used a down-the-throat shot.   US NAVY

The destroyer *Harusame* apparently sinking after the famous down-the-throat shot in Wewak Harbor. *Wahoo*, however, was not given credit for sinking this ship, despite the photo taken through the submarine's periscope.   US NAVY

The Japanese troop transport *Buyo Maru* listing after the first torpedo from *Wahoo*, January 1943. The submarine later used deck guns to fire on survivors in the water.

The control room on *Wahoo* during an attack on a convoy, February 1943.

Crew members from *Wahoo* give food, water, and cigarettes to Malaysian refugees found adrift far from land. They were also supplied with maps to the nearest port.

Captain Morton oversees an attack on a convoy. This photo was taken in the submarine's conning tower.
US NAVY

The Australian crown coin Mush Morton had engraved and presented to his XO, Dick O'Kane, to commemorate O'Kane's perfect hand in a game of cribbage.
JON JAQUES

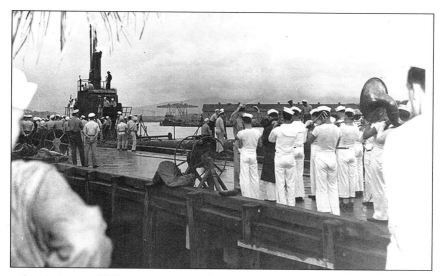

A band plays as *Wahoo* arrives in Pearl Harbor after her historic third war patrol.
US NAVY

Wahoo at the pier shortly after arriving at Pearl Harbor from her third war patrol. The pennants—including the notorious "Shoot the sun za-bitches" one—celebrate the record number of kills on the patrol. US NAVY

Captain Morton shows reporters the locations of the assaults on Japanese shipping made during *Wahoo*'s famous third war patrol. The exploits of the submarine and her colorful skipper made front-page news across America.   US NAVY

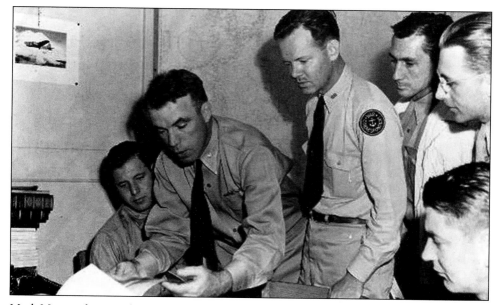

Mush Morton shares with reporters details about where and when *Wahoo* sank a warship, a troop ship, and freighters. The Navy encouraged the unusual sharing of information to improve morale, both among troops and the people back home.   US NAVY

Nitu Maru sinks after being torpedoed by *Wahoo*, March 1943. The crew retrieved a life preserver with the ship's name on it to prove her identity. US NAVY

Wahoo's "commandos" attack an enemy fishing boat using deck guns and Molotov cocktails. US NAVY

Back at Mare Island for an overhaul, May 1943, Morton and *Wahoo* are welcomed by the Navy Yard commandant. In the tweed suit is Morton's father, William, and to the right is Morton's wife, Harriet. US NAVY

Mush Morton, his father, and his wife visit with the commander of the Navy Yard at Mare Island, California. The commander's wife complained about the language on the sub's pennant. US NAVY

Mush and Harriet Morton with Cary Grant. Morton served as technical adviser for the movie *Destination Tokyo*, in which Grant starred as a submarine commander, partly based on Morton's adventures. US NAVY

A censored version of *Wahoo*'s famous battle pennant. This sign at Mare Island Naval Shipyard was part of a war bond sales effort. US NAVY

Wahoo during postoverhaul sea trials in San Francisco Bay, California. US NAVY

With battle flags flying, *Wahoo* prepares to dock at Midway for a refit and R & R for the crew, September 1943. US NAVY

Ensign George Misch, one of *Wahoo*'s officers, points out a kill flag on torpedo tube #3. Misch was one of the eighty men lost when the submarine went down on her seventh war patrol. US NAVY

Three of the young officers aboard *Wahoo* for her fifth patrol, shown in the wardroom reading a letter from home (*left to right*): Lieutenant Richie Henderson, Lieutenant Chandler Jackson, and Ensign John Campbell. Henderson and Campbell were lost on the boat's seventh patrol. US NAVY

Men gather for the dedication of Morton Hall at the Navy's submarine school in New London, Connecticut, in 1945.

Mush Morton's daughter and son, Edwina and Doug, at the ceremony honoring their father and the official naming of Morton Hall at the submarine school, New London, Connecticut, 1945.

when the salvo whistled over our heads, the splashes landing about 500 yards directly ahead.

Before the escort caught up to them, Morton, still convinced the ship was some small, inadequate vessel, crowed, "What a hell of a ship to have as escort of a six-ship convoy! The emperor deserves to lose every damn ship he's got!"

And when the destroyer turned and showed them her side—confirming once and for all that she was the equivalent of the warship that they had sunk at Wewak—Morton was sure the Japanese captain was giving up the chase and returning to protect the convoy from other submarines that might be out there.

"We've dragged her thirty miles from where she's supposed to be," he announced. "She can't afford to leave the convoy unprotected."

When the next shell thundered nearby, he changed his tune. Another boomed just on the other side of them. Now there was no choice. They had to dive and take their chances with a depth charge attack. One well-placed shell on the surface from the destroyer and they would never live to enjoy their heroic and triumphant return to Pearl Harbor.

They went to almost four hundred feet, their maximum safe depth, with the speed log as they passed 250 feet still showing fifteen knots forward speed from their momentum upon diving. They could clearly hear the screws of the warship above them as it circled, and then the enemy destroyer dropped a series of six depth charges on top of them. The booms were loud and they sufficiently frayed the nerves of everyone aboard.

Grider later wrote, "We were plunged into total darkness. A loose piece of metal shot through the void and struck my left ear, causing it to sting sharply. Dishes stacked on the tables were lifted and thrown about. Loose knives and forks flew about at random, their screaming lost in the blasts of the depth charges. Patches of cork showered down, followed by a ventilationless room full of choking dust."

The destroyer soon gave up, likely wanting nothing to do with a crazy submarine driver who would attack on the surface in broad daylight. What would such a man do while submerged?

Morton allowed them to stay submerged after rising to a relatively safe two hundred feet for another half hour or so before bringing them back to periscope depth to look around. Only then did they surface to transmit a message and pick up some radio traffic he had been expecting. Their transmission was a rather unorthodox message to HQ. The received traffic was the reply to their report to headquarters about their successes.

Morton's message:

> **ANOTHER RUNNING GUN BATTLE TODAY... WAHOO RUNNIN', DESTROYER GUNNIN'.**

The confirmation of *Wahoo*'s earlier report, the one announcing the sinking of five ships, was actually disappointing to Morton and O'Kane in its lighthearted simplicity:

> **ADMIRAL HALSEY LIKES YOU FOR GETTING DESTROYER SUNDAY. WE ALL LIKE YOU FOR GETTING ALL FOUR SHIPS OF CONVOY YESTERDAY. YOUR PICTURE IS ON THE PIANO.**

It was typical Charles Lockwood, though.

The next night's broadcast was more glowing, and Sterling typed up a copy to post in the crew's mess, with carbons for other locations throughout the boat. The captain added a copy of his own clever "runnin' and gunnin'" message to hang next to the one from headquarters.

> **COMMANDER IN CHIEF PACIFIC FLEET SENDS WELL-DONE TO WAHOO. THE SHIPS YOU HAVE SUNK WILL DECREASE THE ENEMY'S CAPACITY TO CARRY ON THE WAR.**

> **FOR WAHOO FROM CONTASKFOR42, QUOTE, ADMIRAL HALSEY SENDS CONGRATULATIONS FOR WEWAK JOB. ALSO FROM TASK FORCE 42, FOR NEW EPIC OF SUB-**

MARINE WARFARE COMPLETE DESTRUCTION OF LOADED
CONVOY UNQUOTE. WAHOO LT COMDR MORTON COM-
MANDING TWO DAYS AFTER SINKING DESTROYER AT
WEWAK ENCOUNTERED UNESCORTED CONVOY WHILE
EN ROUTE PALAU. WAHOO SANK ENTIRE CONVOY, TWO
FREIGHTERS, TANKER, AND TRANSPORT, DESTROYING
HER BOATS AND EXPENDING ALL TORPEDOES DURING
FOURTEEN-HOUR BATTLE. TWO MEN WOUNDED.

Now Morton and the rest of the crew were sufficiently satisfied that their efforts were appreciated back at home port.

The captain still wanted to do more damage, though. After perform-ing reconnaissance on Fais Island, Morton proposed a plan to shell the phosphate works on the island, using *Wahoo*'s few remaining four-inch rounds. He wrote that the large refinery, warehouses, and other facilities "offered a splendid target." They were deterred by an interisland steamer with scary guns on her deck moored to a buoy, sitting right in their way.

"She would have made a nice target for one torpedo," the captain wrote. But, of course, they did not have one. Still, he thought about sur-facing and screaming in for an attack.

"Dudley, why don't we just go on back and pick up some torpedoes?" O'Kane asked.

"You're right, Dick. You're right."

And with that, they set a course for Hawaii. But *Wahoo*'s colorful skipper was busy along the way. He wanted to make sure they entered Pearl Harbor in style, and there was work to be done to make certain everyone took note of his boat and her crew when they arrived.

CHAPTER 17

Clean Sweep

"The conduct and discipline of the officers and men of this ship while under fire were superb. They enjoyed nothing better than a good fight."

—Mush Morton in the patrol report, third war patrol, USS *Wahoo*

A fter steaming 6,554 miles and burning 92,000 gallons of diesel fuel *(about fourteen gallons per mile),* Wahoo *ended her third war patrol—"by orders of ComSubPac, after expenditure of all torpedoes"—on February 7, 1943, with her arrival at Pearl Harbor, Hawaii. On the way back and across the international date line, they had two Tuesdays, which fell twice on February 2, Dick O'Kane's birthday.*

Conscious of the criticism—deserved or not—he received for the condition of *Dolphin*, Morton had the crew busy cleaning up all compartments on the boat. O'Kane and the other officers honed their reports, all of which had to be typed up by Yeoman Sterling. Morton wanted every detail of the patrol in the report as accurate as possible.

The captain was especially proud of the section of the narrative in which he praised his officers and crew in general, and Dick O'Kane specifically. When the XO read that section, he was moved. He later wrote:

"I had been reading patrol reports for almost exactly a year, and Morton's narrative was the first that devoted a separate paragraph to his officers and men, the senior by name. But he was a new breed of captain to us, one who exercised the adage of reprimand in private, commend in public."

Morton also included two paragraphs in the "remarks" section of the report on his radical new way of running a submarine's attack process, one not taught at sub school or the Naval Academy. The captain wrote:

The fire control party of this ship was completely reorganized prior to and during this patrol. The Executive Officer, Lieutenant R. H. O'KANE, is the co–approach officer. He made all observations through the periscope and fired all torpedoes. The Commanding Officer studies the various setups by the use of Iswas [usually referred to as an "Is-Was" or, because of its distinctive shape, a "banjo," a circular slide-rule-type device used to calculate approach and attack by a submarine] *and analyzing the TDC and does the conning. A third officer assists the Commanding Officer in analyzing the problem by studying the plot and the data sheets. On the surface the Executive Officer mans the TBT and makes observations and does the firing: The Commanding Officer conns.*

This type of fire control party relieves the Commanding Officer of a lot of strain and it gives excellent training to all hands, especially the Executive Officer. It is recommended that other ships give it consideration and thought.

It was good that Morton and his wardroom spent so much time with the patrol report. As soon as it was submitted and studied by the submarine commanders, copies were made and went directly to the submarine school and other locations for use in teaching others.

In one of the few navigation errors, the submarine completely missed the rendezvous point with its escort, the destroyer USS *Litchfield* (DD-336). Suddenly, there on the horizon was Oahu, and the radio operator hastily issued a message that they hoped would keep friendly aircraft from attacking first and asking questions later. *Litchfield* did come rushing up behind them and ultimately escorted them into the harbor entrance.

But as they rounded one of the big piers that blocked their view of the assigned slip, the crew was surprised to see a huge crowd gathered on the dock, "very much like a peacetime Navy Day," O'Kane noted. And as they drew closer, they could see and hear a band playing over the loudspeakers, and then it was clear that a section was reserved for what were obviously dignitaries and press. Photographers snapped away, and newsreel

cameras were mounted in several locations to capture *Wahoo*'s triumphant arrival home.

On the bridge, Mush Morton looked up and grinned. With the patrol
cut so short, they had not yet had the opportunity to sew together the
usual battle pennant with the Rising Sun emblems arrayed to show the
enemy ships sunk. The captain had a suitable substitute, though. Prior to
leaving Australia, one of the crew had commandeered a large broom
used to sweep off the piers there. Tucked away for the whole trip, it was
now quite visibly lashed to the tip-top of the attack periscope, its bristles
pointed skyward.

All Navy people knew exactly what that meant, and the press soon
informed the entire nation. It was an old tradition, signifying a "clean
sweep of the seas," and it was especially appropriate for *Wahoo*, given her
historic patrol. Several speculated that it was the most photographed
broom in naval history.

For the next several days, as the crew tried to enjoy some R & R, they
had to work around members of the press who were given unprecedented
access to them and their submarine. For the first time in World War II,
photographers were even allowed to take pictures belowdecks. Reporters
were also given details of the boat's action, something that had not happened so far in the war either.

The Silent Service was no longer so silent.

Morton and O'Kane were hustled off to a press conference, and photos of the captain pointing to maps and recounting their adventures
appeared in papers everywhere. It did not end there. They were constantly being interviewed by reporters. Morton sat for a session with *The
March of Time* newsreel cameras and subsequently ended up on movie
screens all over North America. *Wahoo* was front-page news. Headlines
such as WAHOO RUNNING, JAPS A'GUNNING screamed the story of
the boatload of submariner heroes.

Enterprising reporters in Los Angeles even tracked down Harriet
Morton, the captain's wife, and interviewed her, though she could talk
only about how proud she was of her husband. She reminded the reporters that she had no idea where he was or what he was doing.

But there was a cloud over all of the hullabaloo surrounding *Wahoo*. Pacific Submarine Commander Admiral Robert English and three of his senior staff officers had flown off to California on January 20, bound for a visit to the submarine support facilities at Mare Island and to give the men a chance to visit briefly with their families. Their plane went down in a storm, and it was eleven days later, January 31, before the wreckage and their bodies were finally located in a remote area of northern California.

The choice to replace English was Charles Lockwood, who then was the commander of the submarines based at Perth/Fremantle in far western Australia. That was fortuitous for Mush Morton. Lockwood shared his opinions about aggressively running submarines. Lockwood was also a fan of the use of a submarine's deck guns for surface assaults and had equipped most of the Perth boats with upgraded weapons.

As the officers from *Wahoo*'s wardroom compared notes—often while swimming peacefully in the warm waters off Waikiki Beach or working on their suntans—they came to a startling realization. On the boat's second patrol, with Pinky Kennedy at the helm, they had spent over five hundred hours submerged. With Mush Morton in command, *Wahoo* had run submerged a total of less than fifty hours. Not even ten percent as much!

Granted, their patrol had been cut short, and such a radical amount of surface running would not necessarily be the normal practice, even for *Wahoo*. But nothing so forcefully demonstrated how markedly different submarine warfare would now become after Mush Morton's arrival on the bridge of a submarine.

The crew had only sixteen days in port before their next run was scheduled to commence, the shortest period between patrols so far in the war. It came after their patrol of only twenty-four days, which was also the shortest run thus far for any American submarine.

It was a busy couple of weeks, filled with press inquiries and refit crews scrambling all over the boat. Yes, there was R & R, but also refresher training was required. It was also necessary to welcome new crew members who came aboard. Morton made a point of learning their first names, and gave each man a personal pep talk. Of course, this also meant saying good-bye to others who were shipping over to other boats or leaving for new assignments.

Major among those leaving *Wahoo* was George Grider. He was picked to become the XO aboard USS *Pollack* (SS-180). She was another of the older boats that had a reputation of being slow, hard to maneuver, and prone to mechanical problems. She had been on her way back to Pearl from a repair session at Mare Island on December 7, 1941, but was among the first naval units to enter Japanese waters on New Year's Eve, and had completed five patrols by the time Grider came aboard as her number two.

It was not the position he wanted if he had to leave *Wahoo*. He had hoped for new construction.

Morton felt the need to deliver the bad news to his junior officer personally.

"Mush, I know it's a promotion," Grider told his captain. "Truth is, I doubt it's worth it." Grider told Morton he would rather stay on *Wahoo*.

"Hell, George, with you on board, y'all will burn up the Pacific on *Pollack*!"

"But who's going to keep you and Dick out of trouble?" Grider asked with a grin.

Morton's answer was to grab and put Grider in one of his patented wrestling headlocks.

The truth was that the submarine service needed good officers badly, and *Wahoo* had managed to keep its wardroom mostly intact longer than most. There was a growing need for experienced officers, between the rapidly increasing new construction and the necessary replacement of officers who could not make it, those who had been sent to staff duty, or the ones who had been lost in battle—by the time *Wahoo* arrived in Pearl Harbor in February 1943, nine boats had been lost and a total of seventeen would go down in 1943 alone. That would be more than a thousand men lost.

Morton's prediction about Pollack's success turned out to be accurate. Grider would be at the elbow of Bafford Lewellen, *Pollack*'s new skipper, and they would go on to two successful patrols together. Those runs were not without tense moments, some due to problems with the old boat, others provided courtesy of the Japanese. Grider would eventually get his new construction, as XO of USS *Hawkbill* (SS-366), in the summer of 1944. He later commanded USS *Flasher* (SS-249) on her final two patrols before the war ended. There he put to good use his own natural abilities as well as the skills he learned from Mush Morton. Under his command, *Flasher* sank seven enemy ships for a total of almost forty-four thousand tons sent to the bottom, placing him at number fifty-four on the list of skippers. But most of that damage—six ships—came on the boat's fifth patrol, which was the third most productive of the war, based on the number of vessels sunk.

Grider thus joined the list of Morton's officers who would go on to remarkable success at the helm of other boats.

There was one more personnel surprise for the boat. The crew learned that Duncan MacMillan was coming aboard for his PCO cruise. The same Duncan MacMillan that Dick O'Kane was assured would be *Wahoo*'s commissioning skipper before Marvin Kennedy actually got the job. Morton was happy to have him aboard. His engineering background would come in handy with George Grider gone.

Admiral Lockwood, on the job for only a short time, came down to the pier to visit with Morton before they departed. He had only one serious question for *Wahoo*'s skipper: "Mush, at what depth do you set your torpedoes to run?"

Without hesitation, Morton responded, "As shallow as necessary according to the situation."

Lockwood nodded.

Morton had already begun to complain loudly about the dud torpedoes. Or at least the magnetic exploder, which had been an issue with most of the sub skippers but, so far, not with the higher command. He and O'Kane were hopeful now that they had, in Charles Lockwood, someone in high places who would get to the bottom of the problem.

"I wish you Godspeed," the admiral said, and crossed the brow to the pier, where he stood at attention and watched them back away.

As *Wahoo* navigated out of the harbor—with Morton in the conn and PCO MacMillan on the bridge—they passed the rusting hulks of several of the ships damaged in December 1941. The battleships USS *Tennessee*

(BB-43) and USS *Nevada* (BB-36) were gone, back in Washington State being repaired, and would soon return to the war. As did most ships entering and leaving Pearl Harbor, *Wahoo* had a full section of crew members on deck, dressed in clean dungarees, at attention, and facing the damaged ships, all out of respect for those who were lost that terrible day.

As soon as *Wahoo* was under way, the captain requested that charts of the Yellow Sea and South China Sea—their secret destination—be posted all over the boat. In the case of the Yellow Sea, this was an area in which no American submarine had yet operated. Again, this posting of secret information did not follow standard Navy protocol, but Morton figured it was silly to not let his men know where they were headed together. Besides, who were they going to tell besides one another?

There were good reasons why the Yellow Sea, between China and the Korean Peninsula, was what Morton termed "virgin territory" for submarines. It was relatively shallow, averaging less than 120 feet deep, and the Japanese had been taking advantage of the lack of submarines there. The water depth made it tough for submarines to run and hide, but the presence of plenty of enemy targets completely offset that negative in Mush Morton's mind.

That was only one reason Morton was excited about going there: It was also the area where he had once spent many pleasant weeks on summer maneuvers, where he visited Tsingtao, sailed his mahogany boat, met his wife, and ultimately married her. Now he longed for the day when he would be able to tell Harriet and her family that he had been back in the area where so many great memories were born.

Morton also had fun with another brainstorm he had come up with. He put together his own "commando squad," a group of crew members who would be first across should they decide to board an enemy ship or send someone ashore to do some damage against the Japanese. He even had some Molotov-cocktail firebombs the men had constructed, relying on the help of some Marines. The crew members brought them aboard and stored them in the fairwater in the conning tower, just in case they had the opportunity to use them.

We will never know whether Morton actually intended to perform such operations, but the formation of the squad and the prospects for hand-to-hand combat against the enemy had one benefit: It was a tremendous morale booster.

February 23: 1300VW; under way from Pearl for patrol area via MIDWAY. With surface escort until dark.

There had been talk among the crew—and especially with the six new men aboard, all of whom had specifically requested *Wahoo*—about this follow-up act to the boat's most spectacular recent patrol. How could they possibly exceed those record-breaking results? Anything less would be anticlimactic. A bust.

They need not have worried. With Mushmouth at the helm, they were about to not only go where no wartime American submarine had ever gone before.

They were about to accomplish feats no one could have ever thought possible.

CHAPTER 18

The *Smoky Maru*

And the waters returned, and covered the chariots, and the horse-
men, and all the host of Pharaoh that came into the sea after them:
there remained not so much as one of them.

—Exodus 14:28

I suppose we could excuse Mush Morton and Dick O'Kane and the crew of Wahoo *if they became a bit cocky. With all the praise and the atten-tion of the press, it should not be surprising that they had a high opinion of themselves, their boat, and what they would accomplish on their fourth war patrol.*

Back in Pearl Harbor, Morton had all but told a division commander to hush when the man questioned him about the unorthodox way he tended to set his main vents while running submerged.

"It's my boat and I'll run it the way I want to," Morton told him, and that was that.

Now, just to make sure his crew was as optimistic about this patrol as he was, the captain wandered through the boat at all hours, talking up the men, promising them this would be a killer run for *Wahoo.*

They took on 16,000 gallons of diesel fuel and 2,500 gallons of freshwater at the submarine base on Midway and, after only a few hours there, plowed on to the west. They arrived in the South China Sea on March 11 and squatted on what was reported to be the busy shipping lanes between the island of Formosa and the Japanese port city of Nagasaki. Amazingly,

Wahoo had made the entire transit from Midway to the patrol area on the surface, despite rough seas and the possibility of enemy airplanes or ships. They saw none of either.

All that time on the surface caused one minor problem. When the ship's cook tried to make cherry pie for their Washington's Birthday meal, the constant sloshing about made it difficult to keep the filling inside the piecrust. Only the captain could make a change in the menu, so the cook, John Rowls, approached Morton with his complaint.

"We have to have cherry pie," the skipper maintained. "Put some cornstarch in there to make it thicker and it'll stay put."

The quick run had again put them into their assigned area well ahead of schedule, and once again, Morton had every intention of making the most of the head start, as well as the "virgin territory" where they would hunt. The crew had already used several small, spiky, unnamed islands to test and calibrate their radar and the TDC. They seemed to be performing perfectly. It only took the mention of the fact that Honshu, the main Japanese Home Island, was a mere 150 miles north of them at that point to keep the lookouts in the shears and radar and sound operators even more vigilant than usual.

"Remember, boys, they won't expect us to be here," Morton reminded them. "They'll be steaming along, fat and sassy."

They finally got the bridge and shears wet, submerging at dawn on the eleventh, and began searching through the periscope.

Nothing. Nothing but the occasional sampan. None of them seemed to be a worthy target. Some could be picket boats—disguised fishing vessels filled with radio and radar, looking for American ships or planes— but out here, they were more likely to be what they appeared to be. For the first time, the skipper had to adopt at least one tenet of the between-the-wars submarine strategy: remain undetected. The lack of interest among the sampans, their lights all on, and unconcerned about any enemy in the area, and the brightly blazing lighthouse on Bono-misaki indicated that they had so far been able to do just that.

The crew busied themselves as best they could when not on watch. The "*Wahoo* Commandos" prepared their special belts, put together with the help of the Marines back in Pearl, with their machetes and other tools needed if they got a chance to launch an assault. When they were on the surface, they listened to Tokyo Rose, piped throughout the boat. The men hooted at her obvious propaganda snipes but enjoyed very much the popular records she played over the air for them.

Still nothing up there but the sampans and occasional trawler.

Morton was aware that the constant surfacing and diving and dodging of the small vessels, the nearness of the enemy islands, and the lack of deep water beneath them—the captain had taken to calling it a "wading pool"—had everyone on edge. Even the normally placid yeoman Forest Sterling was growing irritated, and especially with Dick O'Kane.

"Hey, I got no problems with the XO. I always get in the last word. I say, 'Yes, sir,' and he walks away," Sterling later wrote.

The captain continued his now familiar trips throughout the boat, wrestling with sailors, joining in their chats, cheering them on, all while washing his clothes in a sudsy bucket or wearing nothing more than a towel, a pair of skivvies, or the red bathrobe.

Morton knew only one thing would get the crew back on track. And that was action.

The chance finally came early on Saturday morning, March 13.

0814I: Sighted smoke. Commenced approach, which lasted almost five hours. The closest we could get was about 8,000 yards. Finally abandoned the approach. A peculiar mirage prevailed. We nicknamed it "SMOKY MARU."

There was great speculation in the conning tower about what the hell that ship was. Some type of interisland steamer, maybe. O'Kane guessed it might be a lightship. Or just a smoking decoy, designed to draw attention away from juicier targets farther away.

Regardless, they continued to track and watch the vessel. Tracked and watched all day until late afternoon. The tense stalking and the iffy nature of their target only added to the case of nerves from which everyone on *Wahoo* was suffering.

"I don't like this," Morton finally said, and uncharacteristically called off the tracking of the smoking specter. "The damn thing could be a Q-ship."

Q-ships were vessels disguised to look like tankers, trawlers, or other types of relatively benign vessels. Once attacked, though, they bared their fangs and countered with their own deadly assault. Such ships were known to be in the area.

The fire control party in the conn exchanged quick glances. Somehow, as it usually did, word spread throughout the boat. "Deadly Dudley" was backing off from a fight. Had he mellowed on his second patrol?

But just then, *Smoky Maru* made a sudden turn and headed straight for *Wahoo*'s periscope.

1640I: Went to battle stations and made approach. At 1704 I fired one torpedo from a stern tube at 1,000-ton ship, range 1,000 yards, 90d port track, speed 12 knots. Missed, a few feet ahead of target. After our long chase this morning and being anxious to shoot something, we let him have just one. He was the type of target worth one torpedo if you sink him, but not worth two torpedoes under any conditions.

Even as the torpedo sped away toward the target, Mush Morton sat at the chart table with his head in his hands. This had been a reluctant attack at best, one he was convinced was not worth the effort or the expense of any of their torpedoes. There was no place nearby to pick up any more. He was still miffed about running out of weapons on the previous patrol and had vowed to make every shot count.

Even if they sank the thing, it would reveal their presence in the area, too. Such news would spread among the enemy immediately.

However, O'Kane and the other officers had insisted they continue tracking all day and eventually try to sink it. When the mystery vessel turned toward them, the skipper finally relented.

To make matters worse, the fish missed. They had guessed range wrong, because, despite watching the ship all day, they had incorrectly estimated its mast height. Tiny errors are magnified many times in submarine warfare. The torpedo broached—popped to the surface—just in front of the target and then disappeared. There was no sign the ship's captain or crew ever suspected an American submarine was shooting at them.

"Captain, let's line up for another shot," O'Kane urged.

"Hell, no!" Morton snapped. "I'm not going to waste another torpedo on the likes of that thing."

The tension in the conn ratcheted up, hanging thick as fog in the cramped compartment. The XO gritted his teeth, his face red with anger.

"We can sink that son of a bitch!" he said, as if biting off and spitting out each word. "Let's don't let him get away."

The look on Morton's face was unlike any man in the compartment had ever seen before. His eyes glowed like coals, his already prominent jaw thrust out even farther, and he pulled himself up to his full height, clenching and unclenching his fists. No man there would have been surprised to see him throw a punch at his XO.

"Goddammit, Dick! That's enough. When you are running your own boat, you can shoot all the torpedoes you want at whatever the hell you want. We are not wasting another one on that bastard! Break off the attack. Secure from battle stations."

And in a voice only slightly less caustic, he ordered a new course, away from the smoking vision on the surface above them.

Over the next several days, *Wahoo* sighted several more similar ships, but they made no effort to track them. And there were still more sampans, their lights blinking away without concern in the nighttime darkness. The notations in the patrol log became a litany, over and over, of "Sighted many lighted sampans during the night." They quickly dubbed the area "Sampan Alley."

O'Kane and Morton quickly got over their spat in the conn, taking out their emotions in heated games of cribbage. At one point, the captain dealt his XO a perfect twenty-nine, a one-in-a-quarter-million-odds event. O'Kane gloated and had all the officers sign one of the cards in the hand to prove it. Crew members stopped by for the rest of the evening to see the winning hand.

Later, the captain threw his exec another winning hand. That one totaled twenty-eight. The ever-competitive skipper totally lost his composure, ripped up the cards, and threw them into the air, vowing he would never play cards with O'Kane again. And he was serious. Serious for the moment, anyway.

Morton later got over it. He had an Australian one-crown coin in his pocket. When they arrived in port after the patrol, he had a message engraved on the back of the coin and presented it to his exec.

"Dick, for your 29 hand, March 18, 1943, *Wahoo*, Mush," it read.

They desperately needed to sink something. Needed to take out their aggression on the enemy, not each other. The success of the previous patrol only made this one more frustrating. So did the high hopes they all had about this new patrol area. Both high-strung men knew it only too well, but the Japanese were simply not obliging.

Then the radar went on the blink. They had to do some fancy maneuvering to avoid numerous junks and small trawlers and fishing boats and, all the while, remain undetected in the process. Referring to Morton and the PCO, MacMillan, who conned them through most of these intricate operations, O'Kane observed, "For sure, no submarine was ever conned through a fishing fleet by more rank or talent."

To add insult to injury, they pulled the plug at what appeared to be the sighting of an airplane. It was later that they realized it was a flight of geese that had chased them down.

Was *Wahoo*'s fourth patrol doomed to failure? Had Mushmouth lost his magic touch?

Finally, early on the morning of March 19, six days after firing the lone torpedo at the smoking ship, their luck changed. And did it ever! They were about to once again do something no submarine had done up to that point in the war.

One of the officers, Chan Jackson, and radioman Jim Buckley—neither of them experienced in radar repair—had managed to get their SJ system back online.

Then, just after 0400, one of the young officers, George Misch, and the lookouts spotted a freighter, sending the boat's crew to battle stations. Misch called for full power and started the race to get out ahead of the first real target they had seen since the end of the third patrol.

0455H: Dived when light enough to see through periscope.

0515H: Fired one torpex torpedo at medium-sized freighter identified as KANKA MARU, 4065 tons, range 750 yards, 120d port track, speed 9 knots. Hit.

It was their first opportunity to use new torpedoes containing a different type of explosive compound. It was Torpex, short for "torpedo explosive," developed by the British and reputed to be fifty percent more powerful than the equivalent amount of TNT.

"Fire only one torpedo," Morton ordered, still conscious of running out of fish on their previous patrol. And fire they did.

In less than a minute, the dawn sky was set ablaze by the blast. The rumble of the thunderous explosion rocked *Wahoo*, even where she floated beneath the surface of the sea.

After part of the ship disintegrated, the forward part sank in two minutes and 26 seconds. These Torpex heads carry an awful wallop.

With no other vessel in sight, Morton brought them up to take a look. There was nothing but debris floating on the water. "No one left to tell on us," Morton later wrote.

The damage done by that single torpedo was sobering, but O'Kane liked the way the math worked out. "Two torpedoes, one ship sunk" was better than "one ship, one miss."

O'Kane was still condensing his notes on the attack, and Morton had hardly finished breakfast when the chiming bells—"the bells of St. Mary's," in submariner slang—again hurried everyone to battle stations.

"Here we go again," the captain said with a grin, still chewing his eggs as he headed for the conn.

It was another freighter. She was at some distance and getting away, but the watch already had them giving chase. Once they got to within shooting range, after running over seven miles in about an hour and a half, Morton ordered them to slow down. They should take their time, maneuver a bit, get a better angle to make sure they did not miss, wasting another one of those deadly torpedoes.

O'Kane's irritation was obvious again, his face once more turning scarlet. He was afraid the ship might make a sudden zig and pull away from them.

Morton noticed, and as soon as he was satisfied they were in the best position, he quietly said, "Okay, Dick. Anytime."

First torpedo hit under his foremast with a terrific blast, but his bow remained intact; however, we could see a tremendous hole up his side. Second torpedo hit him amidships, but it was a dud. The co–approach officer saw a small plume and both sound operators heard the thud of the dud.

The first one hit, but not exactly in the best spot. O'Kane watched through the periscope as the second fish headed exactly for the location on the target that would do the most damage, at the bridge, where it needed to slam in to cut the ship in half.

Jim Buckley reported clearly hearing the metallic clang when the torpedo hit the target's side. The XO saw a plume of water kicked up when the air flask in the torpedo exploded. It made a nice geyser but did no damage whatsoever.

The thud of the dud.

"Damn it to hell!" Morton exploded. The dud torpedoes were really starting to infuriate the skipper.

"She's turning away," O'Kane reported, based on what he saw through the scope. Sound confirmed it.

0921H: Checked the setup and fired another torpedo. The target maneuvered and avoided.

Morton, determined not to allow the ship to get away after such a perfect setup, ordered another torpedo sent her way. The target's captain, despite having a wounded vessel, managed to dance away from it. Then, just to further insult the war's first submarine ace, he did the same thing seconds later on the fourth torpedo from *Wahoo*.

0926H: Fired fourth torpedo right up his rump. Again the target maneuvered and avoided.

"They're shooting back at us, at our scope now," the XO reported calmly.

Sure enough, shells raised columns of water all around where the periscope poked above the calm surface of the sea. The bottom was less than a hundred feet below their keel, so there was not much room to hide. Especially if the captain of the enemy vessel had called for help, if heavily armed patrol boats were speeding their way. They would not have the luxury of trying to shoot at the freighter any more.

The water is so shallow around here, we cannot afford to tangle with a concentration of patrols. That dud cost us one fine ship plus two other pre-cious torpedoes and a chance to shoot at more targets at this spot.

Morton took them to eighty feet—just above the mud and as deep as they dared to go—and headed away to the east. Later, he broke his pencil twice as he entered his commentary about how costly the bad torpedo had proved to be. There was no way to calculate how many potential vic-tims that one dud had cost them. Maybe, at the least, they had caused the enemy to be without a ship for a month or two while they repaired her.

Come nightfall, they would be back to form, though. Finally, the quarry they had anticipated from the day they first read their orders made an appearance.

It came on a quiet night with no other ships spotted. O'Kane was on his way to the wardroom when he passed the captain's stateroom. Mor-ton was lying back on his bed, reading.

"Not a bad day's work," the XO said.

Morton smiled. It was good to be having some success. He had confi-dently predicted five kills on this patrol.

"See anything at all?"

"No, it has been quiet. These captains aren't going to come too close to land at night, but I bet when the sun comes up . . ."

"Ship on the horizon!" a metallic voice on the 1MC public-address sys-tem yelled. Skipper and XO were on the move before the voice clicked off.

March 21, 0510H: (FOURTH ATTACK). OOD picked up ship with a range of 7,000 yards.

0700H: Fired three torpedoes at large freighter identified as SEIWA MARU, 7,210 tons, range 1,600 yards . . . third torpedo hit him amidships and he went down by the bow, attaining a vertical angle, and was out of sight in four minutes. We counted 33 survivors in the water . . . there was debris for the survivors to cling to. Considered they could last but a couple of hours. Took several pictures.

They were not so accustomed to success yet that a kill did not set off cheers, shouting, and singing throughout the boat. The powerful muffled explosion told them what they wanted to know, but the confirmation set off the triumphant shouts again.

The captain made a point of telling every man he met, "Well done!"

Later, they found the force of the blast from the latest target had knocked a washbasin off the wall in the forward torpedo room.

This was a Torpex head and they really blow a ship to pieces and the sound is terrific to us.

But again, there was no time to rest. Two hours later, with breakfast finished and another brutal game of cribbage under way in the wardroom, Morton suddenly stood up after losing another hand.

"It's been over two hours," he announced, stretching. "It's time for another ship. I'm going to the conning tower."

He had taken only a few steps when the "bells of St. Mary's" pealed again.

0958H: Fired a spread of three torpedoes at large freighter identified as NITU MARU, 6543 tons . . . two Torpex torpedoes hit, one under his bridge and the other under the mainmast.

It had been almost too easy. O'Kane reported the ship was either zigzagging narrowly or "steering poorly," and they knew they needed only to put the target between them and the rocky, jagged shoreline behind him. He had no other place to go but into their torpedoes.

This ship went down vertically by the bow and was out of sight in three minutes, 10 seconds. Had the water been deeper he would have sunk faster, because the bow was resting on the bottom as it sank. Two junks were nearby and they appeared to be heading to pick up survivors.

"Battle surface!" Morton ordered. "Let's chase those junks down and show 'em a thing or two!"

Morton was clear: He did not want anyone to rescue the survivors of the ship they had just destroyed. And besides, *Wahoo*'s commandos might finally have a chance to show their stuff!

But instead of coming to try to pick up survivors, the small ships were now running away from the carnage as quickly as they could. They had been spooked by the sudden destruction that had erupted in an otherwise empty, tranquil sea. *Wahoo* gave chase anyway, at the captain's command, until the water beneath them became simply too shallow to allow them to go any farther. They were not only in danger of being spotted by lookouts on the shore, but they might actually have run aground if they kept going.

Mush Morton knew the area well. He had sailed around these islands.

"Reverse course," the captain ordered. "Let's go back to the spot where the *maru* went down and see what we can find."

There was a standing directive to warship skippers to try to secure the codebook used by the Japanese Merchant Marine if possible. There was a chance that there might be other useful stuff floating on the water, too.

And survivors. They knew already there were survivors in the water.

Decided to hunt for anything worth salvaging and pick up a survivor.

There were at least four men they could see who had survived the sinking. Some clung to the bottoms of a couple of overturned lifeboats. One floated nearby, wearing a life jacket. Morton took a long look at them through the scope from a distance.

"It must be colder than hell up there," he said quietly, with a sigh, and even a hint of pity in his voice. He half expected sound to be able to hear the men's teeth chattering. "They are really shivering. You know, next thing, the newspapers will be calling us 'Mush Morton and his Widow Makers.'"

From the captain's grin, the men knew he might actually welcome such a nickname.

As soon as they surfaced and had crew on the deck—several carrying weapons, of course—and the captain on the bridge, Morton turned his attention and the bow of his submarine to the haggard men left floating in the frigid water.

We attempted to pick up at least one of them. They seemed to ignore us entirely.

As they eased the bow of the boat near the lifeboats and to the survivor in the life vest, the survivors seemed to purposely turn their backs or ducked to the other side of the boat to try to hide. One crew member later reported that the survivors appeared to be dazed, that they might well have not understood that *Wahoo* was offering to help them. Crewmen on the deck of the submarine tried, though. They shouted at them, used sign language to offer to throw them a line, but they only turned away.

"To hell with them!" Morton finally yelled.

(There are reports that some of the men on the deck opened fire, that they "used the Japs for target practice." That same report said the captain had deliberately pointed the bow of *Wahoo* at one of the upside-down lifeboats and knocked a survivor into the water. It should be pointed out that those reports were from a spotty, unauthorized diary being kept by an enlisted man who was not even on the deck that day. The secondhand account was based on stories told by men who were. There are no other accounts by anyone—officer or enlisted man—of the submarine deliberately ramming a lifeboat or of crewmen shooting survivors of *Nitu Maru*.)

As *Wahoo* pulled away, crew members shouted back at the Japanese in the cold water, "So solly, please!" and "Tell Tokyo Rose the boys on *Wahoo* said hello!"

Meanwhile, O'Kane oversaw putting swimmers into the water to pick up anything that looked interesting. They did get a water-soaked book that might actually have been the codebook they sought. They also managed to pull in several souvenirs, including flags of the steamship company that owned the boat and a large life preserver with the ship's name painted on it. That item confirmed that the sunken vessel was, indeed, *Nitu Maru*, as they had suspected.

Four enemy ships sunk. One more to go to hit Morton's quota, and plenty of time and torpedoes to get it done.

Now they only needed the Japanese to cooperate and send a parade of potential targets past them.

However, it was no longer a goal of five ships sunk. The captain had already upped the ante.

CHAPTER 19

One-boat Wolf Pack

War! that mad game the world so loves to play.

—Jonathan Swift

*I*t did not take long for Wahoo to bag the fifth victim of her fourth war patrol. Like fishing, it helps to troll where the fish are.

There is, no doubt, a lot of shipping in this area, but one must find it to sink it. We believe we are heading for a good spot.

There is never much water in this "wading pond" known as the Yellow Sea. We have to be careful with our angle on dives to keep from plowing into the bottom. Aircraft and patrols have been scarce, because we are in virgin territory; however, she "ain't" virgin now, and we are expecting trouble soon. We hope to get at least four more ships and then expend our gun ammunition on our way home.

Four more ships? That would give them eight, far and away the most productive patrol thus far in World War II by any submarine. Despite their newfound luck, many felt the captain's new goal was unrealistic.

Number five came along quickly, and she almost begged to be shot. She was a small freighter, ambling along and at an almost perfect angle that required little maneuvering on the part of *Wahoo*. Morton wanted to save his Torpex torpedoes for bigger game, so he used just one of the TNT-carrying fish, shooting from a range of about a thousand yards. The nose of the torpedo hit right under the doomed ship's bridge. The target was immediately enveloped in thick gray coal dust. She was obviously a collier, a ship that hauled coal primarily for naval use. That made her a good kill.

Any fuel or raw materials denied the Japanese would hurt the empire's ability to fight the war. That was a factor of the conflict in the Pacific that had still not sunk in back home. They wanted news of destroyers, aircraft carriers, and battleships that had been sent to the bottom. But with its far-flung colonialism and its resource-starved island homeland, Japan desperately needed the freighters and tankers and their cargo. And that was why the submarines were there, to cut those shipping lanes like the crucial arteries that they were. Yes, enemy warships were highly desirable targets, but by denying the Japanese coal, rubber, oil, and other natural resources that were not available at home, the submarines could hasten the end to the war.

By the time *Wahoo* surfaced to look around, the collier was gone, sunk in less than thirteen minutes. The submarine had to run, though. It would soon be daylight, and they were close enough that they could have easily been seen from the beach.

The shallow water still caused them problems, but it also prompted the captain to try a new feature on his boat. They now had the ability to allow the attack periscope housing to extend all the way down into the control room, below the conning tower. That allowed them to have less scope showing above the surface as they made observations from the control room. At times, with the boat in relatively shallow water, far too much of the periscope poked out of the sea, giving lookouts or aircraft a better chance of spotting it.

1330H: Established the "NIPS" end run route and commenced heading for it . . . we hope to get a couple of ships over on this route within the next day or so and before the "Nips" learn of our presence.

Morton's intimate knowledge of the area was really paying off. They were often in sight of land, and the geography was familiar to the skipper. That especially came in handy when they had to make their way through scores of fishing boats and sampans—vessels that Morton had already taken to derisively calling "fishy *marus*"—that seemed to cover the sea surface all around them. Mush had not spent all his time in the Yellow

Sea wooing Harriet. With all the exercises in which he had taken part, he also knew well the routes that ships in the area would likely be using.

In his few spare moments away from the conn or bridge, Morton took time to write letters to his wife and other relatives, including to his wife's sister, husband, and children, the Avents. They had long since left Tsingtao ahead of the war and were living temporarily in Scarsdale, New York. Even though they would not be mailed until they returned from patrol— if they returned from patrol—it was required that any letters contained no information that might aid the enemy in any way. Censors went over all mail to extract anything that might give the Japanese even a clue about where a submarine had been or what it had done there.

Even so, Morton found a way to let the Avents know that he had visited a place they all had in common. In one letter to them, he included the sentence, "I saw your flagpole today." The family knew at once that their brother-in-law and uncle had been within sight of the flagpole on the Avents' lawn near the beach in Tsingtao.

A ship popped up on radar just after dark on March 24. It showed up at ten thousand yards—more than five and a half miles away—so it had to be something sizable. It quickly claimed *Wahoo*'s attention. Morton began maneuvering on the surface for a stern shot at whatever it was. Radar and the lookouts soon identified the target as a large tanker, coming right at them and making considerable speed. They would need to shoot a good spread and do it quickly, or, if the target got past them, they might never catch up to her to launch a second attack.

"Anytime, Dick."

Morton's calm words had already become as much a part of the language of *Wahoo*'s attack procedure as "mark," "set," and "fire." Three torpedoes were away from the boat's aft torpedo tubes.

The time count had just begun, had made it only to eighteen seconds, when there was the *whoomp!* of a deafening explosion. The submarine rocked mightily. Only O'Kane, gazing through the scope, knew immediately what had happened. Most of the rest of the crew assumed it was a bomb or a shell.

But no. It was their own torpedo, one of the ones they had just launched. Its magnetic exploder—the very device that was drawing the ire of Mush Morton for not exploding when it slammed into a target— had caused the torpedo to blow up prematurely.

And the second one did the same thing. It was a few hundred yards farther along but still packed a staggering punch to *Wahoo*'s jaw.

The agitated sea caused by the two "prematures" deflected the third torpedo off into some entirely wrong direction, certainly not toward the fast-moving tanker.

"Damn! Damn! How the hell are we supposed to fight a war . . . ?" Morton started, but quickly got back to business. A fourth torpedo was sent on its way, but with all the fair warning from the early detonations, the target's commander would certainly have been able to evade anything else sent spinning his way.

About the time it was determined that the fourth torpedo, too, had missed, they saw that the tanker was now shooting back. The prematures and the trail behind the last fish had been more than enough to give the ship an idea of where their attacker was. The lookouts on the tanker had possibly spotted their scope as well, even in the deepening darkness.

2000H: The tanker let go several 4- or 5-inch rounds at a range of about 3,000 yards using the Nips' famous flashless powder. One of the shells landed directly ahead of us and burst with a loud bang. We dived and tracked the target.

They could not chance a lucky shot from their target taking out their shears or opening a leak in the roof. They would go deeper but still try to stay within sight of the tanker. But if they waited too long, they would have to follow her right into Darien Harbor, whose breakwater was not that far away now.

When they did come up to continue the chase with more speed, they saw the tanker was still firing at random, but nowhere close to where the submarine now was. Once they were able to get ahead of the target—the ship making an estimated twelve knots, no match for *Wahoo*'s twenty— and had the tanker lined up in silhouette with a rising moon behind her, Morton took them back to periscope depth. He could tell now that the target was riding low in the water, clearly full of fuel oil, but by then she was also only a few miles from the entrance to Darien Harbor and safety.

2122H: Fired a spread of three torpedoes at target . . . second torpedo with TNT head hit him in the engine room. He sank in 4 minutes, 25 seconds, going down by the stern. The target was loaded to the gills with fuel oil.

They had their sixth kill in seven attacks. But Morton could hardly wait to once again vent his anger with his stubby pencil as he wrote down his frustrations concerning the latest bad torpedoes.

Here again faulty torpedoes frustrated an attack, wasted four valuable torpedoes that we have carried over 5,000 miles, almost caused the WAHOO to be destroyed, and allowed the target the time to open up on its radio and frustrate our newly discovered, fertile shipping route.

Only a few hours later, *Wahoo* relied on the moon once more for its next attack. There was no choice. The radar training gear had jammed, and that left them blind beyond what the lookouts could see from their platforms above the bridge. Commander MacMillan was on the bridge when the lookouts, who actually perched above a stubborn fog that clung to the sea surface, spotted the outline of a ship. MacMillan handled most of the maneuvering to get ready for the attack before the captain was summoned and came to the conn to take over.

This time, their first torpedo ran for forty-eight seconds—about four seconds before she was due to strike the target at that range—before it blew up spectacularly. And early. The second one got even closer to the medium-size freighter they were stalking and exploded, but it, too, was early and inflicted no serious damage.

"She's still going, Captain," O'Kane reported, referring to the target.

"She can't be," Morton said, his face twisted. "That last torpedo . . ."

"Both of them prematured," the XO told him.

"The second one, too?"

O'Kane stepped aside and allowed Morton to take a look through the scope. They had only two torpedoes left, and God only knew whether they would work properly. Based on recent performance, there certainly was some doubt.

But then Morton turned from the scope with a strange look in his eyes. He smiled at his XO.

"Have you seen any guns on her deck, Dick?"

"No, not a one."

"Make all preparations for battle surface!"

Mush Morton would later write, "Anyone who has not witnessed a submarine conduct a battle surface with three 20mm and a four-inch gun in the morning twilight with a calm sea and in crisp clear weather just ain't lived. It is truly spectacular!"

In just over ten minutes, they had gun crews hanging from ladders in the conning tower and ammunition ready at the mess room hatch, prepared to spill out onto *Wahoo*'s deck as soon as they were above water. Then they were on the surface, with men running along the decks even as the seawater streamed off. The very first shot from *Wahoo*'s deck gun hit the afterdeck house on the target, and another soon found the sweet spot on the ship's stern to knock out her steering. Another gun concentrated on where the ship's engines would be as Morton brought them quickly closer.

Lookouts watched for any sign of return fire. Or of an escort of some kind. There was nothing. They bored in for the kill.

Closed in on target and raked him with 20mm and holed him with almost 90 rounds of 4-inch. Target caught fire in several places. Her lifeboat was dangling from the forward davit. Passed about twelve survivors in the water all sorta chattering. The crew yelled to the survivors, "So solly, please."

The rush of adrenaline was felt by every man in the boat, not just the ones on deck doing the damage, as they raced around the stricken ship and continued puncturing her with gunfire. Yes, she was defenseless, but no more so than she had been when they had been firing dud torpedoes at her. The goal was still the same: Sink the sons of bitches!

"Mast on the horizon!" one of the lookouts suddenly sang out. He yelled to be heard between the bursts of gunfire.

"What is it? An escort?" Morton asked.

He could see already that it was a thin mast, so it was not anything as big as what they were effectively destroying. It could be a patrol boat, a corvette. If it was a warship, they could be in big trouble. If they could not outrun it, there was little water to hide beneath when the depth charges started to fall.

But Duncan MacMillan, using the periscope's magnification, was able to quickly tell that it was a small freighter, about a thousand tons. Leaving the first target burning, listing, dead in the water, Morton ordered them to take off after the newcomer. *Wahoo*'s gunfire soon started several blazes on the second target's decks, but her crew managed to put them out.

A *member of her crew was in the foretop waving his arms—maybe he was conning the ship. A few 20mm hits in his vicinity caused him to slide down a guy wire like a monkey.*

At one point, they got close enough to the target that the freighter's machine-gun fire was reaching frighteningly close to *Wahoo*'s deck and to the men on it. They had to ease away, but the tanker was fast, easily making fourteen knots. The submarine was faster if she chose to run away in a straight line. However, she needed to be able to zigzag so the forward deck gun could continue to be used if they hoped to accomplish the two-bagger.

Finally, with some well-placed shots from *Wahoo*, the freighter's engines were disabled, and she, too, was a sitting duck, soon ablaze at multiple points and with sailors spilling off her decks.

Just as the sun was rising, both freighters were going down, sinking rapidly.

Every man on *Wahoo* was elated, cheering, pounding one another on their backs, arguing good-naturedly over who had personally fired the mortal shots. These men had just participated in an action that would have previously been unknown to submarine sailors except in very rare instances. They had claimed two enemy vessels using a running surface attack, employing their ship's deck guns. Previously, submarine warfare required that most of the crew remain belowdecks, doing specific duty, with only the fire control party in the conning tower or on the bridge at the center of the action. Each man played his role, and they were all vital, but he had to rely on sounds and reports on the announcement systems to keep tabs on how the assault was going. Only the captain and XO were typically able to see the damage they were doing in the heat of the battle, and they were too busy to give a play-by-play.

The surface attack allowed many of the crew to actually participate, to fire shots, to see the damage they were dishing out against the enemy. Not only was it an effective way to sink enemy ships, but it was also great for morale.

Assuming things went well, of course.

Mush Morton was likely the happiest man on the submarine when the two freighters were finished. As much as he loved a well-run torpedo attack, it was nowhere close to what he and his crew had just experienced. Nowhere close in excitement or in satisfaction.

But as energizing and effective as the surface deck gun assault was, it was also dangerous.

"At no time during the action had Commander Morton endangered a single member of his crew," Dick O'Kane later wrote.

The XO's statement is true in one respect: Morton never got close enough to either target vessel to be in danger from any gunfire from them.

But there were certainly other hazards he had not mentioned: the possibility of an enemy aircraft or patrol vessel suddenly appearing on the scene; the problematically shallow water that would have offered little cover if that had happened; a deck full of men who would have had to get down the hatches if an emergency dive had been ordered.

War is a dangerous endeavor. Any operation in enemy waters is necessarily a risk. Morton and his crew had willingly taken on those risks and had come out just fine, sinking two enemy ships, making a statement to the Japanese, and, incidentally, having a hell of a good time in the process.

They were not finished, though. The next morning, they spied another small trawler, much like all the other "fishy *marus*" they had been working so hard to avoid ramming. This one could have been assumed to be a fishing boat as well. But there was something curious about the size of the ship's radio antenna.

With that one bit of evidence, the attack was on. Again using the deck guns, the crew riddled the target with gunfire. Despite "resembling a colander," though, the vessel stubbornly remained afloat.

The commandos even retrieved their stock of Molotov cocktails—the ones the Marines back in Pearl had helped them make—and they hurled them onto the ship's decks. When they started fires, though, they quickly burned out. The captain finally decided that the vessel probably was a fishing boat after all, but the antenna meant she had the capability of being a lookout vessel, too.

The seas were too rough to safely attempt a boarding—"otherwise we could have had fresh fish and also opened up some sea valves in her"—so *Wahoo* left the trawler "in pretty much a wrecked condition" and moved on.

The crew had the chance to use most of the rest of their ammunition on a couple more sampans three days after the thrilling experience of the running gun action.

1820H: Secured 20mm guns and crews after expending about 500 rounds on each sampan. They did not sink, but they have a lot of holes in them and are quite wrecked. It was still too rough to go aboard for a mess of fresh fish. Our mouths watered at such a possibility.

But several of the officers noticed that their skipper was not quite as lighthearted as his words in the log might have indicated. He seemed impatient, aggravated by the lack of any more good targets, bored with punching holes in sampans full of fish. It did not matter to him at all that if they had shown up back at Midway with no more kills than they had already notched, theirs would have been a stunningly successful war patrol.

O'Kane found the skipper sitting alone in the wardroom the afternoon after the latest sampan riddling, his head down, seriously studying the chart on the table.

"Dick, look at this," he told his XO, and shoved the chart his way, one finger marking Kagoshima-wan, the large bay at the southern end of the Japanese province of Kyushu. "Look, there are only two routes for ships to get into the bay and to Kagoshima. We could sit there and wait for them to steam right to us. Then we'd only have a short run out to the hundred-fathom curve to get away. What do you think, Dick?"

O'Kane pretended to study the chart for a moment.

"Well, Captain, since you asked for my opinion, I'll give it to you," the XO replied. "I think we ought to save it for the next patrol."

"Okay, why?"

"We only have two torpedoes left, and we have no idea whether they will perform or not. We are out of all but our emergency ammunition for the deck guns. We have some sick batteries that are not making charge. And the currents around Kagoshima-wan are nothing to be trifled with, even with good batteries."

O'Kane sat back and waited for his skipper's reaction. Morton pursed his lips, looking at the chart a few moments longer as if it would show him counters to his XO's arguments.

"I appreciate your frankness, Dick. Tell you what, let's table the idea for a couple of days and see what happens." Then the captain shoved the chart out of the way and reached for the cards. "How about a rubber of cribbage before dinner?"

It would be the first game between the two men since Morton angrily ripped up the cards after O'Kane beat him. O'Kane later noted that in almost every decision Mush Morton made, he had been in full agreement, but for the reasons he cited, he did not think this latest idea was a good one. He took it as a mighty compliment when his captain accepted his assessment.

The XO got good news later that evening. The nightly radio broadcast contained confirmation that O'Kane had received his promotion to lieutenant commander. Now the way was cleared for him to get his own ship's command.

But there was one more chance to do damage on the patrol. Just before three o'clock in the morning, a ship was sighted, a fairly large freighter. Tracking began, and just before dawn *Wahoo* was once again in good firing position. There was even more precision required this time, though. They had to give their torpedoes the absolute best opportunity to hit the target, and pray they did not explode too early or thud harmlessly against the target's hull.

0416H: Fired a spread of two torpedoes . . . 900 yards . . . first torpedo hit under his mainmast, which was our point of aim, and completely disintegrated everything abaft of his stack. The forward section sank two minutes and thirty-two seconds later.

The second torpedo missed, but for a good reason: The first one had completely stopped the ship's forward momentum.

The yelps of the crew were quickly drowned out by the loud creaking and groaning of the wounded target as she sank and was smashed by the force and pressure of seawater.

"Dick, what is the course for the barn?" Morton asked.

"One four five. And we're steering it already."

Morton grinned. At first opportunity outside enemy waters, and after reluctantly skirting around some especially interesting targets, the captain ordered a message be sent to the submarine commanders at Pearl Harbor. He gave the bad torpedoes top billing in a missive that he knew would be seen by many others. Then he let the brass know what *Wahoo* and her crew had accomplished, despite the handicap:

ONE SURFACE RUNNER, ONE DUD, FOUR PREMATURES, ONE TANKER SUNK, ONE FREIGHTER HOLED AND BELIEVED SUNK, FIVE FREIGHTERS SUNK BY TORPE-DOES, TWO FREIGHTERS, TWO SAMPANS SUNK BY GUN-FIRE, AND LARGE TRAWLER WRECKED.

The message back from Pearl—and one that all other submarines would also copy—was short but pithy:

CONGRATULATIONS ON A JOB WELL-DONE. JAPANESE THINK A SUBMARINE WOLF PACK OPERATING IN YEL-LOW SEA, ALL SHIPPING TIED UP.

Another letter Morton took time to write as they made the long run back home was to Captain H. G. Donald. Donald was another staff officer who had gone to bat for Morton with "Babe" Brown when he was about to get deep-sixed off *Dolphin* and shipped out of the submarine service. The thrill of the daring gun attacks showed in his words, but the outwardly valiant skipper also gave candid insight into what he was really feeling as he steered his boat into danger.

"Sank a 2,500 tonner and a 1,000 tonner with our deck guns. And to make the story better, one was sinking while we were plugging the other. The men love to shoot the deck gun. More of the crew feel that they are taking a personal part in the fighting. We fired all our ammunition on both trips."

But then Morton shared his more vulnerable side.

"My nerves are still in knots. I get hell scared out of me constantly, but I reckon all skippers feel the same as I. It is nothing a bit of leave won't cure. They have recommended me for a Medal of Honor. Now won't that be something. Plus a Navy Cross and an Army Distinguished Service Cross. Say, I will burst a button when I strut around!!"

Morton completed his very personal and telling letter to Captain Donald with a sincere acknowledgment.

"Thanks to you, Captain, sometimes a 'feller' does not get a chance like you help [sic] give me. Then too some 'fellers' do not have the luck I have had lately. Here is hoping the *Wahoo* can continue sinking Japs at the rate of one a week for the duration. This has been our average since January, and I hope we can keep it up."

The Medal of Honor never happened, by the way.

So it was that once again, with no torpedoes left to fire and her magazines mostly empty of ammunition, with an unprecedented string of successful attacks recorded in her patrol report, *Wahoo* was headed for home, running boldly and almost exclusively on the surface.

It was as if she were proudly strutting for any enemy that might catch a glimpse of her.

She was now and forevermore to be known as "the One-boat Wolf Pack."

CHAPTER 20

Sucker Punch

"*WAHOO* returned from patrol in very good material condition. While tired and visibly worn by the strain of the patrol, officers and crew were in good health and excellent spirits."

—From the patrol summary, fourth war patrol report, USS *Wahoo*

*M*ush Morton was not a well man.

He continued to have a dull, nagging pain in his prostate, had to urinate often, and regularly had blood in his urine. He was also feverish and had blinding headaches at times. When making port, he was soon off to a hospital for treatment.

Those officers who were aware of his condition sometimes caught him wincing in pain or grunting when he climbed the ladder from the control room to the conn and up to the bridge. Few in the crew knew it or even suspected that their captain had health issues, though. Certainly he seemed to be his usual cocky self as he guided his submarine toward Midway and the submarine base there for the wrap-up of *Wahoo*'s fourth war patrol, arriving there on April 6.

The captain allowed Dick O'Kane to do most of the navigating on the way across the Pacific. Morton had another chore he wanted to accomplish. He put his sewing talents to work crafting together by hand a spectacular pennant in the form of an Indian headdress. On it were arrayed images of a setting sun to represent the ships they had sunk.

Morton was dead set on outdoing their last spectacular return to port. He had the crew lash *two* brooms to the top of their extended peri-scope this time, forming a makeshift yardarm. Then he ordered that the crew install the battle pennant and the two flags they had retrieved from *Nitu Maru*, allowing them to stream out behind the brooms in the wind.

Wahoo made quite an entrance as she steamed through the break in the reef and sidled up to the pier at Midway. But there were few there to appreciate it. No admirals. No covey of reporters. No big band. A small quartet played so quietly the musicians were difficult to hear. Most of their welcome party consisted of line handlers who had no idea who *Wahoo* or Mush Morton was or why they should care. She was just another submarine come to port, and they had to get her tied up.

Forest Sterling observed, "They were so used to successful subma-rines coming in off war patrols that we were just another break in their humdrum life."

Some officers were suspicious of the decision to send what was easily the Navy's most famous submarine to this remote spot, way out in the Pacific beyond Hawaii, for refitting and to allow the crew to rest. Was someone jealous? Or were they wary of giving too much notoriety and attention to the boat and her highly praised skipper?

The base certainly offered none of the amenities or comforts of Hono-lulu. The primary entertainment there was gambling with the cutthroat civilian contractor workers and watching the antics of the island's unique gooney bird population. To protect the crew—and especially the younger men—from the cardsharps, COB Pappy Rau required the sailors to deposit their entire pay into an informal bank he set up before they left the boat. They could withdraw only ten bucks a day. Nobody would get hurt.

There were certainly no accommodations for the officers like the Royal Hawaiian, either. They would stay in rooms at a hotel that been renamed from the regal-sounding "Pan American" to the "Gooney Bird." That is, they could stay there once another boat pulled away, because until those men checked out, all the rooms were taken. The *Wahoo* officers slept in the bunks on board the submarine the first two nights in port.

The endorsement of the run by the commander of Submarine Squad-ron Ten was just as glowing as the previous one had been: "The fourth

war patrol was again outstanding and marked by maximum aggressiveness and cool daring. The intelligent planning and sound judgment of
the Commanding Officer in making his decisions enabled WAHOO to
outsmart the enemy, retain the initiative, and inflict a considerable
amount of damage."

When Morton reported to the squadron commander for his debrief-
ing, he proudly ran down the highlights of the patrol, while continuing
to grouse heatedly about the torpedo failures. In the official patrol report,
the issue took six paragraphs, with Morton noting that while the failure
rate might have appeared to be only twenty percent, the fact was that
"torpedo failures caused the additional expenditure of six good torpedoes and 90 rounds of 4" ammunition." And the captain reiterated,
"Again the Japs' newfound traffic lane was spoiled for further attack."

Then the subject came up of the prospective commanding officer,
Duncan MacMillan, who had already stopped by for a visit. The squadron commander shared the PCO's comments honestly.

MacMillan had reported to him that he had "grave reservations"
about the way Morton and his officers had conducted their patrol. He
had charged the captain and his crew with a lack of proper planning,
poor coordination, and "an absence of discipline in the conning tower"
when Wahoo made attacks on the enemy.

Morton was stunned, for once at a loss for words. MacMillan had
given no indication during the patrol that he had issues or concerns.
Mush's first thought was, "Now I know how Pinky Kennedy felt when I
let him have it in Fremantle." His second impulse was to find MacMillan
and punch his lights out.

Ultimately, Morton decided to simply let the results of the patrol
speak for themselves. They clearly spoke volumes. Nothing more was
ever brought up by Morton's superiors related to MacMillan's statements.
However, that was not the end of it.

Officers from the various submarines in port at Midway always gathered in a meeting room at the Gooney Bird—an informal "wardroom"—
where they could visit, drink cold beer, play cards, and just generally

relax with their contemporaries. Dick O'Kane was there, visiting with a former shipmate, when he overheard someone across the room talking about *Wahoo*.

It was Duncan MacMillan. His words were not kind, "belittling most everything that *Wahoo* had accomplished on patrol and including some disparaging remarks about" O'Kane. The XO felt he knew the reasons for the PCO's disdain. The man had been passed over for command of *Wahoo*, which went instead to a man three years his junior. When Mac-Millan got the PCO ride on the boat, her captain by then was four years his junior. And MacMillan had stood by and watched an officer eight years his junior—O'Kane—as he manned the attack periscope in the conn and the TBT on the bridge, and fired *Wahoo*'s torpedoes.

No wonder the man had gotten his feathers ruffled! He felt as if the brash youngsters were passing him by.

But understanding his motives or not, O'Kane stood and was on the verge of confronting MacMillan when he spotted his skipper, also at a nearby table, and also obviously overhearing the same spiel. Morton motioned O'Kane over.

"Look, let's you and me take a walk before we get into a fight," Morton advised. And they did. It was strikingly similar to the incident in *Wahoo*'s conning tower when Morton prevented his XO from punching out Pinky Kennedy.

But before they got back to the submarine, Morton suddenly pulled up.

"Hell, let's go back and square this away," he said, and spun around, headed back to the Gooney Bird.

However, when they got there, the "wardroom" was empty, the lights out.

"Seeming still a bit riled, Morton headed for the nearest game to take out his anger on a pair of dice," O'Kane later recounted.

MacMillan did get his command, the USS *Thresher* (SS-200), in December 1943. In the process, he became the oldest skipper to command a fleet boat. MacMillan later wrote, "The question of the best age for a submarine skipper is moot. It depends on the characteristics of the officer. Obviously a balance has to be had between the daring of youth and the caution of old age."

However, Mush Morton had little opportunity to throw dice, defend the honor of his boat, her crew, or their methods, or to help get his boat ready for her next patrol. He was summoned to Pearl Harbor by his boss. Admiral Lockwood wanted to talk with him personally about his boat's spectacular success as well as to hear firsthand his thoughts on the malfunctioning torpedoes. The captain left O'Kane in charge and flew to Hawaii.

"The captain will get some time at the Royal Hawaiian after all," the XO noted. But he was wrong. Morton would actually check into the Navy hospital for some attention to his prostate problem between meetings with the brass.

Still mightily impressed with his star skipper, Lockwood seemed more than willing to listen to Morton's complaints. He promised to push the issue. When he left the admiral's office, Morton still was not sure that he had made his point forcefully enough to get something done about it. And this would not be the last time he gave Lockwood the benefit of his opinions on the subject.

For his part, and though he had been at his command only a short time, Lockwood did make the torpedo problem a priority. On his first trip back to the States—shortly after Morton's visit—he told the Submarine Officers' Conference that, "If the Bureau of Ordnance can't provide us with torpedoes that will hit and explode, then for God's sake, get the Bureau of Ships to design a boat hook with which we can rip the plates off a target's side!"

Meanwhile, back on Midway, the squadron commander decided to take a ride with Dick O'Kane and *Wahoo* during her practice drills and while her skipper was away. He wanted to see for himself if what Duncan MacMillan had told him was valid. The XO slid all the personnel up a notch in the pecking order. That had him conning the boat as Morton did, and Roger Paine in O'Kane's spot on the periscope.

The commander strongly expressed his disapproval of such a radical procedure. O'Kane did not blink.

"This is the way we do it on *Wahoo*," he said, and promptly lined up and fired a perfect practice torpedo, right beneath the bridge of a "target" destroyer.

When the captain showed up a few days later, he brought with him a new PCO, Lieutenant Commander John Moore, another former Annapolis athlete. Moore also had an aggressive reputation similar to Morton's, and was arguably just as personable and likable. He also had a personal stake in the war already: Moore's brother had been captured by the Japanese in the Philippines.

Morton also brought something else with him: medals.

With the enlisted men in their dress whites standing in formation on the dock, Dick O'Kane received the Silver Star. Several other officers, chiefs, and enlisted men were also recognized. O'Kane, sporting his new lieutenant commander gold leaves, did the honors.

The captain was not present for the ceremony. He had pointedly asked that he not receive his own second Navy Cross from Admiral Nimitz while he was in Pearl Harbor. Instead, he wanted the formal presentation back in Midway, beside *Wahoo*, with his crew looking on. It was not to be.

When the ceremony was over, Forest Sterling went back aboard the boat. He found the captain in his bunk, his face flushed.

"Captain, you okay?"

"I'm fine, Yeo," he answered, and shakily sat up on the side of his cot. "My kidneys give me a fit every once in a while and I get headaches. I just did not feel up to it today. I'll be fine. How'd it go?"

The patrol earned more than medals. Even after hearing Duncan Mac-Millan's complaints, the squadron commander wrote that the run had been "again outstanding and marked by maximum aggressiveness and cool daring." He specifically praised her skipper: "The intelligent planning and sound judgment of the Commanding Officer in making his decisions enabled the *WAHOO* to outsmart the enemy, retain the initiative, and inflict a considerable amount of damage. The Commander, Submarine Squadron Ten, takes pleasure in extending a 'well-done' to the Commanding Officer and personnel of *WAHOO* for a highly successful patrol."

Admiral Charles Lockwood's endorsement of the report echoed that praise. He went on to single out the surface gun attacks for attention, but with just a bit of caution thrown in.

"It is gratifying to note that all of the WAHOO's gun battles were executed only after a careful estimate of the situation was made; each was carried out with military aggressiveness, professional competence and yet free of foolhardy recklessness. These attacks were carried out when they could be made with the submarine having the definite advantage. It is well to remember that our submarines are very valuable and, at the same time, vulnerable targets when gunfire is used as the attacking weapon."

Lockwood clearly wanted his skippers to emulate his "ace," but to be prudent in how far they went to try to produce the results Mush Morton was achieving. "Mush the Magnificent" was exactly what he wanted every other submarine commander in the fleet to be.

The citation accompanying Morton's second Navy Cross—the award for valor given to naval personnel, second only to the Medal of Honor—mentions his "extraordinary heroism" and says, "The brilliant leadership and valiant devotion to duty displayed by Commander Morton throughout the entire period of action reflect great credit upon his command and the United States Naval Service."

Wahoo had claimed eight kills for 36,700 tons, along with having inflicted heavy damage on one more ship, one that they assumed escaped. In a rarity, postwar analysis would eventually add that damaged ship back into the tally when it was confirmed that it, too, had sunk before reaching port.

Only one other submarine had come close by that point in the war: USS Guardfish (SS-217), with a claim of six ships sunk (later reduced to five). The results would ultimately place Wahoo's fourth patrol at number two on the list of successful World War II patrols, based on number of ships sunk. Only Tang, skippered by Richard "Dick" O'Kane, would later do better, with ten ships confirmed destroyed.

Now, with only fifteen days of rest, a daunting reputation to maintain, a hurting skipper, and sixteen new crew members, Wahoo was ready to depart on her fifth patrol on April 25, 1943. Morton had also brought with him from Hawaii their operation order, and this one sent them to a completely different sort of place.

If Morton and his "widow makers" had most recently been operating in a hot area, they were now bound for a cold one.

Really cold.

And the hallmark of this run would not be what Mush Morton and *Wahoo* accomplished.

It would be what they failed to do.

CHAPTER 21

The Thud of a Dud

"Harriet, you have married an officer without a future."

—Mush Morton in a telephone call to his wife

Wahoo *took special precautions leaving Midway. A broken bit of code, intercepted from the enemy, indicated that a major component of the Japanese fleet was being sent to the Aleutian Islands to counter any U.S. attempt to retake the chain. They were supposed to be located in the northern reaches of the Kuril Islands, a spinelike series of small, rocky spits of land, mostly vertical mountains with little flat space. The chain curled northward from Hokkaido, the northernmost Home Island. They were north of the forty-fifth parallel of latitude. It would be cold there, the sea icy even in May.*

That meant foul-weather gear had to be loaded at night, with as little fuss as possible so nobody on the docks would see them. They also steamed away from Midway on a due-west course until the submarine was over the horizon and a turn to the northwest could be made. No civilian worker could be allowed to make a guess as to *Wahoo*'s destination, say the wrong thing to the wrong person, and allow the Japanese to even suspect that the code had been broken, or that *Wahoo* and three other submarines were on their way to the Kurils to intercept the fleet.

Mush Morton still did not feel well at all. The stress and work of the previous two patrols at the helm and the one as PCO with Kennedy were taking their toll on him. He could not shake the latest flare-up of prostatitis. Still, he kept up a good front, joked with the men, fussed with the officers, and did not let on that he was sick.

The truth was, nobody was comfortable. It was not long before the bitter cold began to affect everyone in the crew. Forest Sterling later remembered, "Every day I added another piece of clothing to go up on lookout. When I came off watch, my teeth were chattering, I was shivering, and my nose and ears were so cold I was afraid to touch them for fear they might shatter into fragments. [Most of the time] it was sleeting and snowing and I stood there trying to peer into a darkness that was not penetrable with the human eye."

Ice had to be chipped away from the bridge and lookout platforms, and it was not unusual to run through a deluge of hail and snow, both falling at the same time and wrapped in thick fog, or to have sleet hissing like a rattlesnake as it struck the deck. Men coming down the ladder quickly took off their wet, cold gear and stuck it into a special locker they had developed so it could be dried and ready for reuse.

Those men who had been in the northern latitudes before in the old S-boats reminded the others of how good they had it. The air-conditioning inside *Wahoo* was far superior to those ancient boats, and everyone below remained relatively comfortable.

When the fog cleared enough for them to get a view of the first islands they encountered, they found little to report beyond one impressive airfield with four hangars and a large landing field. They took pictures and plotted the location for later attention.

The islands observed this far south are barren and completely covered with snow and ice, the installation NATSUWA being the only indication of any activity.

O'Kane suggested—first quietly and then more forcefully—that the captain allow them to move closer on the surface and lob some shells into the hangars. Morton declined. They were supposed to be looking for signs of elements of the enemy fleet. Better for once not to announce their presence. Those warships were the greater prize.

Besides, they were now dealing with a hazard they had not yet experienced.

The harbor was jammed with float ice and no activity could be observed. As the currents were apparently causing the ice floes to surround us, changed course to southeast to get clear.

But if O'Kane had any suspicion that his skipper was getting timid, he soon learned otherwise. On May 4, with PCO Moore at the conn, a ship appeared in the thick mist. Though they could not tell what it was, or even whether it was a single vessel at first, it was of interest. That was especially true when they drew closer and could finally make it out in the cold haze.

An auxiliary seaplane tender, with a complement of aircraft resting on her deck!

When the captain came up the ladder and took a gander at the target, he grinned and winked, completely forgetting about the ache in his lower back and groin. Not only was she a worthy target, but she was clearly more worried about skirting the ice nearer to land than she was about being on the lookout for an American submarine. She was steaming right toward *Wahoo*. All they had to do was wait for her to come within range.

PCO Johnny Moore had heard about how things went in *Wahoo's* conn. He smiled broadly when he heard Morton's patented, "Anytime, Dick."

A three-torpedo spread was away at what amounted to point-blank range. They could not miss!

The first torpedo with Torpex head hit between stack and bridge after sixty-second run. The torpedo fired at his forward goalpost evidently passed ahead and the one fired aft must have been erratic or a dud. It is inconceivable that any normal dispersion could allow this last torpedo to miss a 510-foot target at this range. The target tooted her whistle, commenced firing to port, away from the WAHOO, and then turned away, dropping four depth charges.

The first fish had hit, did explode, but apparently did little damage. The other two missed, though there had been a perfect setup.

"Son of a bitch doesn't even know what direction we are!" Morton exclaimed. "And thanks to the damn duds, she's getting away!"

Morton thought for a quick moment about surfacing, giving chase. But it was bright daylight up there. The ship had certainly broadcast the presence of an American submarine, even if they had no idea what direction it was from them. And she could hug the island in water too shallow for *Wahoo* to dive into.

Trying to angle for another shot while submerged was out of the question, too. They had some bad batteries that could not be replaced at Midway and that left them short on the juice—having only about half the normal power—it would have taken.

"I just hope we put them out of commission for a while," the captain said quietly, gritting his teeth.

They found a picture of a similar ship in the identification manual. That class should have been able to make over twenty knots. This one was running away at about eleven. Maybe that indicated she was wounded, at least.

After winding around among the Kurils, they saw no sign of the predicted enemy warships and turned south, off the main island of Honshu. Not only did it turn noticeably warmer, but suddenly potential targets were everywhere.

The well-oiled fire control party soon had six torpedoes headed toward a couple of freighters, one of which—a smaller one—had all indications of being armed, carrying freight but acting as an escort, too. Of the six torpedoes fired, only one did any damage. It struck the larger freighter in a sweet spot.

The first torpedo hit the YUKI MARU *under the stack and broke her back.*

The smaller, more maneuverable vessel managed to wend its way through the torpedoes that were aimed her way. She was now heading for *Wahoo* full charge. Morton took the submarine down quickly and steered away, but the crew still had their fillings rattled by four well-placed depth charges. Depth charges that were not really all that close, but still close enough to fray nerves.

Later that afternoon, O'Kane was in his cramped quarters, door closed, catching up on transcribing his notes on the attack. There was a knock. Morton came in and sat down heavily on his XO's bunk. The skipper clearly had something on his mind.

"Dick, we've been a bust so far on this run," he said.

"We started slow last time, too, Captain. We got a good one today. It'll pick up now that we're farther south."

Morton rubbed the whiskers on his rather sizable jaw.

"I've been thinking. I may have been too careful staying out twelve miles or more. They're staying close to shore here. You and I . . . sometimes we cancel out each other. Neither one of us is as decisive as we would be alone. I know you wanted to chase that son of a bitch this morning, and I took us the other way." He looked sideways at his XO. "Starting in the morning, I want you to take us in close. Call me when you have a ship."

O'Kane could not believe what he was hearing, but he certainly was not going to argue. It was exactly what he wanted to do.

"Aye, sir," he told his skipper.

The exec was also aware that the captain had just conceded that his second was ready for his own boat, and that he had complete confidence in him to accept more responsibility on *Wahoo*—far more than a typical submarine captain, with a typical submarine captain's ego, would have ever considered doing.

O'Kane was up early the next morning, joined by Johnny Moore, who was proving to deserve his reputation for aggressiveness. Soon they were just over a mile from the shore. Land was clearly visible through the scope. So were several smaller ships. They would almost certainly be aware that there was a submarine lurking out there after the previous day's attack. They stayed ridiculously close to the beach, mirroring the shoreline, even steering into coves.

O'Kane noted that when the captain arrived in the conn, he appeared to be well rested for the first time in months, and in an especially jovial mood. Once he was convinced there would be no attempt to go after the small and hardly worthwhile shore hugger, he went back down the ladder, back to his stateroom and bunk for more rest.

Finally, midafternoon, three more ships appeared, still relatively close to shore, but not so close that they weren't worth the effort. Morton, O'Kane, Moore, and Paine soon had them into position, and three torpedoes were on their way toward the largest target of the three.

No way to miss these guys!

The first torpedo (Torpex) aimed at MOT, prematured after 50-second run halfway to the target. The second torpedo aimed at mainmast, and down practically the same track as the first, was evidently deflected by the premature or failed to explode. The third torpedo fired at the foremast hit the point of aim but failed to explode.

A premature and a dud. Damn!

Rested or not, Mush Morton was furious, and loudly and profanely said so. Everyone in the conn, and those below in the control room—who could hear him clearly—was well accustomed to his disgust with the duds and how vociferously he expressed it. Even if he was preaching to the choir.

Both sound operators reported the thud of the dud at the same time that a column of water about ten feet was observed at the target's side abreast of her foremast as the air flask exploded.

1510K: Received first of the series of depth charges expected under these circumstances.

The two smaller freighters—similarly armed to the one the day before—proceeded to give them all a good headache with some too-close-for-comfort depth charges. This was a relatively new experience for most of them. Those who had been with Morton for all three runs knew that their skipper was especially adept at outrunning or outguessing antisubmarine efforts. They had mostly had only random and distant "ash cans" of TNT intended for them.

The captain's command to steer a new course up the coast sounded almost halfhearted, as if he were saying, "For all the damn good it'll do!"

There was a rousing discussion of their torpedo woes that evening over dinner in the wardroom. What had changed? Why were they suddenly finding so many worthless fish?

O'Kane had an idea or two. So did Roger Paine. The captain was in his stateroom and not available to express his opinions.

The Mark XIV torpedo was lighter, smaller, and more powerful than its predecessors, using steam to power it toward its target. It carried a five-hundred-pound warhead. But early in the war, and under the assumption that most targets would be large metal warships, a new top-secret exploder—the Mark VI—was developed. It employed a magnetic detector, which was supposed to sense the steel hulls of the enemy ships and detonate.

Several of the officers on *Wahoo* were convinced, based on far more observation than they really wanted, that there were several problems with the exploder. First, it was too heavy and tended to make the torpedoes run much deeper than the depth that had been set for them. They were often simply running beneath targets. Second, they had not been tested properly, and there was too little known about the magnetic fields of ships in the first place. Some submariners were convinced that the detonators did not work unless they struck a target at precisely the right angle. That was crucial, since so many of their potential victims were actually merchant ships and not necessarily ships with solid iron hulls. Early success was due to skippers' using the existing supply of older Mark X torpedoes with contact exploders. Or Mark XIVs with the older exploder. Now those were mostly gone.

The next morning, the XO took his coffee with him up to the bridge and was soon joined by Johnny Moore, who had become a good like-minded partner. It was not long before they had pips on the radar, potential targets, and the captain was summoned. By the time Morton popped up the ladder, Moore and O'Kane had already settled on a good approach on what appeared to be a large tanker and a freighter.

Of the six torpedoes fired, three hit.

Just after the fifth torpedo was fired the first hit the tanker amidships, breaking her back. She sank by the bow and caught fire aft. The fourth torpedo hit the freighter under the bridge, breaking its back, and the fifth torpedo hit her aft.

Crew members tried to get photos of the sinking ships, but there was not much light, and besides that, the dead ducks had slipped beneath the surface too quickly. Morton told the ecstatic crew to run and hide at three hundred feet, finding a nice temperature inversion to crouch beneath. Differences in water temperature can actually prevent sound-probing equipment from penetrating past that point. Submarines often used that to their advantage. *Wahoo*'s crew took great delight in listening to far-distant explosions all day as the enemy futilely attempted to make a lucky strike against them.

The nightly broadcast on May 10 brought interesting news. Dick O'Kane had orders to report to Mare Island when they got back to Pearl Harbor. He was to assume command of a new boat then under construction there. It was *Tang*. Roger Paine would move up in the natural order of progression to replace him as XO on *Wahoo*. The changing of the guard started immediately with O'Kane passing off some of his exec responsibilities to the much younger but very eager Paine.

Mush Morton was like a proud papa seeing one of his kids off. It had been obvious all along that his XO would soon have his own boat. The orders came as no surprise to Morton. And he told O'Kane and anybody else who would listen that his second would make one hell of a skipper.

O'Kane was thrilled, too. But also happy that he had gotten a Mare Island boat. His family was there, riding out the storm of war. He would have several months with them as he got his new ride ready.

It was about this time, too, that Morton had to acknowledge that all the shooting they had been doing within sight of the Japanese mainland had kicked over an anthill. Antisubmarine units—aircraft and patrol vessels—were suddenly in sight just about every time they punched up the periscope or swept the area with a radar scan. He reluctantly reverted to more traditional submarine operations: run on the surface at night and attack in the darkness, stay submerged during the day, popping up occasionally to take a look with the scope or radar.

Those safer tactics lasted only a couple of days, and the old burr under the skipper's saddle—the damned dud torpedoes—was the main reason he went back to his preferred methods.

Two ships came into sight beneath their smoke the evening of May 12. It was a small freighter and another much larger one, a good ten-thousand-tonner. O'Kane, conducting what would be his last attack while aboard *Wahoo*, angled to get them into a position where the targets would be between the submarine and the streak on the water from a bright, full moon.

Soon four torpedoes were away. Buckley on sound called out, "All hot, straight, and normal!"

The captain's frustration with the results is obvious in his description in the patrol report:

The first torpedo fired at the mainmast hit. The second torpedo, fired at his stack amidships, is believed to have been erratic or a dud. The target course and speed had been most accurately determined and it is inconceivable that a normal dispersion could cause it to miss.

"Battle surface!" Morton suddenly yelled. One of the ships—the larger one—seemed to be falling behind, and the captain had made the instant decision.

To hell with being conservative! They would go after the son of a bitch with some speed and maneuverability, on the surface, full moon or no full moon.

Mush Morton loved being on the bridge of his submarine, running on the surface. It reminded him of being at the tiller of his mahogany sailboat, the wind and spray in his face.

They quickly caught up to the target ship and spun about to shoot a torpedo from the bow, the last left one they had remaining up there. Johnny Moore, below them in the conning tower, was the man who actually hit the firing plunger.

Morton and O'Kane watched for the phosphorescence in the water so they could see weapon and target coincide in the distance. So did Forest Sterling and a couple of young lookouts on the platform above.

"You see anything, Dick? Yeo? Where'd it go?"

Both men said, "No, sir."

The torpedo had simply whooshed out of the tube and inexplicably sunk to the bottom.

"Goddammit! Set up for a stern shot."

They had only one torpedo left back there, too, and soon it was on its way. This time they could easily see the long streak of green light that marked its path.

It hit under the bridge with a dull thud, much louder than the duds we have heard only on sound, but lacking the "whacking" which accompanies a wholehearted explosion. It is considered that this torpedo had a low order detonation. Some sparks were observed on the target above the impact, but he turned away, apparently under control, belching smoke.

"Let's get the gun crews on deck! We'll sink that crippled Nip bastard one way or the other!"

"Captain . . . the other *maru* . . . she's shooting at us!" one of the lookouts called down.

The other vessel, the smaller freighter, had circled back to help its sister, and opened fire from a distance, but she was getting closer and more accurate. That forced *Wahoo* down.

But Morton did not give up easily. Six minutes later, he sent them back to the surface. The big freighter, still limping from the one good hit, had fallen behind the other ship once again.

Morton ordered gun crews out onto the deck, toting ammunition. But once again, and before they could make a run at the big target, the smaller armed freighter turned and headed back, her guns blazing and shells already making geysers in the water that were splashing closer and closer to *Wahoo*'s hull.

"That whole lousy *maru* is not worth a single member of our crew," the captain said, his lips a thin line, his eyes flashing in the moonlight.

Two blasts on the dive Klaxon sent everyone belowdecks yet again, and the sea swallowed up *Wahoo*. The bow was pointed east. With all torpedoes expended for the third straight patrol, Morton had few options left. He headed for home, for Hawaii.

Three ships sunk, 24,700 tons (later reduced to 10,500 tons), in twenty-six days. The best total tonnage of any of the boats that had left in the same general time period. A respectable patrol in anybody's book.

Anybody's but Dudley "Mush" Morton's.

The Squadron Ten commander used terms such as "outstanding in aggressiveness and efficiency" and "action-packed" when he later described the run in his endorsement of the patrol report. Charles Lockwood was even more effusive.

"These three patrols establish a record not only in damage inflicted on the enemy for three successive patrols, but also for accomplishing this feat in the shortest time on patrol. Once again *WAHOO* utilized all the weapons available in conjunction with sound strategic and tactical judgment. This combined with teamwork of personnel made this fifth war patrol another outstanding example of how to conduct submarine warfare."

Mush Morton was still Lockwood's superstar skipper. And there was a third Navy Cross in the works for the skipper. A second Silver Star for Dick O'Kane. But Lockwood had no idea the earful he was about to get from his best captain.

This time, as the ship entered Pearl Harbor, there was only a small pennant flying and no brooms lashed to the periscope. Morton did not feel it appropriate, considering they had sunk only three ships.

The welcome at the pier was more muted, too. Maybe the band and dignitaries were growing tired of greeting returning submarines.

But Admiral Lockwood was there, a broad smile on his face, and he came on board to shake the hands of officers and enlisted men alike. He was clearly proud of *Wahoo* and the men who had made her so successful.

After spending a few minutes below with Morton and O'Kane, the admiral emerged and led the way across the brow, up the pier, and toward his office. Morton walked beside his boss, a grim expression on his handsome face. He had already told O'Kane that he was going to give Lockwood a piece of his mind, maybe wrecking his own naval career in the process. But he was going to see that something was done about the torpedoes.

O'Kane remained behind. There were rumors that *Wahoo* was not long for Pearl, that she would be headed to Mare Island to finally get her faulty batteries repaired and for a general refit. The fact that there was no paymaster there to meet them and pay them seemed a pretty good sign that the rumors were true. When no bus showed up to haul them to the Royal Hawaiian, it all but confirmed it.

That evening, Morton placed a telephone call to Harriet in California. Though he could not, for security reasons, directly tell her the good news that they would be heading stateside in a few days, he did give her a predetermined code word or two that let her know. She fought to keep the excitement out of her voice, just in case the call was being monitored.

Then he shared with her the gist of his heated one-on-one meeting with Admiral Lockwood.

"I may not be in submarines that much longer," he told her. "My Navy career is probably over. A subordinate just can't speak to his superior that way, much less the commander of the submarine force in the Pacific."

Harriet did not doubt him. She did not know Admiral Lockwood or his disposition, but she certainly knew how her husband could be if he was agitated about something. But she had heard this before, this "My Navy career is over." Twice already, in fact.

Once after the incident with the U-boat, when his commander thought he should have been more aggressive, and again when Mush balked at taking *Dolphin* out on patrol. She reassured him as best she could, told him he was just exaggerating, but she could hear in his voice that he was more serious this time.

"Harriet, you have married an officer without a future," he told her.

To his wife, the dashing, daring captain of *Wahoo* sounded about as depressed and beaten down as she had ever heard him.

At that moment, the most famous and effective submarine skipper in the U.S. Navy was convinced he had just ended his career.

He need not have worried.

CHAPTER 22

Errol Flynn and Cary Grant

"Explosive! As big as the broad Pacific!"

—From the theatrical trailer for the movie
Destination Tokyo

*H*ad Mush Morton been the only submarine skipper who was grousing *about the ineffectiveness of their torpedoes, his dire prediction about his naval future might have come true. Or if the Navy had not made him a bona fide hero, a symbol of how the Americans were winning the war. Or if his big boss had been anyone other than Charles Lockwood. If, instead of Lockwood, Admiral Ralph Waldo Christie had gotten the job of submarine commander in the Pacific when Admiral English was killed. Christie had desperately wanted the job and lobbied hard for it. And after all, he was an ordnance engineer by training and had been one of the developers of the problematic exploder. Christie had complete faith in the unit and had openly challenged any sub captains who reported problems with them.*

But the people Lockwood was listening to—in addition to Morton— were some of those other aggressive and mostly effective captains— effective in spite of the duds they were firing out of their torpedo tubes. Lawson "Red" Ramage in USS *Trout* (SS-202). William J. "Moke" Millican in USS *Thresher* (SS-200). Like Morton, both men had openly challenged their commander—Ralph Christie—on the subject, risking their commands.

Millican actually lost his. In his patrol reports, as well as in conversations with anyone who would listen, Millican had coined the expression "We clinked them with a clunk." Christie relieved him as well as his division commander, who had backed his skipper and his grousing.

Christie was already irritated with Ramage for his criticism of torpedo reliability in his formal patrol report. Ramage pointedly used all capital letters and many exclamation points in the reports when referring to torpedoes that failed to explode, writing, "DUDS!!!" Christie brought up the subject when Ramage stopped by his office just before taking *Trout* back out on patrol.

"Red, with that boat and crew and with you at the helm, I expect you to sink one ship for every torpedo you fire," the admiral told him, only half joking. "Sixteen torpedoes, sixteen ships."

Ramage, according to reports, did not blink. Instead, with his boss sitting right there across the desk from him, he fired right back.

"If I find that your torpedoes are twenty-five percent reliable, I'll be lucky. And you will bless me!"

Christie returned fire, not even trying to hide his own anger, and the conversation was immediately in danger of becoming a full-blown fistfight. The squadron commander stepped in and prudently concluded the meeting.

But the point was that Lockwood was now the main man, and he was firmly convinced that his skippers were reporting a true problem with the bullets in their guns. He began to push for better torpedoes, not hesitating to step on toes or ignore military courtesy in the process. There is no way we will ever know how much more damage American submarines could have done in the Pacific had they been properly armed from the beginning. Because men like Morton, Ramage, and Millican stuck to their guns—and had the track records to give their complaints even more clout—the problem was eventually addressed.

Morton told everyone who would listen that if he survived the fit he threw in Lockwood's office, then he was confident his boss would get the problem solved. He only hoped it would happen in time for him and his crew to become as effective as they could be on their future patrols.

After Morton's heated visit to Lockwood's office in Pearl Harbor, the admiral told one of his aides that Morton looked tired and pale. He had already agreed—partially due to Morton's direct request—to send *Wahoo* to Mare Island for an overhaul. He also hoped that his superstar skipper would get some rest while he was in the States. Rest and medical attention.

There was another ceremony at which the latest bunch of medals was presented to *Wahoo*'s crew. Admiral Nimitz pinned on Morton another Gold Star to signify another Navy Cross. When Nimitz shook Morton's hand, the crew, which had been standing at attention, still managed to get off a cheer that was heard up and down the pier. O'Kane got his Silver Star. The entire boat was presented with the Presidential Unit Citation, but this one was for the first patrol under Morton, not the most recent. *Wahoo* had been using up all her torpedoes and cutting her patrols so short that the award citations could not keep up with them.

As the crew off-loaded everything not necessary for the trip from Pearl Harbor to San Francisco Bay, the captain did something he rarely did. As soon as the medal-presentation ceremony was finished, he began a stem-to-stern inspection, with O'Kane trailing close behind, making note of any problems the skipper found.

The mood on the boat was almost giddy. They were headed stateside. For a while, they would not have to dodge radar pips or patrol boats or be ready to duck out of the sight of airplanes. The cooks were busy preparing a special meal for the evening, and the aroma of baking ham filled the submarine.

As usual, the captain made a point of stopping to talk, to joke, even to wrestle playfully with the men along the way. At one point, Dick O'Kane decided to quickly open a hatch and drop down to the battery compartment to check on progress in jury-rigging the bad cells for the run to California.

Morton had not noticed. He turned to continue the inspection and promptly stepped into the open hatch. He was fortunate not to be hurt badly, but he did strain some muscles in his leg and had some nasty bruises on his chest and abdomen. He was also furious at his XO, stopped the inspection right there, and stormed back toward his stateroom.

O'Kane, who was mortified, was up the ladder in a flash and chasing after his captain.

The two men apparently made up and there were no signs of their relationship changing after that incident. But they both knew O'Kane's tenure on *Wahoo* was dwindling. Morton also continued to tell everyone that his second would be one hell of a sub skipper when he got *Tang*.

Just to show there were no hard feelings, Morton made a point of giving O'Kane the helm as they left Hawaii the next morning.

Johnny Moore had finished his PCO cruise and did not make the trip with them. He was off to take command of USS *Grayback* (SS-208). Moore was especially pleased that his first boat would be equipped with a new five-inch deck gun. His was one of the first of the Pearl Harbor boats to follow the lead of the Australian boats and add more surface firepower to the submarines. He and Morton had had many conversations in the wardroom about how effective submarines could be on the surface if they aggressively used their deck guns. Though they had had little opportunity to do any of the swashbuckling stuff on his PCO cruise, Moore was still anxious to give it a try.

Moore would prove to be another Morton protégé to become an especially skillful and effective submarine commander. He and *Grayback* would go on to sink nine ships and damage another for a total of nearly fifty-five thousand tons. In February 1944, a Japanese aircraft caught *Grayback* on the surface. According to enemy records recovered after the war, the plane hit the submarine with a bomb and "she exploded and sank immediately." Moore and his crew on *Grayback* were all lost.

On the way to California, Mush Morton decided he would revert to his old ways. *Wahoo* would make a grand entrance into the base at Mare Island. After a little updating by the captain with his needle and thread, the battle pennants were hung from the makeshift broom yardarms so the wind would catch them perfectly as they passed beneath the Golden Gate Bridge. The house flags from *Nitu Maru* were pulled out and attached to the shears once again.

But there was more. The skipper had secretly sewn together another flag. The crew had been told to keep it handy but to not hang it until they had passed Alcatraz and were well on their way to the mouth of the Napa River, where the Mare Island naval facility awaited them.

Their escort had already welcomed them, thirty miles out from the entrance to the bay, and flashed them the message: CONGRATULA-TIONS AND WELCOME TO THE STATES.

The captain's special flag, dangling from the periscope enclosure, hung limp as they neared the pier where they were assigned. It was a beautiful day, without the usual fog, so they had a good view ahead of them. The crowd on the dock, waiting to welcome the now legendary *Wahoo*, could see them coming from a distance. They began waving and cheering from the moment the submarine came into sight. If her return to Midway or Pearl was no longer a big deal, *Wahoo* was still a star back in the States. A Navy band played a vigorous version of "California, Here I Come." It was obvious even from a distance that many of the people there to greet them were brass, important officers. Every *Wahoo* crew member not on watch belowdecks was in his whites, topside.

Just as they maneuvered the boat and made the turn to moor her, the wind caught Morton's new flag, probably just the way the skipper knew it would. A crewman held a rope that was designed to assist it, just in case.

When it was unfurled, everybody on the dock could read the message Morton had sewn on it:

SHOOT THE SONZA BITCHES

The crowd cheered wildly, as if Morton had just scored the winning touchdown.

As he, O'Kane, and the other officers stepped across the brow to meet the official welcoming party, one of the first to approach and shake their hands was the Navy Yard commandant. At his side was his wife, who was still staring intently through her ornate opera glasses at Mush Morton's banner.

"What does it say?" she asked her husband.

When he told her, her hand went to her mouth and she had a horrified look on her face. She would later complain to her husband. He asked Morton to remove the flag and not display it again. It was offensive to some, he told the captain.

Mush obliged. The message had been sent successfully.

Also on the dock that day was Dick O'Kane's wife, Ernestine, as well as Harriet Morton. She, too, had received the coded message from her husband that they were headed to Mare Island.

It was a wonderful homecoming for the submarine sailors. Mush and Harriet left almost immediately, bound for a luncheon in San Francisco and the opportunity to catch up on everything, including Doug and Edwina. O'Kane visited with his wife but had to stay nearby for a few more days as work began on *Wahoo*. Shortly, he would take a quick walk down to where his new boat would soon be ready for sea trials. At that point, he would say good-bye to *Wahoo* and devote his full time to *Tang*.

As soon as the crowds dispersed and the band finished playing, the relief crew was busy, overhauling *Wahoo*'s engines, repairing the pesky batteries, and adding reinforcement to the conning tower. The Japanese were becoming more effective with their depth charges. Although *Wahoo* had had limited exposure so far, it was prudent to make sure she would stand a better chance should she find herself there again. By the time they left for their next patrol, *Wahoo* would virtually be a new boat.

The truth was, the captain used his considerable charm and clout, including the favor with which Charles Lockwood treated him, to get much more work done to *Wahoo* than the typical commander might have been able to do. In addition to the heavying-up for the conning tower, she got an auxiliary gyrocompass, some newly developed sound gear, and a state-of-the-art radar upgrade. The Mare Island group also did considerable work to reduce the profile of the boat's bridge and fair-water. O'Kane noted that it made his old boat look very much like the new model he was about to take over. He also recognized that his captain had done much more in that meeting in Pearl Harbor with Lockwood than rant about the torpedoes. He had gotten approval for a complete makeover for the submarine service's most recognized boat.

Except for essential personnel, all crew members were granted as much leave time as possible during their seven weeks at Mare Island. Since Morton was out of pocket at the time—or because no one wanted to challenge Lockwood's fair-haired boy—it was O'Kane who caught heat for allowing so many of the crew to be gone. Captain J. B. Griggs, the commander of Submarine Administration, summoned the soon-to-be-ex-XO to his office and chewed him out.

"Can you explain to me why you allowed everybody on *Wahoo* to leave?" Griggs asked.

"Not everybody, Captain. The Yard personnel have taken over all watches, but the captain and I did allow anyone we didn't need to take leave."

O'Kane's point was that the boat was in dry dock and there was not much that could happen to her that the crew could do anything about.

"What if the dry dock should flood?" Griggs continued, stretching.

"That is not going to happen," O'Kane shot back.

"It'd better not!"

O'Kane later said, "I was not invited to stay for coffee."

Ironically, Griggs's son, Jack, who had been on *Wahoo* but left for a tour on another boat, would be back in Mush Morton's wardroom for the sixth patrol. The incident confirmed that many in the submarine service had begun to resent the publicity and praise being thrown at Morton, his boat, and his crew. The Navy's public relations efforts had needed a "hero," and Morton fit the bill perfectly, with his flamboyance, his looks, and, of course, his remarkable success. *Wahoo*'s return to the States only set off a new round of publicity about her heroic captain and crew, their clean-sweep brooms in the shears, and the mighty blow they were inflicting against the "Japs." The short-lived flag even found its way into many stories written about *Wahoo* and Morton.

Though he did enjoy some leave, Morton was not able to spend as much time as he would have liked visiting with his family, either. Nor did he follow his commander's admonition to get plenty of rest. He was at the boat some of the time, taking care of the many details of getting the big, complicated overhaul completed and the new systems properly tested. In order to continue drawing his submarine pay, he had to stay on active duty a certain number of days while in port. And frankly, his family needed the money.

But the most famous submarine officer in the Navy had other chores to do while there, too. They were more in keeping with his considerable stardom as well. And they came partly due to the relationship he had built with people in the movie business.

One of those commitments was a quick jaunt down to Los Angeles to appear on the *Command Performance* network radio show, hosted by big-band singer Ginny Simms. The program was broadcast to servicemen all over the globe as well across the United States. Harriet, Doug, and Edwina were there in the audience as Mush chatted with the show's famous host.

At one point in the broadcast, Morton said, "People ask me why I go to war and fight. Right out there is the reason."

He pointed toward his wife and children and had them stand up for applause.

Back at Mare Island, Morton was asked to be a technical adviser on a Hollywood film that was already well into preproduction. The Navy also asked one of *Wahoo*'s chiefs, Andrew Lennox, to assist the film crew during their time in the area, both at Mare Island and in Los Angeles. We do not have information on how much actual technical advice Morton or Lennox gave on the making of the film, to be titled *Destination Tokyo*, but we do know the studio made the most of the association with the captain and crew member from the famous submarine. So did the Navy.

Publicity shots were circulated showing Morton and the movie's star, Cary Grant, together. These appear to mostly have been taken in the San Francisco area when the movie crew and stars visited Mare Island to familiarize themselves with submarines and their tactics. Newspapers across the country, including the *New York Herald Tribune*, did feature stories on how the colorful *Wahoo* skipper was helping Hollywood tell the story of the brave men in the Silent Service. The Navy encouraged the speculation that the film would be based on the actual exploits of Morton and *Wahoo*, though there turned out to be little similarity between Hollywood fiction and reality.

The Warner Bros. picture was directed by Delmer Daves and also starred John Garfield and Alan Hale—who, as previously noted, had starred in another submarine picture that featured a submarine with a Mush Morton connection. The advice from Morton and Lennox and the visit to Mare Island must have been beneficial, because the Navy would actually use the film later in the war to help teach submarine operations.

There was one problem initially with the realistic sets used. The equipment and interior of the submarine were so accurate that the Navy required the film crew to change some of it out. They came up with a mishmash of gear that would never have actually existed inside a submarine, just so the enemy would not learn too much from the movie. While they sacrificed some accuracy, any Japanese spies seeing the feature would have been confused by how the submarine—the fictional USS *Copperfin*—was equipped.

Destination Tokyo proved inspiring to those who saw it, and served the exact purpose that made the Navy so willing to participate in its production. One young New Yorker was especially moved when he saw the picture at a theater near his home in the Bronx. Bernard Schwartz was so excited when he watched Cary Grant spying on Tokyo Bay through *Copperfin*'s periscope that he decided to enlist in the Navy and volunteer for submarines. Schwartz did just that, serving on a submarine tender. That young man eventually became an actor better known as Tony Curtis. He would one day costar with Cary Grant in a successful comedy about submarines called *Operation Petticoat*.

The major overhaul on *Wahoo* was completed to everyone's satisfaction on July 11, 1943. Crew changes were now finished as well. Roger Paine was installed as executive officer. Chandler Jackson slid into position as third officer. William Carr, who had been on *Wahoo* from the beginning and was thus dubbed a "plank owner," was now chief of the boat.

Mush Morton was delighted with the makeup of the crew, and especially its officers and COB. While he hated to lose O'Kane to *Tang*, he was confident that the boat would not miss a beat, and especially with Paine as XO. Even before they left Mare Island, he had already begun discussing with Paine, Jackson, and the other officers a new and radical idea he had been noodling over. An idea so radical that he asked them not to mention it to anyone outside the wardroom of *Wahoo*. He could only imagine what his superiors would think of it.

Sea trials and training for new crew members continued until July 20. The star power of *Wahoo* and Mush Morton continued. The captain invited Errol Flynn to host a party for the crew the night before they departed Mare Island. The famous actor accepted, but did not stop there. The next morning, on the twenty-first, with the boat deemed ready to return to the war, *Wahoo* departed San Francisco Bay headed back across the Pacific to Pearl Harbor. Flynn rode aboard the submarine, enjoying the view from the bridge and cigarette deck, all the way out to about twenty miles from the mouth of the bay. Flynn went back over to the pilot boat with the harbor pilot for the ride back to San Francisco.

During wartime, there was no such thing as a routine passage anywhere in the Pacific, but in what one of the crew described as "yachting weather," the cruise from California to Hawaii was most pleasant. As they left their escort behind, the crew in *Wahoo*'s shears and on her bridge watched hopefully for dolphins that might play in the wake of their bow. That was a long-established nautical omen that meant good fortune.

Try as they might, they saw none.

CHAPTER 23

Damn the Torpedoes

"This is bad. It is daylight now and we cannot clear the scene of action and the target will disclose our presence. Damn the torpedoes."

—From the patrol report, sixth war patrol, USS *Wahoo*

"**M**ush, I don't feel very well."

"Damn, Roger, you eat too much last night?"

"Maybe. I'll see the corpsman and see if he's got anything. It feels like somebody's sticking me in my side with a red-hot poker."

They were not even back in Pearl Harbor yet after an eventless cruise from California when Paine suddenly took sick. Chan Jackson had to take over and navigate them into port. Once there, they would be hurrying, getting fuel tanks topped off, taking on torpedoes and ammunition along with replenishing stores. They were scheduled to depart for Midway and their sixth patrol only three days later.

The report on Roger Paine, his new XO and a key part of his team, was bad. He had acute appendicitis and was transferred immediately to the naval hospital for emergency surgery. Had it been a week or two later, Paine might have joined the growing list of submariners who had emergency appendectomies while at sea. That would have been similar to a scene that Morton had actually observed being filmed for *Destination Tokyo*.

A replacement for Paine was identified quickly, and before he knew it,

Lieutenant Commander Verne Skjonsby was vacating a desk at a staff job in Pearl Harbor with Admiral Lockwood and was headed for second in command on the boat he had heard so much about. Despite the recommendations of people he trusted at Pearl, Morton still had his reservations about Skjonsby. First among them was the fact that he had not yet made a war patrol. Offsetting that, though, was his standing near the top of the class of '34 at the academy, and his training in ordnance with emphasis on torpedoes.

Besides that, Morton found him to be friendly, outgoing, and someone the men could accept, despite his desk-jockey pedigree. Forest Sterling was immediately impressed with his likable personality, as well as his asking the yeoman to sit down with him and go over every single man in the crew so he could get to know them better.

"I want to learn how to do things the *Wahoo* way," he told both Morton and Sterling. "Looks like it works pretty well."

But XO Paine was only one of Morton's new team to be taken away from him. On the run from the States, a radio message informed him that Chan Jackson, his third officer, would make a U-turn in Hawaii and head right back to the mainland to help place a new boat into construction as her executive officer. Roger Paine had gone from officer to XO—a path that normally took half a decade—in only a little over a year, so it should not have been a surprise that a promising young officer like Chandler Jackson would do likewise. For his part, Jackson was thrilled with the quick promotion. He, like several crew members, had gotten married while at Mare Island. Now, with his new construction assignment, he would be able to continue his brief honeymoon.

Still, the promotion cost Morton someone else on whom he was going to rely to help him execute his radical new idea.

The skipper's idea was as simple as it was unorthodox. When firing torpedoes at targets, it was normal procedure to shoot a "spread," several torpedoes at a time, to increase the likelihood of at least one of them hitting home. Since *Wahoo* had now had to cut short her patrols after running out of torpedoes, and because they still carried plenty of duds, Morton wanted to adopt a new strategy.

He proposed firing only a single torpedo at a time at each target. No more spreads.

Morton felt that with the expertise of his fire control party—and especially with Paine and Jackson—they could shoot directly at where the center of the target would be by calculation. Despite the duds, if they did what he thought they could do in aiming at the ships, he figured that they could sink fifteen ships before they exhausted their supply of two dozen torpedoes.

There was one other development that further convinced Morton his one-shot-per-target plan would work. Admiral Nimitz—mostly due to Charles Lockwood's urging, based on the pointed reports from Morton, Ramage, Millican, and others—had ordered that Admiral Christie's magnetic exploder be deactivated on torpedoes carried by all submarines under his command. And that was most of them.

Paine had not questioned his skipper's kill estimate. He figured it was worth a try, and if anybody could do it, Mush Morton could. And if it didn't work, they would change tactics and do something that did. They would not have wasted many torpedoes while experimenting either.

Wahoo's luck continued to be bad.

While in port at Pearl Harbor, and while performing the routine task of venting the boat to remove bad air, Bill Carr was overcome by fumes and fell deathly ill. He, too, headed for the hospital in an ambulance, and while it was touch-and-go for a while, the doctors finally reported he would be okay. But he would not be sailing with *Wahoo* on the sixth patrol.

Morton called in favors and managed to draft Chief Boatswain's Mate James Lane as his new COB. Lane had been aboard on *Wahoo*'s third and fourth patrols, and Morton knew him well. With the addition of Lane, the captain felt better about the situation.

There was another reason that Morton felt confident as they steamed away from Hawaii on August 2. He and other crew members had visited Paine and Carr at the hospital and were heartened that both were on the way to recovery. Also, in three days of testing, and to get the new XO up to speed on how *Wahoo* did things, every test torpedo they fired had run straight and true, passing directly under the middle of the target at which they were shooting. Skjonsby seemed to fit in perfectly, too.

But once they were out of Midway and in a hot area for potential targets, things went bad in a hurry. *Wahoo* was assigned to operate jointly with USS *Plunger* (SS-179) and her skipper, Benny Bass. Bass had only recently returned from the Sea of Japan and reported good hunting there, with ships that persisted in running with their lights on and not really doing any serious zigzagging. There were no indications of mines in the area either. Although that might have changed after Bass and his boat had stirred things up in the neighborhood, Morton was excited about getting there and trying out his new plan.

Plunger was another of the older boats and prone to mechanical problems. Sure enough, she developed engine and motor problems early in the patrol and lagged behind her sister.

Morton plowed ahead, still licking his chops at the prospects for doing serious damage out there in the waters between Japan and where Russia and Korea came together. Again, these were Morton's old haunts.

He took *Wahoo* through La Pérouse Strait, just north of the Japanese islands, and into the Sea of Japan, running at top speed on the surface in the dark of night. Bass followed, two days later, submerged because it was daylight.

Once in the Sea of Japan, Mush was still in a hurry to get to where he was supposed to be, to where the targets swam. He kept the ship on the surface, despite brilliant sunshine, few clouds, and great visibility.

August 14th; 1535K; Believe it is wise to make a run on the surface for our assigned area, which is about 150 miles south. Will likely reward us with a target during the night. It is a beautiful day.

We arrived in the SEA OF JAPAN in a little over six days with 70,000 gallons of fuel remaining. This is most satisfactory. Good weather combined with FAIRBANKS-MORSE engines is really wonderful.

Wahoo immediately spotted a convoy, three freighters. One lagged behind. She was a lovely target.

2217; Decided to attack the trailing ship. It could be sunk without the next ship ahead (distance between the last two ships, 6,000 yards) knowing what it was all about, thus we could get both ships.

"One at a time, boys! One at a time! And we'll have enough torpedoes left for the next convoy!"

The log entries for this and for the next three days of attacks tell the story of Mush Morton's grand experiment:

15 August. Fired one torpedo at a freighter. Miss.
Fired one torpedo at a freighter. Dud.
Fired two torpedoes at a freighter. Both missed.
Fired one torpedo at same freighter. Miss.
17 August. Fired one torpedo at a freighter. Miss.
Fired one torpedo at a freighter. Miss.
18 August. Fired one torpedo at a freighter. Miss.
Fired one torpedo at a freighter. Miss.
Fired one torpedo at same freighter. Broach.

Morton, though, blamed their lack of hits on the torpedoes, not his drastic one-shot-only tactic. In his notes on the final attack, he wrote:

Torpedo must have broached and exploded before reaching end of run. This is bad, as it is daylight now and we cannot clear the scene of action and the target will disclose our presence. Damn the torpedoes.

Morton later called these the most frustrating days of his submarine career. The lack of results was certainly not due to restraint or conservative approaches. As usual, Morton made bold approaches, sometimes firing from as close as six hundred yards. They were often launching the assaults on the surface, using the more accurate radar to do end runs and maneuvers to get into perfect firing position. They even reverted to the old-fashioned "angle solver" instead of the TDC, but nothing seemed to work.

Morton, Skjonsby, and the others were certain their fish were swimming true, but that something either made them run deeper than they were supposed to or that they simply were not exploding when they hit something. Somewhere along the way, Skjonsby, whose training was in this very field, decided that the contact exploders—the devices that should have caused the torpedoes to detonate on contact now that the faulty magnetic exploders had been deactivated—might be bad as well.

In the remarks on the patrol report, Morton requested giving skippers the option of using either type of exploder. "This will give the various submarines more flexibility in torpedo firing."

Morton finally surfaced and requested permission from Lockwood to come back to base and get more torpedoes. The admiral agreed and *Wahoo* pulled out of the area, again running mostly on the surface, ignoring challenge lights from Japanese shore emplacements when they went back through La Pérouse Strait. Forest Sterling later wrote of a conversation with a clearly disconsolate skipper in the conning tower. Morton was not his usual self that evening. He had his head in his hands, a sour look on his face. The yeoman had never seen Morton in such a mood.

"Yeo, I thought we would set records out here this run," he told Sterling sadly. "Instead, we drew a zero."

Plunger had better luck, despite its own troubles with the torpedoes. Bass and his crew were eventually credited with sinking three ships.

After the war, records indicated that *Wahoo* and her crew had done better than they thought. Two of the dud torpedoes still packed enough wallop to damage a couple of ships.

Shortly after *Wahoo* cleared the strait, lookouts spotted smoke on the horizon and the ship moved closer to see what it was. It turned out to be a sampan. The vessel was in the wrong place at the wrong time. Mush Morton was just looking for something on which to vent his frustration. He ordered a shot across the bow of the tiny vessel, but the sampan kept moving.

With the deck guns manned, Morton gave the order to shoot, riddling the boat with twenty-millimeter and four-inch gunfire. Then he steered them close enough to send across a boarding party, but with the bow of *Wahoo* almost touching what was left of the sampan, six people emerged from inside, holding up their hands in surrender.

No one would have been surprised if their captain had ordered the gun crews to open up on the men. He did not.

"Take them prisoner," he told them.

Gave prisoners clean, dry clothes, baths and a round of brandy. Pharmacist Mate examined all prisoners and found only one with a slight shrapnel wound on his knee. Prisoners seemed grateful for being picked up.

The crew took them to the after torpedo room, where they would remain as prisoners of war until they reached Midway. Through sign language, they learned that five of their shipmates had been killed in the attack by *Wahoo.*

Later that day, they spotted several other sampans and promptly destroyed them with deck gun fire as well. After splintering one of the boats, the captain made an idle statement that prompted several members of the crew to take quick action.

"I sure wish I had one of those glass fishing balls," he said, watching the debris from the sampan floating in the water. "It would make a good souvenir for my children."

Immediately, two men dived off the deck and into the freezing water to try to grab a souvenir for their skipper.

Morton was stunned.

"Get those men back on deck!" he ordered. "They'll freeze their asses off in that water!"

The captain was angry at the men's lack of judgment and had them brought to the conning tower, their clothes dripping and their teeth chattering.

"Men, what the hell were you thinking?"

"We just wanted to get you the souvenir, Captain," one of them said, shaking so badly he could hardly speak.

Forest Sterling, who witnessed the whole thing, said the captain was suddenly overcome with emotion, moved by the devotion the men had just shown to him.

"Somebody get these men some blankets and some dry clothes," Morton said, his voice breaking. "And a ration of medicinal whiskey for each. Boys, thank you, but please don't ever do that again."

Sterling said the skipper had to stand there for a moment, bracing himself on the rail, struggling to get his emotions in check.

There had been an odd request attached to the radio message that gave approval for *Wahoo* to return to base. They were to drop off ten of their remaining torpedoes at Midway, but only after recording their serial numbers. Sometimes when a submarine returned from patrol with torpedoes remaining, they were asked to leave them off while passing by Midway. That was so the base would always have some available for other boats that could use them. But the recording of the serial numbers made this order curious.

"If they are going to give these duds to somebody else, they need not bother," Morton told his XO. But the captain did not want to break radio silence to ask headquarters their intent. "Hell, we'll just have to let them work it out."

When they off-loaded the weapons during a brief stop at Midway, the captain made his thoughts very clearly known. The commander there assured him they were not destined for the replenishment, that they were to be shipped to Pearl Harbor for testing. Morton was relieved and told him so.

There were no brooms in the shears, no pennants flying this time when *Wahoo* moored at sub base Pearl Harbor at the end of August 1943. No newsreel cameras or reporters, either.

For the first time in her stellar history, even going all the way back to Pinky Kennedy, *Wahoo* was returning to home port with a "zero run."

CHAPTER 24

"He Wants *Wahoo* the Worst"

"Far better it is to dare mighty things, to win glorious triumphs, even though checkered by failure, than to rank with those poor spirits who neither enjoy nor suffer much, because they live in the gray twilight that knows neither victory nor defeat."

—Theodore Roosevelt

Both *the Submarine Division Forty-two commander and Admiral Charles Lockwood strongly backed up Mush Morton's contention that the torpedoes were primarily to blame for* Wahoo's *sixth-patrol shutout. However, they also noted that their favorite skipper's one-shot-per-target tactic was not working either.*

The division commander wrote in his endorsement to the patrol report, "A skillful commander with precise instruments for obtaining target data has a natural reluctance to waste torpedoes on slow speed, small or even medium-sized merchant vessels. Why use two torpedoes when one may easily finish the job? Considering all factors including torpedo performance it is essential that spreads be used to insure [*sic*] destruction of the target."

Lockwood was more blunt, writing, "The decision of the commanding officer to fire single torpedoes, while understandable, is not concurred in [*sic*]. A minimum of two, preferably three torpedoes, using a spread, should be fired at any target worthy of torpedo expenditure. . . ."

The patrol report, all typed up by Forest Sterling and ready for distribution upon arrival in Pearl, told the story in detail. There was page after page of detail on each attack.

Then, when Morton met with his commanders, he pulled no punches. Though not as angrily as in his previous meeting with Lockwood, the skipper made his case once again that the bad torpedoes were getting American skippers and their crews killed out there. They were also drastically reducing the possible number of ships they were sinking.

Morton was just one member of a choir—though a very loud one— and they were all singing the same tune. The sub base commander shared a recent top-secret dispatch from USS *Tinosa* (SS-283), operating in *Wahoo*'s old stalking grounds around Truk. He had experienced eight straight duds while attacking two large freighters.

Ultimately, to show his continued and total confidence in his "ace," Lockwood approved *Wahoo* to receive a supply of a brand-new torpedo, the Mark XVIII electric. While their development had been problematic so far, these torpedoes—based on a German design copied from several that had been salvaged after they ran ashore on the East Coast of the United States—were the latest and best hope to overcome the continuing troubles.

Though aware of the issues with the new weapon, Morton was thrilled with the opportunity to see what they could do. He was of the belief that anything would be better than what they had been using.

There was another meeting between Lockwood and Morton during *Wahoo*'s quick week and a half in Pearl Harbor. In that conference, the admiral told Morton that he was worried about him.

"Mush, you look tired," he told him. "You feeling okay?"

"Aw, I'm doing fine, Admiral. My gut gives me a little bit of a problem sometimes, but it's nothing I can't ignore when there are Jap ships to sink."

After the dud of a patrol to the Sea of Japan, Morton told his XO and others that there was the possibility that Lockwood would pull him off the boat for some R & R. He knew he could use some rest, too, but he desperately wanted to go back there right away and one more time so he could show what *Wahoo* could do. He had his case all ready to make his plea to the big man.

If Lockwood showed an inclination to take him out of the game, he would agree to take a rest, but only after one more trip to the prime hunting grounds between Hokkaido and the mainland. If need be, he would beg for one more chance in that prime area.

For his part, Lockwood had quite a quandary. Morton was one of his top stars, a true inspiration not only to other submariners but to all fighting men. To the folks back home, too. There was no doubt Morton was due for another spectacular run, similar to *Wahoo*'s third and fourth. Those adventures were still getting play in the press back home.

Lockwood had been forced to use younger, less experienced skippers to helm all the new boats coming over. He also had been giving his more experienced captains a break, some of whom had been at war for almost two years now. The numbers were further complicated by the traditional Navy seniority issue. Having skippers who had less tenure meant the rest of the officers on the submarines were younger.

Submarine commanders had to be senior to their officers. Sometimes seniority had to be based on class rank when both men were equal in years of service. It led to some real juggling by Lockwood and his squadron commanders.

Regardless of that, when Lockwood saw Morton for the first time after *Wahoo*'s sixth patrol, he was shocked by the change in the man, both physically and in mood. Morton seemed tired, bordering on exhaustion, and even his handshake was markedly weaker. He appeared to have aged years; his face was pale and lined, his grin not nearly as broad, and there was little of the old flinty spark in his eyes.

That is until he started describing the maneuvering they had done for the attacks on all those beautiful targets in the Sea of Japan, arms waving, moving objects on Lockwood's desk around to show where all the vessels had been. Until he spit and spewed about the duds and all the damage *Wahoo* could have done to the Japs if they had been armed with torpedoes that would actually blow up.

That was when that old fighting spirit emerged again. Though he was past due for a rest, Morton convinced Lockwood to allow him one more run.

"You know, Mush, I ought to take you off the boat and let you cool off a bit," he told Morton. "But I just can't do it."

He okayed one more run.

The skipper also got word on September 1 that he had been promoted to the rank of commander, effective October 15. As with most of this brief stay in Hawaii, there was no pomp or ceremony surrounding the promotion, and Morton hardly took note of it, other than letting Harriet know he had moved up a pay grade.

Once he sold Lockwood on one more patrol in enemy waters, Morton got busy trying to put together the strongest crew he could round up for what he was already calling his "redemption run." Eight men had left, most headed back stateside for new construction. Jack Griggs had a new assignment as well, a new boat being built on the East Coast. Morton lobbied with the staffing officer to make sure he got top-notch replacements for each.

Chief Carr came back aboard as COB, feeling fine after his hospital stay. Chief Lane had done just fine, but Carr was a plank owner and one of the key men when they launched one of Morton's patented surface attacks.

At the last minute, Mush managed to get an excellent torpedoman shipped over. Robert Logue had been to school on the new torpedoes they would be carrying and was already considered to be an expert. Morton pulled some strings and got him off the tender and onto *Wahoo*.

Yeoman Forest Sterling was also due to rotate off the boat. After a long wait, he was finally scheduled to attend steno school back in the States starting the first of November. With a typical patrol, they would not get back home in time for him to start school.

In a one-on-one meeting with Sterling, Morton turned on the charm to try to convince him to take another ride on *Wahoo*.

"So how's about it, Yeo? As a favor to me? You make one more patrol with me and we'll be back in October with plenty of time to spare. You know, we get out there and use our torpedoes and come on back with the battle pennant flying. I'll even guarantee you a plane ride to San Diego so you can start your class on time."

Sterling was moved that his skipper wanted him badly enough to make a personal plea. He told him he would stay aboard for one more trip.

Next on the list was his short-time XO, Roger Paine, who had now fully recovered from the bum appendix. The skipper visited with him and made the same plea he had to Sterling: Come on back to *Wahoo* and continue his turn as his exec that had been so rudely interrupted. *Wahoo* would make news again.

Oh, make no mistake about it: Vern Skjonsby had done a fine job, and Morton liked him, but he was convinced that having as many plank owners as possible on this pivotal patrol was essential if he was to return the 238 boat to its previous glory.

"Roger, you were a key man in what we've done so far," Morton said, selling hard. "With you back as my second, we'll be back in stride, I promise you."

Paine, too, was flattered. He had a good reason not to accept the skipper's invitation, though.

"Mush, you know how much I loved my time on *Wahoo*, and how much I appreciate you and all you taught me," he told his former skipper. "I don't think I would go out as exec under anybody else. But I have a command waiting for me. That will set me up for a long career in the Navy after this damn war is over. This will give me time with Bebe and my boy, and I have hardly seen the little fellow since he was born. He just had his first birthday and he doesn't even know who I am."

Paine had seen his captain angry plenty of times, but never so much as at that moment. And never with those piercing eyes directed at him.

"Fine!" Morton said, his face red. "Fine!"

He spun on his heels and stormed out of the room.

Paine started to call him back, to wish him good luck on the patrol, to say something to make this parting more amicable until they could share lunch and beers and cribbage again after he and *Wahoo* got back.

But Morton was gone.

The quick turnaround meant they had little time to swim in the Pacific off Waikiki or lounge in the makeshift and continual party room at the Royal Hawaiian. The torpedomen were especially busy, taking classes on the new torpedoes, but not able to talk about it with any of their shipmates due to the weapons' top-secret nature.

As with their previous patrol, they were once again to be accompanied by USS *Sawfish* (SS-276), commanded by Eugene Sands. And they were to follow the same route as before, through La Pérouse Strait north of Hokkaido and into the Sea of Japan, between the Home Islands and Russia.

Despite his fatigue and the ache in his lower abdomen and back, Mush Morton was visibly excited about returning to that area. He knew—and Admiral Lockwood emphasized again—that with all the thunder and lightning *Wahoo* and other boats had set loose there already, and whether it was as effective as everyone had wanted it to be or not, the Japanese were now ready with their own hailstorm. Intelligence had reported more patrol craft, and significantly more airplanes, all watching for American submarines. Shore batteries had been strengthened, too, and were more vigilant now that the submarines were daring to go there.

Mush Morton had seen for himself how many potential targets steamed into the crosshairs of his periscopes, though. He knew the area so well based on his prewar experience in the region. He was convinced they could still enjoy great success there if the torpedoes worked.

There was no way they could miss setting a new record.

As *Wahoo* left Diamond Head behind, they carried a famous passenger with them from Hawaii to Midway. The heavyweight boxing champion Gene Tunney had joined the Navy and, under direct orders from President Franklin Roosevelt, was to head a physical fitness program. Someone decided submariners, out of all the men in the Navy, needed help most in that department. Tunney first declared that incoming submarine crews could have all the fun they wanted the first night, but there would be early reveille and calisthenics each morning thereafter. Then Morton and his crew found out that the boxer-turned-commander would be riding along with them as far as Midway.

The captain took the opportunity to show Tunney the true life of a submariner. That included the usual indoctrinational depth charging to acclimate new crew members to what it felt like. But Morton told nobody but his XO that this particular time, he had asked that they be extra close to the blasts, to give everyone—including Tunney—the full benefit of the experience. One crewman described it as a "tooth rattler."

When Tunney left *Wahoo* at Midway, he had a new respect for submariners, and his policy on their physical fitness softened considerably.

The stay at Midway would be a quick one, just long enough to top off the diesel fuel tanks and replenish the stores. But an hour before they were due to leave, Mush Morton popped into the yeoman's office and greeted Forest Sterling with a hard slap on the back. Painful as Morton's "greetings" could be, everyone knew they were the way the man demonstrated his affection.

While Sterling got his breath back, Morton asked, "Yeo, have you got your orders to steno school made up yet?"

"Well . . . no, sir . . . but . . ."

"We just picked up your assignment. Think you can get 'em done in a hurry?"

"Pretty damn quick if you give me word, Captain."

"I'll make it your choice. If you want to finish the patrol, my offer of the plane ride when we get back still stands. But if you want to take off, and we can find a relief who you think can do the job, you can go."

For the entire walk to the squadron commander's office, Sterling felt this was all a really cruel practical joke. The captain had been so determined for him to make this run, and now, with less than an hour to go before they left Midway, he was allowing him to leave *Wahoo*.

"I can never understand why Captain Morton changed his mind and transferred me at the last minute," he would later say.

When they reached the commander's office, Morton removed any doubt about whether the transfer was for real or not.

"I'm about to give up the best damn yeoman in the Navy so he can go back to steno school," he told the duty officer there. "I need to trade the best for the best. What you got?"

There were three yeomen in the office, all busy at their desks. They came running when the commander called them. They knew Sterling and they certainly knew Morton and his boat. If this was a chance to ship out on *Wahoo,* they wanted in.

Morton left it up to Sterling.

"Which one is the best, Yeo?"

He pointed to William T. White, a yeoman second class, who had spent a little time on *Wahoo* as a relief.

"Why did you pick this man?"

Sterling grinned.

"Because he wants *Wahoo* the worst. And he did a damn fine job before."

"Then he's my man. Commander, can we get him ready to go in forty-five minutes or not?"

"We can."

Sterling, with mixed emotions and still dizzy from the quick turn of events, ran all the way down to *Wahoo* and quickly typed up his own orders. XO Verne Skjonsby signed them.

Word spread throughout the boat and everybody who was not busy shook his hand, kidded him, slapped him on the back, and wished him well.

With his relief arriving just in time to hustle across the brow with his seabag, Sterling watched with sadness as the line handlers did their job. He saw the officers on the bridge and the lookouts in the shears. He even reached and grabbed the bowline, and when Morton told him to, he unwound the final turn off the mooring post and tossed the line into the murky water.

Mush Morton touched the brim of his hat and tossed an informal salute in the direction of his former yeoman.

"Good luck, Yeo. Take care of yourself," he called back to him, yelling over the sound of the boat's diesels.

"Good hunting!" Sterling yelled to those men topside, still fighting the feeling that his boat was leaving him behind and he was supposed to be aboard.

Sterling had noticed something else as he made his quick exit from

Wahoo. There were a few odd glances his way by some of his former ship-mates. They had a look in their eyes that could best be described as fear.

Sterling knew exactly what it was. Many on the boat that day believed that the sudden departure of a key crewman only minutes before casting off lines was a bad omen. A jinx if there ever was one.

The yeoman sat there on his seabag, taking a moment to catch his breath and smoke a cigarette, watching his former boat and his former shipmates depart the relative safety of Midway.

Wahoo was soon little more than a gray silhouette on the distant western horizon.

Then she disappeared completely, swallowed up by a shadowy tropical rainstorm.

CHAPTER 25

On Eternal Patrol

"**Died**: Presumptive 7 January 1946—Officially determined to be Missing in Action as of 1 November 1943, having been serving aboard the USS *WAHOO* when that submarine failed to return from a war patrol in the Sea of Japan. In compliance with Section 5 of Public Law 490, as amended, death is presumed to have occurred on 7 January 1946.

Place: Sea of Japan. (Asiatic area)

Next of kin: Harriet Nelson Morton, Wife"

—From official service record, Commander Dudley Walker
Morton, U.S. Navy, Active

*F*rom the moment he heard that Mush Morton was going back out with *Wahoo, George Grider was worried. He later wrote, "Wahoo left on its seventh patrol for waters so perilous they were shortly to be abandoned as a patrol area, and with a skipper so enraged he was ready to take any chance to redeem his boat's proud record, and with a fire control party that did not know him well enough to try to hold him in check."*

Maybe if Roger Paine had made the trip. Or Jack Griggs had not left. Or Grider was not on another submarine.

Maybe if Admiral Lockwood had not relented, if he had not ignored his own instincts and had assigned a relief captain for *Wahoo* so his ace could get some rest and medical attention.

Maybe if Mush Morton had not been so pissed off about his last two patrols, about those damned torpedoes. If those last two runs had just been more successful.

Maybe if he had agreed to Lockwood's request, gone back to California, spent some time with Harriet and the kids, made some speeches and helped sell some war bonds, done some interviews, hobnobbed with some movie stars, and gotten the disappointment and frustration out of his system.

As was typical, Morton and *Wahoo* drove off and left Sands and *Sawfish*. *Wahoo*, usually running at top speed on the surface, was through the strait two days ahead of her sister boat, but not before a guns-blazing surface attack on a large Japanese fishing boat. Thirty fishermen were killed, but the enemy was effectively alerted by that assault that another American submarine was headed back through La Pérouse and toward the Sea of Japan.

Four days later, she took down a freighter, and then, over the next several days, claimed two more ships. Postwar accounting would give *Wahoo* credit for sinking four ships, for thirteen thousand tons on her seventh patrol.

News sources reported the sinking of what they called an interisland steamer with the loss of over 540 lives. Tokyo Rose denounced the brutal attack and loss of civilian lives. *Time* magazine reported the sinking, but with a spin entirely different from the Japanese propaganda. The article's title, "Knock at the Door," was a reference to the fact that the sinking occurred in waters that were "Japan's historic door to the mainland of Asia." It went on to call the American submarine patrol in the Sea of Japan "one of World War II's most daring penetrations of enemy waters, a feat ranking with . . . the Japanese invasion of Pearl Harbor, the U.S. raid in Tokyo Bay." The Associated Press circulated a story that ran in all the papers, quoting a spokesperson at the Office of War Information: "An Allied submarine would have to dare risks almost if not as great as those that confronted the U.S. submarine that made its way into Tokyo Harbor."

(The reference to a submarine operating in Tokyo Harbor was a well-publicized myth, and one not discouraged by the Navy. Though many made the comparison, it was not USS *Copperfin* with Cary Grant at the helm in *Destination Tokyo*. Still, many claimed the fictional boat's entrance into Tokyo Bay was based on classified reality, with the movie offering a thinly veiled warning to the Japanese.

The lore was likely based on USS *Trigger* (SS-237) and her attack on the Japanese carrier *Hiyo* at the mouth of the bay. Rumors soon spread that the submarine had been lying on the bottom of the bay, watching the carrier while she was under construction, waiting for her to be launched so she could be effectively aborted before she left the womb. That was not the case.

There was another incident—well publicized by legendary war correspondent Ernie Pyle—in which a submarine doing lifeguard duty entered Tokyo Bay to rescue a downed bomber pilot. The headline of Pyle's article was "Even If You Was Shot Down in Tokyo Harbor, the Navy Would Be in to Get You.")

Naval commanders, including Admiral Lockwood himself, were certain the sinking of the Japanese ship—be it ferry or troop transport—had been Morton and his boat's work. Citing the Associated Press story as part of the report on *Wahoo*'s loss, Lockwood wrote, "No other submarine of this command was in the vicinity specified above in the time given and it must be presumed that this attack was made by the USS WAHOO. It is in keeping with the high standard of daring and aggressiveness displayed by Commander Morton on previous patrols."

Everyone back at Pearl Harbor and in Washington anxiously awaited one of the skipper's typical lighthearted, braggadocio reports.

It never came.

Just as sinking the fishing boat on the way into the strait alerted the Japanese that submarines were coming in, sinking the transport signaled that a submarine was heading back out of the Sea of Japan on a return course. *Sawfish*, which had finally overcome more dud torpedoes of her own, including the uniform failure of all of her Mark XVIIIs, had still managed to strike several fatal blows, too.

As she ran the strait ahead of *Wahoo*, headed eastward, *Sawfish* was spotted by enemy shore batteries and challenged by the Japanese. While they were not able to sink her, they did launch aircraft and conducted a brutal air attack against Sands and his boat. This further indicated to the enemy that the second American submarine they knew had been fishing in the pond to the west would likely be coming along behind the first, heading home.

There has been much speculation about what actually happened to *Wahoo*. Part of that conjecture is simply the result of the fact that most who knew him—including Charles Lockwood—found it difficult to fathom that Morton could be caught and sunk. He was invulnerable, a real-life Superman, like the character in the newly available comic book that all the sailors were reading.

Some maintain that the submarine was on the surface on a bright, sunny day, trying to make the run through La Pérouse Strait on October 11. Dick O'Kane believed the boat may have been damaged, possibly by one of her own circling torpedoes, the new and unproven ones. That theory has been discounted. Such an occurrence would likely have finished *Wahoo* right then and there.

Others suspect there may have been mechanical problems. *Wahoo* had had her share of those, though mostly nagging ones, nothing serious. Some think she may have struck a mine and suffered damage that kept her from going down any deeper than about periscope depth. Or maybe Morton was just being Morton, taking the quickest and most direct route toward home to replenish his torpedoes and return to the fray, and boldly going where the enemy least expected him to run. Thumbing his nose at them as he did.

Some Japanese war records claimed that the submarine was initially spotted by a shore battery, which began firing, causing *Wahoo* to submerge as far as she was able to go. Others in the Imperial Japanese Navy at the time disagree. They say the shore batteries were too far away from where *Wahoo* ran and never fired a shot. Even if they had, they would likely not have caused the submarine any real concerns from that distance. Nor do they think the shore installations ever spotted the submarine.

Others who have studied the Japanese pilots' accounts of *Wahoo*'s sinking disagree that the submarine was even running on the surface. Instead, they maintain, *Wahoo* was submerged as deeply as she dared go, hampered by either mine damage or mechanical problems. A small leak produced a telltale oil slick and allowed the first airplane to spot and bomb her.

Thanks to later efforts to find the wreck of *Wahoo*, and extensive interviews with the Japanese pilots and the men who manned the patrol craft, we now have a more complete picture of what actually happened.

A patrol aircraft spotted a small but lengthy oil slick on the surface, giving credence to the theory that the submarine was having some kind of mechanical problems or had been damaged in some way. Passing overhead, the aircraft's pilot could clearly see the outline of a submarine, not far below the surface, silhouetted in the clear, cold water.

The pilot made one more pass, lined up, and dropped a bomb. It was placed perfectly. The force of the blast brought the boat to the surface for a moment, giving the pilot a good view of her decks and propellers as her crew fought to get her back down and as close to out of sight as they could manage.

The Japanese pilot swooped around in a tight turn and dropped a second bomb, and this one appeared to do more damage to the boat's fuel tanks. *Wahoo*, wounded, was emitting a thick stream of oil and air bubbles to the surface, making her even easier to track from the air.

She had turned by then and appeared to have set a course for what many believed to be the Russian coast. Morton would not have been one to surrender. If they could make it close to land, they could scuttle the ship and have some chance of making it to shore.

Forest Sterling later wrote of a casual conversation he had had with his skipper. Morton talked about what it would be like to spend the rest of the war in Russia should they have to abandon *Wahoo*. Mush had made it clear that would be the absolute last option he would consider.

The first patrol plane returned to base for fuel and more bombs, while a second one pounded the helpless victim. The oil trail gave them a good indication of where the submerged vessel was. Even without that, air bubbles and the clear water offered the aircraft a relatively easy target.

We can only guess what the crew was doing during this terrible time. Probably working to stop leaks, trying to keep the motors online as long as the batteries would last. But they certainly knew how desperate their situation was.

The submarine had finally slowed to only a knot or two of forward speed. The planes dropped markers on the sea surface, and patrol boats moved in with their depth charges. The pounding was intense. At one point, a chunk of metal, later identified as a portion of the submarine's propeller, bobbed to the surface. The oil was thicker, too, indicating massive leaks in the boat's fuel tanks.

Dick O'Kane always believed that Morton was taking extraordinary measures to save his boat and crew, probably trying to dump enough fuel from his heavily damaged submarine to get her buoyant enough to get to the surface. There, he would try to shoot it out with his attackers while scuttle charges were set and the boat was blown out from beneath them.

If that was the commander's plan, it did not work.

Wahoo remained just deep enough to be out of sight but not so deep that she could hide from the airplanes circling above. In total, over five dozen depth charges and forty bombs were expended on the U.S. Navy's most famous submarine, though the enemy almost certainly had no idea who they had in their sights. It was just an American submarine, and one that had just inflicted severe damage in the enemy's backyard.

Wahoo finally stopped completely.

With a last gush of oil—maybe Morton's last-ditch effort to blow the tanks and pop up for a final fight to the death, maybe just an indication that the submarine had come totally apart, sinking deeper—*Wahoo* was gone.

Eighty men were lost.

It can now be reported that those who have since dived on, photographed, and studied *Wahoo*'s remains found the likely fatal damage occurred to the submarine just aft of the conning tower. It came with the very first bomb dropped. That blast left a huge rupture from the conning tower all the way down to the boat's keel. The subsequent bombs and depth charges were unnecessary.

There is also reason to believe that the mortally wounded submarine somehow managed to creep along, even after the Japanese had assumed she was done for, maybe just on the force of will of her skipper. It appears she may have limped another ten miles before the flood finally took her down forever.

Back in Pearl Harbor, Charles Lockwood was worried. He hoped against hope that his "ace" would turn up. *Sawfish* reported in east of the

Kurils, but there was no word whatsoever from *Wahoo*. The next required update from Morton was supposed to be on October 26.

Nothing.

Lockwood ordered aircraft to run along the most likely routes the submarine might have taken on the way home. Maybe they were dead in the water, radio busted, waiting for help to come.

The admiral waited as long as he could to make it official. On November 9, Lockwood declared USS *Wahoo* overdue, presumed lost with all hands. That set loose the sad duty of notifying the crew's next of kin.

Lockwood's official report on the incident was impassive, straightforward.

"It is with deep regret that the Commander, Submarine Force, Pacific Fleet, reports that the USS *WAHOO* has not been heard from since her departure from Midway on 13 September 1943, and it is presumed that this vessel is lost."

Unofficially, though, the main boss of submarines in the Pacific was shaken, taking the loss personally. It had to be worse for him, considering he had ignored his own better judgment and allowed Mush Morton to take *Wahoo* out again.

"It was difficult for me to imagine that Morton and his boat could be lost," Lockwood later wrote. "I just did not think the Japanese were smart enough to get him. He would never come steaming in again with a broom in the masthead and Mush Morton's fighting face, with its wide grin, showing above the bridge rail."

He was convinced that it had taken a mine to damage *Wahoo* so severely that Morton could not bring her home, even using all her stealthy attributes. That led Lockwood to immediately stop all submarine action in the Sea of Japan.

George Grider heard the news even before the official announcement came. It depressed him greatly. As noted, he felt the loss was the result of the new personnel in the fire control party. If he, O'Kane, and Paine had been there, things might have been different. They knew how to keep Morton focused. They were the perfect team for what they were supposed to be doing.

Like so many before and after him who left a ship just before it was lost, Roger Paine felt intense guilt. It was a double blow for him, because his other previous boat, *Pompano*, had also just been reported lost, taking seventy-six men down, including many of his former shipmates.

Paine, too, wondered whether he could have done something—anything—to have helped save *Wahoo*. If he had only had a change of heart and returned as Mush's exec, as his skipper had so desperately wanted him to do. That angry final visit with his skipper haunted him the rest of his days.

George Logue was a teenager in the hills of Central Pennsylvania when his family got the news that their brother, Bobby, had gone down with the legendary submarine onto which he had just shipped over.

"I come home from school one day," he remembers. "My mother was ironing and she was crying. I asked her what was wrong. She showed me the newspaper, the story that *Wahoo* was overdue and presumed lost."

The newspaper had the story before Logue's mother heard the news from the Navy.

Robert Logue was not even supposed to be on the boat for that patrol. He had other duty pending, but the decision was made to send him out with *Wahoo* due to his extensive training with the new Mark XVIII torpedoes.

Then, a few days later, the family got word that Bobby was not aboard *Wahoo* after all, that the Navy decided they needed his expertise as part of the crew of the new submarine tender USS *Orion* (AS-18), which had just arrived at Pearl Harbor. They had sent a relief torpedoman to Midway to take his place.

Only later would the Logues learn that *Wahoo* had just pulled away from the dock at Midway when the relief arrived. Bobby Logue had, indeed, been aboard the missing submarine after all.

"We were overjoyed when the Navy told us he had been transferred off. Then we got a telegram days later apologizing for the mistake," George Logue remembers.

Back in California, Harriet Morton received the news the way most families did: in a message delivered by a representative of the Navy. Then it was in all the papers. Like some of the others, she had her doubts.

"Presumed lost" did not at all mean that he was dead. Few knew as well as she how determined her husband was. If anybody could bring back a distressed submarine, Mush could. And he would do it with style, too.

For a long while, Harriet still expected to get the word that he and his crew had survived, that he had somehow found a way to get his boat to safety. He would call and tell her how mad Admiral Lockwood was that he had made a mess of his boat. At worst, he was a POW. And God help those guards! They had no idea whom they were messing with!

Only after receiving his third Gold Star, signifying the awarding of his fourth Navy Cross by President Roosevelt—presented posthumously in May 1944—and his Purple Heart in March 1946 did it finally sink in that she was a widow, that her children would never really get to know their father.

Douglas Morton vaguely remembers his mother telling him and his younger sister that his father was "lost."

"I was four years old," he says. "My response was, 'Why don't they find him?'"

Interestingly, George Logue and others would one day attempt to do just that very thing.

The celebrity status the Navy had worked so hard to achieve for *Wahoo* and "Mush the Magnificent" meant that their loss sent shock waves through not only the Navy but the whole country. Headlines delivered the terrible news that the "runnin', gunnin'" *Wahoo* was missing, and with it, the man who epitomized the dashing, daring, Jap-killing submarine skipper.

Until the day he died in February 1994, Dick O'Kane pushed hard to have Mush Morton awarded the Congressional Medal of Honor—the one Mush was certain was coming his way when he wrote the letter to Captain H. G. Donald at the end of the fourth patrol. O'Kane was not successful. The country's highest award for valor has still not been awarded to Morton.

An early citation for the award was drafted shortly after the loss of *Wahoo* and its skipper, but it never received any action. O'Kane felt it was premature and poorly written. Little was known about the submarine's final patrol, and the updated information, mostly from Japanese records, would have confirmed that Morton had returned to form, that he deserved the medal for his final run, if not for his complete and amazing body of work.

Later, Morton's daughter, Edwina, would gain the assistance of a member of Congress from her home district in Connecticut in trying to get her father the medal. She felt she was making progress when the congressman was defeated for reelection and the project stopped cold.

O'Kane also felt *Wahoo* and her crew had not been properly recognized for all they accomplished. The submarine had received only one Presidential Unit Citation (PUC), an award for extraordinary bravery in accomplishing a mission under difficult and hazardous conditions above and beyond what other units might have experienced in the same campaign. The one PUC came after *Wahoo*'s third patrol, its first with Mush Morton in command. O'Kane was convinced things were just happening too fast for the Navy's slow and bureaucratic award process to keep up with what this remarkable submarine and crew were accomplishing. Morton and his guys were using up their torpedoes and coming home before the paperwork could catch up.

And once *Wahoo* and Morton were gone, thoughts of awarding additional PUCs were simply overlooked. Or it was too painful to pursue.

Despite O'Kane's efforts, *Wahoo* never received a Presidential Unit Citation beyond that first one, despite a record far superior to many of the other boats that were awarded the honor multiple times.

Speculation today is that the incident in which *Wahoo* fired at survivors of the torpedoed troopship is the primary reason for Morton's not receiving the Congressional Medal of Honor. Some say Morton was simply too controversial a figure, a flashpoint. Many in the higher reaches of the Navy did not share Charles Lockwood's high opinion of the man or his unorthodox tactics, or they resented Lockwood's open affection and praise for him. They did not like his singling out Morton and a few other of his favorites over many of the other submarine skippers who were not as flashy but still got the job done.

Morton also had a knack for rubbing the wrong way many of the more conservative naval brass. That was especially the case when they did not approve of his full-speed-ahead mentality or in-your-face demeanor when he did not get his way. Others maintain that his celebrity status was a negative, causing jealousy among some elements.

Still, it is difficult to understand why Mush Morton, of all potential recipients of the highest award for valor, has not yet received serious consideration for the award.

As previously noted, a number of men from Morton's wardroom went on to accomplish amazing things in the war.

Richard Hetherington O'Kane took *Tang* on one of the wildest rides of World War II. O'Kane did receive the Medal of Honor for his actions. Additionally, his total tally of sinkings and tonnage made him the highest-scoring submarine commander of World War II. He eventually achieved the rank of rear admiral upon retiring from the Navy in 1957. He remained married to Ernestine until his death in 1994, and was survived by his children, James and Marsha. Admiral O'Kane was buried in Arlington National Cemetery.

The destroyer USS *O'Kane* (DDG-77) was named for him in December 1994.

George Grider went on to skipper two submarines in World War II. He received a Bronze Star and the Navy Cross for his service. A heart attack shortened his naval career, and he returned to school to earn his law degree. Grider later served in Congress from his home state of Tennessee. He died in March 1991.

After his appendectomy, Roger Paine went on to helm USS *S-34* and then was executive officer on USS *Tinosa*. Later, he became skipper of the newly constructed USS *Cubera* (SS-347). Paine was active in the Navy's early nuclear efforts and captained several other vessels before becoming commander of a destroyer group and a destroyer flotilla. After a turn on the staff of the chief of naval operations, he retired in 1972. Paine died in November 2008 at Annapolis, Maryland. He was the last surviving officer to have served on *Wahoo*.

Yeoman Forest Sterling eventually achieved the rank of chief petty officer and served in the Navy until August 1956. He later wrote, "At midnight, January 1, 2000, in keeping with my predictions to my *Wahoo* shipmates, I expect to hoist a few beers and say to them, 'Sorry, fellows, I should have been with you. My spirit has been with you all these years!'"

He was able to keep that promise. Sterling did not pass away until May 2002, shortly after celebrating his ninety-first birthday.

Harriet Morton remarried in 1948 to Robert Bradford. She had already moved to the suburbs just north of New York City with her two children, near her sister, Jeanette. Starting in November of 1947, she began receiving the benefits from Mush's veterans' insurance of $10,000 as a monthly payment of $39.70 for the next 120 months.

Like Forest Sterling, Harriet had a pact with friends that she would live to see the year 2000. She did, but passed away shortly thereafter.

Though he was skipper of *Wahoo* for only ten months and took her on just five war patrols, Mush Morton ended up at number three on the list of top submarine skippers of World War II, based on number of confirmed ships sunk. He was behind only Dick O'Kane and Slade Cutter. Out of the top five sub skippers of the war, three received the Congressional Medal of Honor: O'Kane, Eugene Fluckey, and Samuel Dealey.

Wahoo's fourth patrol is number two on the list of best war patrols by number of ships sunk. Only *Tang*'s third patrol—with Dick O'Kane at the helm—was better, and that was by only one ship.

The destroyer USS *Morton* (DD-948), commissioned in May 1949, was named for Commander Morton. His daughter, Edwina, was the ship's sponsor at its official launch. She was only sixteen years old at the time, the second-youngest person ever to christen a ship for the U.S. Navy. Her mother, Harriet, had been called upon to christen the submarine USS *Volador* (SS-490) the year before. This gave them the distinction of being the only mother and daughter ever to sponsor new ships.

Morton Field, an athletic facility at Mare Island, and the gym at the submarine base at New London, Connecticut, were also named in his honor.

One of the bas relief panels at the U.S. Navy Memorial on Pennsylvania Avenue in Washington, D.C., depicts the "clean sweep" arrival in Pearl Harbor by USS *Wahoo*.

The cribbage board—the one on which Dick O'Kane made his perfect hand and over which some of *Wahoo*'s most audacious assaults were plotted and replayed—still rides the seas today, always aboard the oldest attack submarine in the fleet. As of this writing, that is USS *Greeneville* (SSN-772).

Wahoo and her crew would lie undisturbed in their final resting place, her exact whereabouts still a mystery, for almost sixty years.

Then, in the fall of 2006, the dedication of a group of doggedly determined people and the advent of modern ocean exploration technology once again put Mush Morton and the legendary *Wahoo* right back in the headlines.

EPILOGUE

"On a submarine, everyone has to work together, fight together and when their time comes, they are lost together. That is the way it was with *WAHOO* on her seventh war patrol as she ended her career, probably in the Sea of Japan late in 1943. It was the last chapter in the story of a fine ship and an heroic crew."

—From official history of USS *Wahoo*, Office of Naval Records and History, Ships' Histories Section, U.S. Navy Department

"*It was the last chapter in the story of a fine ship and an heroic crew.*"
Wrong!

Oh, it was a "fine ship" and "heroic crew" for sure, but the official account of *Wahoo*'s story and her ultimate loss—or at least as detailed by the Office of Naval Records and History—was not correct. Not when it concluded with that statement.

There most certainly was a very compelling and inspirational chapter yet to be written. In truth, that final chapter deserves a book of its own.

The rest of *Wahoo*'s story would begin to be written by George Logue, all the way back in 1943. That was when he found his mother crying at the ironing board after learning of his brother Bobby's loss on the submarine. About the time he heard that no, Bobby was safe after all. And then, ultimately, that he was gone.

George Logue vowed then that he would find his brother someday. He had no idea where to look or how long and difficult that quest would prove to be. There is no doubt he would have pursued it anyway, even if he had known then what shoaling waters lay ahead.

Then along came George's nephew, Thomas, who, as a kid, read everything he could get his hands on concerning his uncle and the remarkable submarine on which he died. He read books by Dick O'Kane and Forest Sterling and George Grider. The submarine bug bit him hard. Tom Logue was a young man so fascinated by the story of his lost relative that he eventually entered the Naval Academy, graduated, volunteered for submarines, and then served in Admiral Hyman Rickover's "nuclear Navy." He went on to become chairman of the computer science department at Annapolis.

Also contributing to the effort was Douglas Morton, who, as a child, wondered why, if his dad was missing, nobody was out there looking for him.

And Bryan MacKinnon, Mush Morton's grandnephew, who fortuitously was living and working in Japan in the 1990s (as he still does today), in a perfect position to assist in the effort when he learned what the others were trying to accomplish.

And Marty Schaffer, a World War II sub veteran. He was a man who could not tolerate the thought of brother submariners lying dead out there without a proper funeral. Without their families enjoying the peace that that would come with knowing exactly where their final resting place was.

Then the effort would be moved along by a Japanese admiral, by the crew members from World War II Japanese minisubmarines, by an Australian deep-sea explorer, by a high-tech petroleum exploration vessel and its crew, by Russian diplomats, by workers at the museum for the USS *Bowfin* (SS-287) at Pearl Harbor, by a Baptist missionary in Japan, and ultimately, by a team of Russian deep-sea divers.

This final chapter even includes the pilots of the aircraft who actually bombed *Wahoo* that day.

With little money and even less time or resources, George Logue kept the promise he made himself as a teenager. He got serious about the search in 1947, even though he was a college student at the time with little money, no resources, and not a clue where to start looking.

"When I heard 'overdue and lost,' I said, 'Like hell! I'm not going to rest until I find out what happened to *Wahoo*.' I was just a kid," he later told a newspaper reporter.

Maybe, but the kid did not give up, even though he kept running into brick walls. That was especially true when the search was tantalizingly close to paying off. It was years later, when he was contacted out of the blue by an energetic former World War II sub sailor—Marty Schaffer—that things started to happen. Schaffer had maintained his great interest in the diesel submarines on which he had served. In those fifty-two vessels and approximately 375 officers and 3,100 enlisted men who had been lost during the war. When Schaffer got wind of Logue and his mission, he contacted him to compare notes, to see what Logue had been able to find out about *Wahoo*.

Eventually, the two men realized that they would have to travel to Wakkanai, the northernmost city on the northernmost Japanese island of Hokkaido. It was the area from which the attack on *Wahoo* had been launched, and it was the waters surrounding the area in which Mush and his crew went down. That made it the logical place to go to dig up some solid clues about exactly what happened to her and precisely where she might lie.

Logue had exchanged correspondence with researchers in the area, but in 1993 he decided—boosted by Schaffer's enthusiasm and offer to go with him—that he needed to visit the area to jump-start his search. Never mind that neither he nor Schaffer spoke a word of Japanese.

The two men could not have anticipated what eddies in the stream their presence would cause. Or what a welcoming and hospitable group they would eventually encounter.

Logue and Schaffer had two goals they wanted to accomplish. One, of course, was to learn more about what happened to *Wahoo* in her last hours, and where, in the cold waters off Hokkaido, her remains might be. But they also wanted to put up some sort of memorial there. And it would not just be for the American submarine. It would also be in memory of the people lost on the ships Morton and his crew sank in the seas just before their own loss. In their minds, it would be a true "peace memorial." They had no idea how receptive the Japanese would be to such a thing.

Fortunately, they met up with Larry Hagen, a Baptist missionary in the area, who was able to translate for them and introduce them to local officials who might be willing to help. The researchers with whom Logue had already been exchanging information put them in touch with representatives from the Japanese Maritime Self-Defense Force, the strictly defensive peacetime version of the Imperial Japanese Navy.

Logue and Schaffer learned a great deal during their stay. They also managed to organize a private wreath-laying ceremony—thanks to the JMSDF—at a spot off Hokkaido where locals and some of the Japanese involved with the attack had always assumed *Wahoo* was. Even if it turned out not to be the right spot, the wreath-laying ceremony was a worthwhile and very moving effort.

They also learned that, luckily, the Japanese were receptive and eager to help them with the peace memorial idea. They were just as happy to help find *Wahoo* and put together the story of her loss, as best they could.

Armed with those contacts and information, and with considerable help from Hagen and others, Logue and Schaffer put together a public memorial service for 1995. Out of the peace memorial effort emerged a friendship with IJN submarine veteran Satoru Saga, who lives in Wakkanai. He introduced them to Vice Admiral Kazuo Ueda, another former Imperial Japanese Navy submariner. Saga had been a crewman on one of the tiny five-man submarines that were being stationed all over the Home Islands in anticipation of what the Japanese assumed would be an eventual D-day-like invasion by the Allies.

Ueda had done considerable research on military action in the area during the war. He knew everyone at the Japanese war archives department. That meant he was able to offer unprecedented access to the historical records and introduce the growing group looking for *Wahoo* to some key individuals who could help further the cause.

Among those Saga was able to introduce them to were some of the actual participants in the attack on *Wahoo*. That included the pilot of the airplane that dropped the first bomb on the legendary vessel. With remarkable clarity, those men were able to supply firsthand accounts of what happened that day, at least from their perspective.

For his part, Admiral Ueda had his own ideas, based on his knowledge and considerable research, about where the American submarine most likely lay.

The Japanese submariners were especially interested in helping in the quest. The brotherhood among submariners is a close one, even among former enemies. Now no longer adversaries, these "brothers in the 'phin" (a reference to the dolphin, the symbol adopted by submariners) knew all too well what it would mean to family members to know where their men had died. They could finally say a proper good-bye.

Despite language and distance, the memorial conceived and champi-oned by Logue, Schaffer, and Saga soon came to pass. With the help of their newly found Japanese friends, it was officially dedicated on Septem-ber 9, 1995. Mush Morton's widow and his grandchild, Chrissy, were present, as was Bryan MacKinnon, Morton's grandnephew. He did not know it then, but MacKinnon would soon be deeply involved in the quest to find the boat. Also at the dedication were George and Tom Logue, Marty Schaffer, Larry Hagen, Satoru Saga, and representatives from the U.S. embassy and Navy. There were also numerous Japanese representa-tives, including at least one survivor of one of the ships sunk by Mush Morton and his crew on that final run.

Logue and Schaffer kept their promise. The peace memorial honors both sides.

Also present were two other men who had a vested interest in the fate of *Wahoo*: the pilots of the two airplanes that bombed her.

Afterward, one of the pilots said, through a translator, "Mrs. Morton has been giving us bad looks until the day before the memorial event. Of course, she could not help it. The actual people who attacked her hus-band were right in front of her. We are all human. But on the day of the memorial, I saw her expression relax. I was amazed. Although we did have a big celebration right after the attack, that was only because of the war. We had no personal hate toward any of them. It made me feel like a burden was finally off my shoulders, now that the former enemies got together, and swore that such war should never happen again."

At a reception attended by Japanese and Americans, Harriet Nelson Morton Bradford gave a short speech in which she declared that without forgiveness there can be no peace. Her remarks were well received.

Bryan MacKinnon would later describe the memorial dedication cer-emony.

"[It] began at Cape Soya at three o'clock, and lasted an hour. The sight of Japanese and American naval officers sitting together in their formal dress whites was impressive. More impressive were the old foes, arm in arm, unveiling the memorial, laying wreaths, and voicing the strong desire for peace between our two countries."

Many reporters were present, and NHK, the Japanese national television network, ran two separate stories on the event, with video of the ceremony. Harriet, George, and several others were prominently featured in the reports. Harriet is shown placing a wreath on the memorial. Logue told the Japanese reporter, "I was very upset, but it has completely turned around. I am very, very happy to be here."

The memorial is in the form of a six-foot-high pyramid, made of granite, topped with an orange ball representing the sun. There is a small "window" in the pyramid just beneath the "sun." Through that window, visitors can see the waters beneath which *Wahoo* sleeps.

A plaque on the monument bears the following inscription, in English and Japanese:

ON OCTOBER 11, 1943, THE JAPANESE NAVY SANK THE AMERICAN SUBMARINE *WAHOO* SS-238 IN A FIVE-HOUR AIR AND SEA ATTACK. *WAHOO* WAS LEAVING THE SEA OF JAPAN AFTER HAVING SUNK SEVERAL SHIPS IN A TWO-WEEK RAID. WHEN THE *WAHOO* WAS LOST IT WAS THE HIGHEST-SCORING SUBMARINE IN THE U.S. NAVY. EIGHTY AMERICANS SLEEP IN THE SŌYA STRAIT 12 MILES NORTHEAST OF HERE. MANY JAPANESE SLEEP IN THE SEA OF JAPAN FROM *WAHOO* ATTACKS.

THIS MONUMENT WAS ERECTED BY THE MEMBERS OF THE JAPANESE ATTACK GROUP AND RELATIVES OF AMERICANS LYING IN *WAHOO*. OLD ENEMIES MET AS BROTHERS TO DEDICATE THAT OUR COUNTRIES WILL HAVE LASTING PEACE AND WAR WILL NEVER AGAIN DESTROY THE FRIENDSHIP WE NOW ENJOY TODAY.

("Sōya Strait" is how La Pérouse Strait is listed on Japanese maps.)

The memorial is located not far from the Tower of Prayer, a monument to Korean Air Lines flight 007, which was shot down by the Soviet Union when the passenger plane strayed into Soviet airspace during a planned missile test. A hundred and sixty-nine people died in that tragedy, which also occurred in the waters off Hokkaido.

About the time of the 1995 memorial dedication and the establishment of the *Wahoo* memorial in northern Japan, Bryan MacKinnon joined up with the others who were looking for the boat. MacKinnon, who was working in Tokyo for Merrill Lynch Japan, created a nonprofit organization to provide a central group to help continue the effort. The MacKinnon Organization served as a clearinghouse for all the information that was being uncovered, a place where families of lost submariners, researchers, archivists, and the media could see the latest information on the boats on "eternal patrol."

Besides distance and lack of funding, there were other reasons why the search for *Wahoo* stalled out for several years, even with so many dedicated people shepherding the effort.

First, it was very difficult to get access to the area. The geography of the region was a considerable hindrance. Though the waters in the area are relatively shallow, they are very treacherous, with dangerous currents, and the seawater is extremely cold.

The region was also a political hot spot at the time. Both Japan and Russia have, in the past, staked claim to the waters in the area, as well as to the Kuril chain of islands that stretch northward from Hokkaido. That has caused considerable tension. The specific location where *Wahoo* most likely lay was considered to be Russian territorial waters, due to their proximity to the Russian island of Sakhalin across the strait. The spot did belong to Japan during World War II and was only a dozen miles off the Japanese coast.

And it was also a prime exploration region for undersea petroleum. That made the territorial claims on that little sliver of the globe even more contentious. And even more problematic for those who sought *Wahoo*.

The next major development came in 2002, when Australian Wayne Sampey contacted Bryan MacKinnon with an offer of help. Sampey was head of the Ocean Wilderness Group and became project director with the Australian arm of the National Underwater and Marine Agency. NUMA, founded in 1979 by author Clive Cussler, has as its mission "preserving our maritime heritage through the discovery, archaeological survey and conservation of shipwreck artifacts." The group has been instrumental in locating several World War II aircraft, but is probably best-known for its efforts in locating and bringing to the surface the Confederate submarine CSS *Hunley* off Charleston, South Carolina. The *Hunley* was the first submarine to successfully sink an enemy vessel during wartime, but she and her crew of eight men were lost under mysterious circumstances shortly after accomplishing that feat in Charleston Harbor in 1864.

Sampey and MacKinnon jointly created the *Wahoo* Project Group. Their explicit goal was locating Mush Morton's submarine. From that point on, all activities were done under the group's auspices, and the Russians later joined in.

Besides technical expertise, Sampey and NUMA were able to assist with locating sponsors, and to get both the American and Russian governments excited about the search for *Wahoo*. That political cooperation was a major step in the eventual success of the mission. The end of the Soviet Union also made greater assistance from Russia possible, and Sampey, MacKinnon, and the others took advantage of that fortunate turn.

At this point, staff members from the USS *Bowfin* museum ship at Pearl Harbor were contacted and asked to help. Strict standards have been established for activities permitted in the vicinity of sunken vessels in which lives were lost, civilian or military. MacKinnon and the group were determined to follow those guidelines explicitly.

They also obtained the blessing of the U.S. Navy to search not only for *Wahoo* but four other lost World War II submarines. The Navy is understandably reluctant to have unauthorized groups diving on what amounts to the tombs of lost servicemen. Maritime law prohibits such exploration without permission of the country whose vessel is the subject of such activities. Once convinced there would be no effort for salvage or to remove bodies from the wreck, the Navy gave the venture a thumbs-up.

The real breakthrough came in 2004, but the going was still slow, tedious. Sakhalin Energy Investment Company (SEIC), a joint venture between Russia and Shell Oil Company, was formed to explore for and exploit the petroleum in Russian waters in the area, as well as to conduct extensive research into military and naval activities in the Sakhalin and Wakkanai region. The venture's Explosive Ordnance Disposal Coordination Centre (EODCC) was also charged with locating and neutralizing weapons that were dumped in the area during the war.

During this time, EODCC member Ian Bullpitt became interested in locating *Wahoo* and visited MacKinnon's *Wahoo* Web site. He contacted the *Wahoo* Project Group to offer his assistance.

A Russian subcontractor, Romona, while conducting a subsea survey of La Pérouse Strait, diverted from their normal survey route to search the "Ueda location," the spot where Vice Admiral Ueda's research had convinced him that *Wahoo* most likely rested. They also scanned another area considered to be a possible site because Japanese fishermen had been snagging their nets on something down there for years.

SEIC produced side-scan sonar readings and images of both of those promising locations. The first images from the Ueda location immediately raised the interest of those who saw them. They were consistent with a submarine matching the dimensions of a *Gato*-class submarine. And they were within a few hundred feet of where Ueda thought *Wahoo* to be.

Bullpitt informed the *Wahoo* Project Group of these very interesting side-scan images. They were the first real validation that Vice Admiral Ueda's spot was likely the location of the *Wahoo*.

Still, with this exciting new evidence, progress was maddeningly slow. Later in 2005, a Russian team led by Vladimir Kartashev attempted to take a closer look at the site but ran into equipment problems. Kartashev's group subsequently contacted MacKinnon and his team and offered to help look for *Wahoo* if they could get additional funding in their search for *L-19*, a missing Russian submarine, also from World War II.

Another year passed after the team received and got so excited over the promising images, but the long, frustrating search was finally about to pay off.

In a press release, the *Wahoo* Project Group said, "[We] are now preparing a complete, nonintrusive subsea survey. [The group] has a thorough understanding of the responsibilities with regard to the USS *Wahoo* site and other sites. The group has no intention of either releasing the location of, or interfering in any way with, the site. Their primary aim is to verify, document, and to provide a record of the USS *Wahoo* and her resting place as the tomb of eighty brave souls, entrusting all gathered materials to the USS *Bowfin* Submarine Museum and the appropriate authorities for historic and commemorative purposes, and to close another mystery in the chapter of events known as World War II."

In July of 2006, Kartashev's team of Russian divers from Vladivostok, using the same images that SEIC had made available to MacKinnon, converged on the Ueda site. Funding remained a problem, so theirs was a decidedly low-tech operation, using a small sailboat as a platform and a crew of only a half dozen men. Their diving gear was very basic, too. That meant divers going down to two hundred feet in very cold water, where the images showed the submarine to be, had to make quick trips. Their photographic equipment was just as basic, too, limiting them to relatively close-up stills and rudimentary video.

But the evidence was enough. They were convinced that they had finally found *Wahoo*.

Or at least they had unofficially found the submarine. Now the U.S. Navy had to be convinced, and everyone knew that would be difficult, if not impossible. The Navy had a reputation for being skeptical about evidence or reports of lost warships that had reportedly been located.

For several months, the *Wahoo* Project Group had been gearing up for a U.S. Navy–sponsored dive on the sunken submarine in order to solidly prove or disprove that it was *Wahoo* down there. That would turn out not to be necessary. Charles Hinman and Jerry Hofwolt of the *Bowfin* Museum at Pearl Harbor spent a great deal of time poring over the images the group had provided them. They were able to conclude without question that the dim, rusting hulk was the *Wahoo*.

As it turned out, *Wahoo* was the middle boat in a series of three American wrecks discovered in a few short years, and over sixty years after their loss. USS *Lagarto* (SS-371) had been found and officially identified the previous year in the Gulf of Siam. The remains of USS *Grunion* (SS-216) were found in the Bering Sea in August 2007. *Grunion* sank in July 1942. She was on her very first war patrol. *Lagarto* was lost in August 1945.

On October 31, 2006, the Navy issued a press release with the headline: NAVY SAYS WRECK FOUND OFF JAPAN IS LEGENDARY SUB USS *WAHOO*.

It was finally, gratefully official. The photos from the Russian dive team were clear and the evidence compelling. The wreck had "characteristics consistent with USS *Wahoo*, and the submarine was found very near those reported in Imperial Japanese records."

The news release, whether intentionally or not, corrected the "last chapter" statement in *Wahoo*'s official history, saying, "After an extensive review of evidence, the last chapters [in *Wahoo*'s story] are being written as the Commander, U.S. Pacific Fleet, declared today that the sunken submarine recently discovered by divers in the Western Pacific is, indeed, the World War II submarine USS *Wahoo* (SS-238)."

Admiral Gary Roughead went on to say, "This brings closure to the families of the men of *Wahoo*, one of the greatest fighting submarines in the history of the U.S. Navy."

There were mixed emotions among all those who had so long sought the lost submarine. Jubilation over finally knowing, sadness still for those brave men who died there that day.

Doug Morton, who noted that he was speaking on behalf of his sister and the rest of the family, was quoted in the release as saying, "The Morton family is thrilled that there will be closure to the loss of our father. The loss of a famous submariner who was loved by his family and crew has been very difficult."

On July 8, 2007, the U.S. Navy paused long enough while conducting routine operations off the coast of Wakkanai to hold a ceremony at sea for *Wahoo* and the lost crew. Rear Admiral Douglas McAneny, commander of Submarine Group Seven, oversaw the event from aboard USS *Frank Cable* (AS-40), a submarine tender home ported in Guam.

Accompanying the *Frank Cable* was a Russian LST. She was there on a similar memorial mission in memory of the *L-19*, which has, as of this writing, still not been precisely located.

The United States Navy and the USS *Bowfin* Submarine Museum had provided family members the opportunity to make their own personal remembrances of loved ones who had been lost on *Wahoo*. As part of the Navy's ceremony in La Pérouse Strait, the Navy put together a large, coin-shaped container that held all those remembrances and placed it in the water there at the final resting place of "Mush Morton and his Widow Makers."

Among those present for the wreath-laying and remembrance were Captain Tom Logue and another relative of Torpedoman Bobby Logue, Rear Admiral John Christenson, another nephew, who also has a long and proud record of service in the Navy.

On the sixty-fourth anniversary of *Wahoo*'s loss, October 11, 2007, a moving memorial service was held at the USS *Bowfin* Submarine Museum in Hawaii. More than two hundred attended, mostly surviving family members, U.S. Navy personnel, including senior officers, and other dignitaries. The ceremony included a twenty-one-gun salute and the playing of "Taps." The family members of the crewmen also had the opportunity to step up and ring *Wahoo*'s ship bell.

It was normal practice for submarines to leave their ship bell behind when they went to sea. *Wahoo*'s is on display at the museum—adjacent to the USS *Arizona* Memorial at Pearl Harbor—at a special exhibit in honor of the boat and its crew.

When Ruth Anders Taylor, brother of crewman Floyd Anders, rang the bell, she gave it an especially vigorous peal.

"This one's for you, brother!" she shouted.

She had expressed to a reporter her welcome relief now that *Wahoo* had been found. She and other family members had never been sure whether the boat might have been captured, its crew put into a POW camp and left to die there, or maybe tortured to death by the Japanese.

Now they finally knew his fate, their fate.

"I had a good cry," Taylor told the reporter. "Now I know Floyd and his crewmates are all resting at the bottom of the sea together."

In a recent radio interview, Doug Morton says he is still in awe of the reverence and respect with which people talk to him about his father. That is especially true of submarine sailors, regardless of their rank.

Doug Morton had always found it difficult to talk about his father.

"I was so young when he died, and people are surprised to hear that I still cried at night, even as an adult, when I thought about him," he says. "It has been a big part of my life. People find me somehow and want to tell me how much they admire and appreciate my father. It was difficult for me to even speak about it for years, but now, after over sixty-five years, it is getting better. And after the ceremony, I felt great relief. I don't cry at night anymore."

In the mid-1960s, a verse was added to "The Navy Hymn," one that specifically included submariners. It was too late for Mush Morton, the crew of *Wahoo*, and the other fifty-one boats lost in World War II. But it still offers comfort to the families of the men—and now women—who pull a hatch cover over their heads and deliberately sink their ship in order to protect you and me:

> *Lord God, our power evermore,*
> *Whose arm doth reach the ocean floor,*
> *Dive with our men beneath the sea;*
> *Traverse the depths protectively.*
> *O hear us when we pray, and keep*
> *them safe from peril in the deep.*

AUTHOR'S NOTES

*A*s I was considering my next book project after War Beneath the Waves—*and not necessarily one about submarines—I found myself in Jacksonville, Florida, on business. I was early for my departing flight and, on a whim, decided to run up to St. Marys, Georgia, and spend a few minutes at the submarine museum there. The real reason for the detour was that I wanted to meet in person the museum's manager, John Crouse, who had been such a great help to me during my research on several previous books.*

The nice lady who opened the door early for me gave me the news that John had recently suffered a heart attack and was home recuperating. She was kind enough to give me the run of the place, and I was amazed at the number of sub-related items John and his group had been able to collect and display in a small but historic building there on the town's waterfront. (The museum is across the street from where tourists catch the boat out to Cumberland Island. It is easy to miss, but you should not.)

As I wandered around looking at the various exhibits—many of them obvious works in progress—I eventually wandered up to the second floor and the museum's library. There were several out-of-print books there and, even with frequent glances at my watch, I became engrossed in a recurring theme in a couple of them: the not-so-subtle change in the nature of submarine warfare during the early years of World War II, a metamorphosis that was led by a group of colorful, outspoken skippers who literally rewrote the manuals as they went. Primary among them was Dudley "Mush" Morton. I quickly thumbed through the *Wahoo* patrol reports that John and his crew have typed up, bound, and made available to museum visitors and researchers. The imaginative and descriptive prose in those reports—drafted by Morton, XO Dick O'Kane, and Yeoman Forest Sterling—was even more intriguing to me.

By the time I left St. Marys and rushed down I-95 to catch my flight, I knew I had to learn more about this enigmatic, dynamic, and creative man. The more I searched, the more I realized that his complete story has never been brought together in one place. Additionally, there is an entire generation of people who are unaware not only of his influence on history and accomplishments in the war, but of his remarkable character.

Still, I was not sure there was a book there.

One reason for my doubts was that various parts of Morton's story have been recounted in several books since the war. Dick O'Kane's excellent work *Wahoo* is the most detailed, but it is more the history of the submarine and the XO's personal experiences aboard her than it is a definitive look at Morton. Forest Sterling's *Wake of the Wahoo* was a great retelling of his own time aboard the boat, well written from an enlisted man's perspective. Again, though, Morton was only a part of that. George Grider's *War Fish* was another well-done memoir of wartime experiences, with Mush and *Wahoo* a key part. Then, as I have mentioned in other books, there is Clay Blair Jr.'s *Silent Victory*, the definitive source for information on the submarine war. Mush makes quite a few appearances, but gets lost in all the detail.

James F. DeRose's *Unrestricted Warfare*, first published in 2000, finally pursues the premise that the skippers who came along after the start of World War II radically changed the nature of the Silent Service and thus were key to America's success in the Pacific. Morton is obviously a big part of that proposition. DeRose's research on the *Buyo Maru* incident brought us new information and rekindled the controversy. A more recent book, *Battle Surface* by Michael Sturma, which I was able to read and review in manuscript form, had a very helpful chapter on Morton, his unprecedented use of *Wahoo*'s deck guns, and the *Buyo Maru* assault. Professor Sturma has also pulled together additional new information on surface submarine assaults.

Once I realized there was no book out there on Morton himself, each of these works would prove to be useful in piecing together and confirming events, time lines, facts, and perspectives. Something else kept nagging at me. When I mentioned to people that I was considering doing a book on Mush Morton, I often got a blank stare. Most people, including many familiar with submarines, know little of the details of his story. Despite his immense popularity at the time and his influence on the war itself, even many submarine buffs are unfamiliar with the full story. He was in command of the Navy's most famous submarine of its time and the skipper who best personified the swashbuckling submarine ace, yet few now know much beyond the basics.

I still did not know whether I could add anything to what had already been written, or whether I would be able to do the research necessary to contribute to our understanding of the man.

I was talking with my friend Jon Jaques, a former submariner and a national officer with United States Submarine Veterans Inc. (USSVI), and I mentioned my interest in Morton. He encouraged me to go with it, primarily because nobody else had done it, and from what he knew, the tale would be compelling. It should not just be for sub buffs and historians but for anyone who loves a good story populated with strong and interesting characters.

Well, that was the closer. A good story! Interesting characters! I have always been a sucker for those things. Fortunately, so are my literary agent, former diesel-boat submariner Bob Robison, and my editor at NAL Caliber, Brent Howard.

Jon, who is a CPA, has compiled a very helpful monograph on the records of all U.S. World War II submarines and their skippers. He also put me in touch with Paul Sniegon, an associate member of the Volunteer

Base, USSVI, and an amateur submarine historian and researcher. Paul was as excited about the prospects as Jon and I were. He promptly filed a Freedom of Information Act request on our behalf and obtained myriad documents that were extremely valuable in piecing together details of Morton's naval career before *Wahoo*, his family, and more. Paul also sent me other bits of research and tracked down Web sites that assisted in telling this story. He put together and sent me a binder with the complete war patrol reports from all the boats in World War II on CD. I had some of them already in various forms, but this made it extremely easy to more quickly locate particular boat information.

Then I contacted Myrna Hayes at the Mare Island Historic Park museum in California. She was kind enough to put me in touch with a former "yardbird" there named Larry Maggini. Larry had been collecting information and photos on the facility for years and was very helpful in providing me with higher-resolution scans of official Navy photographs related to *Wahoo* and Morton. Many of those that appear in this book are thanks to Larry's hard work, along with that of his friend Joe Kendall, who spent a great deal of time and effort at the Naval Archives scanning images.

To really tell the story, though, I knew I needed to speak with members of the Morton family. I cannot thank enough Doug Morton, Edwina Morton Thirsher, and Mayna Avent Nance for so generously spending time with me and graciously answering all my questions.

I am also grateful to Bryan MacKinnon, who has been a tremendous help from the other side of the world in assisting me in contacting family members. He was also kind enough to spend time giving me details and then proofing and correcting the story of the search for *Wahoo*'s resting place and the memorial ceremonies that have followed. But mostly I want to thank Bryan for all he has done to help find *Wahoo* and give peaceful closure to so many who lost men on the submarine.

Without all these folks, this story could not have been told.

The book, though, is primarily dedicated to John Crouse. John had a dream of a museum that would house artifacts from the diesel submarines, and in a place where everyone—the general public and boat sailors—could come see them, smell them, and touch them. It would also be a place where nonquals like myself could come and lay hands on the hardware that made up those marvelous vessels. The museum at St. Marys was his dream, his life, and ultimately his legacy.

In 2010, my plan was to track down John while we were both at the annual submarine veterans' convention, that year in Cincinnati. My intentions were to buy him a cup of coffee, finally meet him face-to-face, and thank him for his help. I also wanted to let him know his museum was the seed from which this book grew. I did not get the chance.

John suffered another heart attack in the hotel lobby during the convention and, surrounded by his sub buddies, was wheeled out and put into an ambulance. He died in the hospital a few days later.

Thank you, John. You may now rest your oars.

APPENDIX

Few prize-courts sit upon their claims.
They seldom tow their targets in.
They follow certain secret aims
Down under, far from strife or din.
When they are ready to begin
No flag is flown, no fuss is made
No more than the shearing of a pin
That is the custom of "the Trade" . . .
Their feats, their fortunes, and their fames
Are hidden from their nearest kin;
No eager public backs or blames,
No journal prints the yarns they spin,
(The Censor would not let it in!)
When they return from run or raid.
Unheard they work, unseen they win.
That is the custom of "the Trade."

—From "The Trade" by Rudyard Kipling, 1916

CITATIONS FOR DUDLEY MORTON'S NAVY CROSSES AND PURPLE HEART

Signed June 21, 1943

The President of the United States takes pleasure in presenting the NAVY CROSS to LIEUTENANT COMMANDER DUDLEY W. MORTON, UNITED STATES NAVY, for service as set forth in the following

CITATION:

"For extraordinary heroism and outstanding courage as Commanding Officer of the U.S.S. WAHOO during action against enemy Japanese forces in the Pacific Area which resulted in the sinking of 31,890 tons of enemy shipping. Ingeniously devising an improvised chart of a little-known hostile territory, Lieutenant Commander Morton, displaying fearless initiative, utilized the chart as his guide and entered hazardous waters, where he attacked and sank an enemy destroyer. Later, he engaged an unescorted Japanese convoy in a fourteen-hour running battle and, tirelessly pursuing his objective in the face of heavy gunfire, successfully accomplished the destruction of four important vessels. His inspiring leadership, keen judgment, and daring aggressiveness were in keeping with the highest traditions of the United States Naval Service."

> For the President,
> Frank Knox
> Secretary of the Navy

Signed September 25, 1943

The President of the United States takes pleasure in presenting the GOLD STAR in lieu of the Second Navy Cross to COMMANDER DUDLEY W. MORTON, UNITED STATES NAVY, for service as set forth in the following

CITATION:

"For extraordinary heroism as Commanding Officer of a United States submarine in action against enemy Japanese forces in dangerous hostile-patrolled waters. During vital operations in an extremely hazardous area, Commander Morton directed the effective torpedo and gunfire of his ship with outstanding professional skill and excellent judgment, accounting for eight enemy vessels, a trawler and two sampans, a total of 36,693 tons, as well as damaging a 5,973-ton freighter. The brilliant leadership and valiant devotion to duty displayed by Commander Morton throughout the entire period of action reflect great credit upon his command and the United States Naval Service."

> For the President,
> James Forrestal
> Acting Secretary of the Navy

Signed October 15, 1943

The President of the United States takes pleasure in presenting the GOLD Star in lieu of the Third Navy Cross to COM-MANDER DUDLEY W. MORTON, UNITED STATES NAVY, for service as set forth in the following

CITATION:

"For extraordinary heroism as Commanding Officer of a submarine on patrol in enemy Japanese-controlled waters. With outstanding skill and courage, Commander Morton delivered aggressive torpedo attacks against hostile vessels and succeeded in damaging or sinking a large amount of enemy shipping. His daring leadership and indomitable fighting spirit and the gallant devotion to duty of his command were in keeping with the highest traditions of the United States Naval Service."

> For the President,
> Frank Knox
> Secretary of the Navy

Signed May 17, 1944 (awarded posthumously)

The President of the United States takes pleasure in presenting the GOLD STAR in lieu of the Fourth Navy Cross to COMMANDER DUDLEY W. MORTON, UNITED STATES NAVY for service as set forth in the following

CITATION:

"For extraordinary heroism in the line of duty as Commanding Officer of a United States submarine in action against enemy vessels. With the utmost skill and daring, Commander Morton conducted three highly successful war patrols in Japanese-controlled waters, inflicting heavy losses on enemy shipping, and, courageously entering dangerous, confined and shallow waters on a subsequent vital mission, accomplished the complete destruction of at least one important hostile ship. Commander Morton's brilliant tactical ability and inspiring leadership throughout these extremely hazardous operations reflect great credit upon himself, his command and the United States Naval Service."

> For the President,
> James Forrestal
> Secretary of the Navy

Navy Department
Bureau of Naval Personnel
Washington 25, D.C.
Mrs. Harriet N. Morton
1189 California Road
Tuckahoe 7, New York

Dear Mrs. Morton:

The Bureau has the honor to inform you of the award of the Purple Heart and certificate to your late husband, COMMANDER DUDLEY W. MORTON, U.S. NAVY, in accordance with General Order 186 of January 21, 1943, which reads in part as follows:

"The Secretary of the Navy is further authorized and directed to award the Purple Heart posthumously, in the name of the President of the United States, to any persons who, while serving in any capacity with the Navy, Marine Corps or Coast Guard of the United States, since December 6, 1941, are killed in action or who die as a direct result of wounds received in action with an enemy of the United States, or as a result of an act of such enemy."

By direction of the Chief of Naval Personnel.

Sincerely yours,
W. C. Palmer Jr.
Lieutenant Commander, USNR
Medals and Awards

EARLY PROPOSED CITATION FOR CONGRESSIONAL MEDAL OF HONOR FOR COMMANDER DUDLEY MORTON (THE MEDAL WAS NEVER GRANTED)

MORTON, Dudley W.   Comdr. USN Pacific

USS *WAHOO*

Recommended for MEDAL OF HONOR by Sub Bd. of Awds Ltr FB-5-102/P15 Serial 0085 SECRET ltr dated 2 Dec. 1943 Red'd Bd. D&M 3-27-44

Awarded: NAVY CROSS—5 April 1944 Bd. Awds. Mtg.

"For extraordinary heroism above and beyond the call of duty and conspicuous intrepidity as commanding officer of a submarine in action against enemy vessels in patrolled enemy waters. With great courage, aggressiveness and submarine warfare efficiency, he entered dangerous, confined and shallow waters where he sank at least one important enemy vessel. This feat alone ranks with the most daring operations of any submarine exploit of World Navies to date. Other successes in this area are unknown, since his submarine failed to return from this patrol and it is presumed that he gave his life and his ship to the service of his country. His courage, initiative, resourcefulness, and inspiring leadership combined with excellent judgment and skill during this and three previous patrols have served as an inspiration to all submarine personnel. His conduct on this, as well as on all his previous patrols, is in keeping with the highest traditions of the Naval Service."

PRESIDENTIAL UNIT CITATION, AWARDED TO USS *WAHOO* AT THE COMPLETION OF HER THIRD WAR PATROL, THE FIRST UNDER THE COMMAND OF DUDLEY MORTON

The President of the United States takes pleasure in presenting the PRESIDENTIAL UNIT CITATION to the UNITED STATES SHIP *WAHOO*

For service as set forth in the following

CITATION:

"For distinctive performance in combat in the New Guinea Area, January 16 to February 7, 1943. In bold defiance of an enemy destroyer attempting to run her down in a confined harbor, the WAHOO remained at periscope depth to counter with a daring attack, sinking the Japanese vessel by her torpedo fire. Pursuing similar tactics while under sustained fire, she fought a fourteen-hour battle, attacking an unescorted armed enemy convoy and destroying the entire force, two freighters, one tanker and one transport and their personnel. The high combat efficiency of the WAHOO, her officers and men, is exemplified in the destruction of 31,890 tons of enemy shipping during a War Patrol from which she escaped intact."

For the President,
Frank Knox
Secretary of the Navy

SAILING LIST, USS *WAHOO*, SEVENTH WAR PATROL, SEPTEMBER 9, 1943—PRESUMED LOST, OCTOBER 11, 1943 (AND THE PATROLS ON WHICH THE MEN SERVED)

Name	Patrol
Floyd Roland Anders	2–7
Joseph Stephen Andrews	6–7
Robert Edmund Bailey	7
Arthur Irvin Blair	2–7
Jimmie Clark Berg	2–7
Donald Raymond Brown	7
Chester Eugene Browning	6–7
Clifford Leslie Bruce	5–7
James Parr Buckley*	1–7
William Wilson Burgan	7
John Stephenson Campbell	3–7
William John Carr*	1–5, 7
James Edward Carter*	1–7
William Emery Davison	2–7
Lynwood Norman Deaton*	1–7
Joseph Steve Erdey	7
Eugene Francis Fiedler	5–7
Oscar Finkelstein	6–7
Walter Oswald Galli	7
Cecil Edward Garmon	6–7
George Caleb Garrett Jr.	4–7
Wesley Lawrence Gerlacher	2–7

*Denotes "plank owners" (crewmen who helped put USS *Wahoo* into commission, May 15, 1942).

Richard Pickering Goss	4–7
Hiram Moe Greene	7
William Reeves Hand	6–7
Leon Myron Hartman	7
Dean Marriott Hayes	2–7
Richie Neale Henderson*	1–7
William Howell Holmes	7
Van Andrew House	6–7
Howard James Howe	6–7
Olin Jacobs	6–7
Robert Lee Jasa	5–7
Juan Oro Jayson	3–7
Kindred Bernelle Johnson*	1–7
Dalton Christopher Keeter*	1–4, 6–7
Wendell Wayne Kemp	5–7
Paul Kessock	7
Eugene Thomas Kirk	5–7
Paul Henry Krebs	5–7
Arthur Delno Lape	7
Clarence Albert Lindemann	7
Robert Baier Logue	7
Walter Lawrence Lynch	7
Stuart Emerson MacAlman	5–7
Thomas Jamieson Kennedy MacGowen	6–7
Albert John Magyar	6–7
Jesus Chargualaf Manalisay	3–7
Paul Anthony Mandjiak	6–7
Edward Eugene Massa	6–7
Ernest Cletus Maulding	6–7
George Evans Maulding	6–7
Thomas Judson McGill Jr.*	1–7
Howard Eugene McGilton	6–7
Donald Jay McSpadden*	1–7

*Denotes "plank owners" (crewmen who helped put USS *Wahoo* into commission, May 15, 1942).

Max Leroy Mills	6–7
George Arthur Misch	2–7
Dudley Walker Morton	2–7
Percy Neel	5–7
Forest Lee O'Brien*	1–7
Roy Lester O'Neal	6–7
Edwin Eldon Ostrander	6–7
Paul Daniel Phillips*	1–7
Juano Lavell Rennels	4–7
Henry Renno	5–7
Enoch Howard Seal Jr.	3–7
Alfred Russell Simonetti*	1–7
Verne Leslie Skjonsby	6–7
Donald Owen Smith*	1–7
George Vernon Stevens*	1–7
William Clifton Terrell	6–7
William Thomas	6–7
Ralph Oley Tyler*	1–7
Joe Vidick*	1–7
Ludwig Joseph Wach*	1–7
Wilbur Edward Waldron	5–7
Norman Conna Ware*	1–7
Kenneth Lloyd Whipp*	1–7
William Thomas White	7
Roy Leonard Witting*	1–7

*Denotes "plank owners" (crewmen who helped put USS *Wahoo* into commission, May 15, 1942).

SAILING LISTS FOR USS *WAHOO*, WAR PATROLS ONE THROUGH SIX (BUT NOT ABOARD FOR THE SEVENTH AND FINAL PATROL)

Name	Patrol
John H. Allen	2
Jesse L. Appel*	1–5
Richard W. Ater*	1–5
John F. August	6
Raymond O. J. Baldes*	1–2
Charles J. Ballman	5
Raymond G. Beatty*	1–3
Edward L. Bland Jr.*	1–2
Carl A. Brockhauser*	1–3
Clyde A. Burnum*	1–2
Orville F. Chick*	1
Fred B. Chisholm	3
John W. Clary	3
Jack E. Clough	3
Harry Collins	5–6
Kenneth R. Cook	5
William E. Coultas*	1–2
Helmit O. Dietrich	5–6
David E. Dooley*	1–3
Ira Dye*	1
Dennis L. Erickson	3–6
Dale E. Eyman*	1

*Denotes "plank owners" (crewmen who helped put USS *Wahoo* into commission, May 15, 1942).

Sidney F. Flateau*	1
Oakley R. Frash*	1–4
Donald W. Gilbert	5
Henry P. Glinski	2–3
George W. Grider*	1–3
John B. Griggs	2–4, 6
James C. Hall*	1–5
William J. Hanrahan*	1–2
Marius S. Hansen*	1–2
Daniel J. Hargrave*	1–4
Theodore L. Hartman*	1–4
Walter C. E. Heiden*	1
William H. Hodges	5–6
Earl T. Holman	4–5
Carl C. Hood	5
Deville G. Hunter*	1–4
Chandler C. Jackson*	1–5
Willie James	2
Clifford T. Janicek	5
Edward Jesser*	1–3
Clarence E. Johnson*	1–2
Donald O. Jonson	6
Marvin G. Kennedy*	1–2
John Kochis*	1–2
Jerome T. Kohl	4
Stephen Kohut*	1–5
Fertig B. Krause Jr.*	1–5
Sylvester J. Laftin	2
Joseph R. LaMaye*	1
James E. Lane	3, 4, 6
James E. Lavine*	1, 5
Richard H. Lemert	2–6
Andrew K. Lennox*	1–3, 5

*Denotes "plank owners" (crewmen who helped put USS *Wahoo* into commission, May 15, 1942).

Leslie J. Lindhe*	1–3
Stanley A. Lokey*	1
Duncan R. MacMillan	4
Clyde C. Mayberry	4
Henry J. Meditz*	1
James H. Miller*	1–4
John A. Moore	5
James Morris*	1–4
Edward F. Muller*	1–5
Chester M. Myers*	1
Richard O'Kane*	1–5
Lester L. Osborn*	1
Roger W. Paine Jr.*	1–5
Joe D. Parks*	1–5
Walter P. Patrick	3–5
Ralph R. Pruett*	1–5
Russell H. Rau*	1–4
Burrell A. Record	4, 5
Cecil Robertson	3–5
John C. Rowls*	1–5
Earl C. Schreier*	1
C. J. Smith*	1
Edward A. Smith*	1
Forest J. Sterling	2–6
Kelly R. Thaxton*	1–2
Maurice J. Valliancourt*	1
David A. Veder	2–4
Lonnie L. Vogler*	1–2
Harlan C. Whaley	2
William F. Young	2–4
Charles A. Zimmerman	3–6

*Denotes "plank owners" (crewmen who helped put USS *Wahoo* into commission, May 15, 1942).

WORLD WAR II PATROLS OF USS *WAHOO*

No.	From	Date	Duration	Score (claimed)	Score JANAC	Return
1*	Pearl Harbor	8/23/42	55 days	1/6,400	0/0	Pearl Harbor
2*	Pearl Harbor	11/8/42	48 days	2/7,600	1/5,400	Brisbane
3**	Brisbane	1/16/43	23 days	5/31,900	3/11,300	Pearl Harbor
4**	Pearl Harbor	2/23/43	42 days	8/36,700	9/20,000	Midway
5**	Midway	4/25/43	26 days	3/24,700	3/10,500	Pearl Harbor
6**	Pearl Harbor	8/2/43	27 days	0/0	0/0	Pearl Harbor
7**	Pearl Harbor	9/9/43	32 days	1/7,100	4/13,000	Lost 10/11/43

*Marvin Kennedy was skipper.
**Dudley Morton was skipper.

INDEX

Photo courtesy of the *Birmingham Post-Herald*

Award-winning author **Don Keith** has twice been named Broadcast Personality of the Year by *Billboard* magazine. He cowrote *Firing Point* with former submarine skipper George Wallace. *Gallant Lady*, Keith's "biography" of the USS *Archerfish*, was a featured selection of the Military Book Club, along with *In the Course of Duty* and *Final Patrol*. He is also the author of *War Beneath the Waves*. Keith lives in Alabama with his wife, Charlene.